IDENTITY, POWER, AND CHANGE

MICHAEL A. WEINSTEIN
Purdue University

IDENTITY, POWER, AND CHANGE

Selected Readings in Political Theory

Scott, Foresman and Company

Preface

This book, which is designed principally for courses in political theory, grew out of a conviction that the study of political theory can make a significant contribution to the development of the good human life. In a time in which disciplined thought about the proper orientation of an individual to his community is scorned in many quarters, my conviction may appear extravagant. However, I believe that only a commitment to the humanizing function of political theory can make the study of theory meaningful. If we do not expect the political theorist to provide us with significant information about how we can, should, and do relate to the issues that concern the communities to which we belong, we have not been fair to the theorist and have wasted our time reading his work. While the elegance of mathematics and the beauty of poetry make the study of these two pursuits worthwhile, political theory must finally be judged by its ability to aid people in clarifying the choices that they face in their public lives. As you, the student, read this book, keep in mind that it is designed to present alternative ways in which people can relate themselves to the concerns of their communities. If, after reading it, you see new options or deepen your insight into old alternatives, my purpose will have been fulfilled. Of course, you can read this book to realize other purposes. It provides an introduction to political theory as an academic discipline, some thoughts on contemporary political problems, and readings from important works in political theory. However, the ultimate aim is to make some contribution to the way you lead your life.

In preparing this book, I have depended upon conversations with my colleague and my wife, Deena. During the last several years we have frequently discussed the problems treated in this book and have attempted to think out different orientations to public affairs. Since we have developed our political ideas together, in discussion and action, Deena's contribution to this book has been great. Also, I am indebted to friends, students, relatives, colleagues, and teachers who have been kind enough to talk with me about political theory. Even if books in this field are usually written or compiled by individuals, the pursuit of political theory has always been a cooperative endeavor. Nonetheless, I am accountable for what I have written and the selections that I have made.

M.A.W.

Table of Contents

General Introduction

A person reading, without any preconceived notions, the works of writers identified as political theorists would doubtless find himself hopelessly confused about the nature of the subjects of their concern. He would learn that some political theorists are interested in such unrelated topics as the virtues of drinking parties and the proper sauces to put on meats. Many people have lost sleep over this chaotic situation; they have begged for a clear definition of political theory and sometimes have even attempted to supply one. Unfortunately, no definition of the subject has gained universal acceptance. Thus, you may hear that political theorists are concerned with the definition of and conditions for the "common good" of a community. Then, however, someone will ask you what the "common good" means. After watching you squirm, he will probably tell you that the "common good" is the figment of a fool's imagination. He will say that there is only "good" in relation to individuals and that what political theroists are trying to describe and explain are the struggles of people to obtain more of the things they want. This definition may seem more realistic to you than the first one until you learn that other "authorities" are sure that political theorists study the activities of the world spirit, the proletariat, the technostructure, chemicals in the brain, or the child from ages one to three. If you have taken political theory at all seriously, at some point you will become convinced that there is no truth to theory and that its study is merely a more or less enjoyable game. This is a stage through which most theorists pass and from which some never escape.

What accounts for the variety of topics and problems which political theorists treat? For one thing, political theorists often discuss the issues in human relations which most perplex their generation. Since each generation is confronted with unique challenges, the subjects of theory tend to change historically. Thus, the generation which experienced the Great Depression was preoccupied with the ideal of social justice and the means to its realization, while the generation which suffered through World War II and its aftermath became concerned with defining and justifying a democracy in a world which threatened to become totalitarian. The generation currently maturing has its own special concerns, which are partly conditioned by the existence of nuclear weapons, the growth of sophisticated technologies, the movement for social justice, and the emergence of youth as a self-conscious political group. This is not to say that the same concepts do not recur over time in the writings of political theorists. The notions of justice, equality, rights, power, human nature, revolution, and peaceful change, among others, have always concerned political theorists. However, these concepts have undergone a wide range of interpretations by different cultures and in different historical periods. Indeed, one problem which some political theorists discuss is the separation of that which is universal in political life from that which is dependent on particular historical events.

Another reason for the diversity in political theory is the fact that theorists have done their work in a variety of cultures. Confucius, writing in ancient China where eating habits had religious significance, was more likely to be concerned with meat sauces than an American habituated to eating fifteen-cent hamburgers. Plato, who lived in ancient Greece where drinking meant more than a weekend escape from the drudgery of classes, was more likely to employ the drinking party as an analogy for politics than a modern-day Westerner. As long as there are different cultures which emphasize different values and practices, political theories will probably vary at least in detail.

Finally, despite endless efforts to define political theory, the most prominent writers in the field have taken the entire area of human relations as their province of study. Since there are a multitude of human relationships in each society, each theorist has paid attention to the ones which he considered most significant. For example, Karl Marx emphasized the means of producing economic goods as a decisive factor in determining political and other social relationships; Marshall McLuhan argues that the media of communication condition much of social life; and Arnold Toynbee has stressed the broad social significance of religious beliefs and institutions.

At this point there are bound to be doubts, complaints, and objections expressed by those who wonder whether political theory is political. If most political theorists consider a variety of social relationships, do their theories have any distinguishing characteristics? The answer is affirmative. First, political theorists usually deal with public problems or issues which affect entire communities of human beings. Thus, Marx has a place in political theory because, unlike many other economists, he attempted to identify the connection between economic activities and other human pursuits. Second, because political theorists are interested in the whole community, they have often been preoccupied with the question of how ordered relationships are possible in communities at all. How do rules arise in communities? Why do some people obey them and others disobey them? How can they be changed? Are rules merely reflections of more important and basic factors? If so, what are these factors? What kinds of rules are necessary if communities are to continue to exist? To what extent are rules a product of force and fraud; to what extent are they reasonable; what does "reasonable" mean? Can rules and systems of rules be judged according to their desirability? If so, what are the criteria for good rules? These are the types of questions which political theorists are almost inevitably forced to treat when they examine the problems of entire communities. Still, this minimal definition of political theory does not clearly distinguish the field for sociological theory, anthropological theory, jurisprudence, and philosophy of history. This, however, is as it should be. Human affairs do not arrange themselves to suit the needs of traditional academic disciplines.

The issues in political theory which could be discussed in this book range from the divine right of kings to the generation gap. The decision to treat personal identity, organized power, and political change was determined by my estimation of the problems which concern politically aware (not necessarily active) people in the currently maturing generation. In bars, coffeehouses, student unions, dormitories, and sometimes even classes, certain questions occur with a predictably high frequency. Who am I? How can I communicate what I am? Can I lead a satisfying life in this society the way things are? What is a satisfying life? What can I do about military power? What will it do to me? Should I spend my life following orders in a bureaucracy? Will the requirements of the job I take force me to behave immorally? If I don't like some aspects of the society, or all of it, how can it be changed? What kinds of changes do I want and what part can I play in bringing them about? Is a revolution possible or desirable? What are the chances of obtaining the changes I want by "working within the system"? Anybody who has discussed these questions realizes that the debates are more often frustrating than enlightening. People feed on their own ignorance, become dogmatic, begin to attack each other personally, and their conversations soon degenerate from the promise of mutual stimulation to the reality of boredom and gossip about particular people and ideas. Everybody complains about this situation, but the conversations seem to go on with as great a futility as ever. Incongruously, the people participating in the discussions have often just returned from classes in history, English, philosophy, or one of the social sciences. But their scholastic experiences do not seem to significantly enlighten their conversation. Nevertheless, almost every political theorist who is read in the schools has significant insights, distinctions, and concepts to offer this generation of university students. Each has written about identity, power, and change after disciplined thought. While none can provide an individual with absolute guideposts for the critical choices in his life, the theorist can at least make one aware of the alternatives from which he can choose. Such freedom should not be foregone before it is tasted.

The Problem of Personal Identity

The words "self," "individuality," "personality," and "identity" connote profound mysteries to be explored and significant conquests to be won. Sometimes they also mean unattainable goals, endless hang-ups, and visits to the counseling service. In either case, the words refer to problems which have become dominant in twentieth-century literature, philosophy, and social science. We are often told that we "create" ourselves through our actions. Each situation we confront supposedly presents us with a choice, and the choices we make reputedly determine our personalities. Like it or not, so this theory goes, we cannot escape from the ultimate freedom to say no to any demand. People who claim that they are not responsible for their actions are "copping out"; they are letting others determine their fate when they could control their own destinies. However, existentialists, who hold these views, are not the only voices in the discussion. From others, we also learn that our personalities are shaped by the rewards and punishments we receive from birth onward. We are conditioned to act and even to feel in socially favored ways. We are always searching for praise, affection, and pleasures, and we will do almost anything to receive them. We learn about our personalities from what others say about us and what others do to us; meanwhile, we are molding the personalities of our associates by rewarding and punishing them. For behaviorists who entertain these doctrines, our lives are vicious, yet democratic, circles. In addition to the existentialists and the behaviorists, there are people who claim that the "self" is a product of the secretions of endocrine glands, the "instinct" to protect territory, and a multitude of other forces. Anyone who attempts to answer the classical identity question "Who am I?" is likely to be frustrated if he looks for intellectual guidance. Each of the arguments appears plausible, at least in some respects. We feel that we have freedom, yet we notice ourselves automatically conforming to the standards of superiors or peers. The situation was not always like this.

Before the nineteenth century, political and social theorists did not often talk about identity. Instead, they discussed human nature, i.e., the essential characteristics which all human beings have in common. Are men basically self-seeking, are they altruistic, or do they have a dual, selfish-loving nature? For writers in the Catholic tradition, human beings could freely choose to descend either to the level of beasts governed by carnal appetites or persons living according to the law of love. Realists like Hobbes and Machiavelli judged that men were hopelessly selfish, while believers in progress thought that men might become benevolent. For readers today, this debate seems to lack the elements of excitement and seriousness. Where, after all, are the discussions about the differences between and among people?

During the nineteenth century, writers began to pay more attention to the variations among individuals and groups than they had in the past. In part, this tendency was due to the rise of nationalism in Europe and the search for qualities in history and culture that would differentiate one's own nation from others. Also, the appearance of romanticism, with its cult of the free expression of the unique potentialities of each individual, indicated an increasing concern with the particular in man rather than the universal. Both of these movements, along with such things as the progressively greater social differentiation in industrializing societies, frequently resulted in the view that the differences among men and among nations were more important than their similarities. The most striking examples of this type of thought are the extreme racist ideologies which hold that members of certain groups are not worthy of the treatment given to "full" human beings. Of course, placing stress on the particular characteristics of individuals and groups by no means classifies one as a racist. Variety can be embraced just as easily as it can be loathed. Interest in unique qualities, however, does seem to lead to a preoccupation with the problem of identity. Nineteenth-century writers increasingly began to find that they could not answer the question

"Who am I?" by confidently saying, "I am a soul in search of salvation," "I am a bundle of selfish desires,"or"I am a being capable of love and self-sacrifice." Perhaps one was really an Italian, an "Aryan," or a dynamic, spontaneous, unique, and sacred individual. At the present time, the problem and the confusion have become intensified. Many doubt that they can ever understand their essential nature or the natures of those around them. Ironically, nationalism, romanticism, and industrialism, which were, in part, aimed at helping people discover themselves, often seem to have resulted instead in the *loss* of self.

The study of identity is a challenge to explore what makes one a specific person. The study of human nature is a challenge to explore the characteristics of man in general. When people become more interested in identity than in human nature, they begin to believe that human beings in large part create themselves through their actions. As much as behaviorists and existentialists differ about the actual ways in which personalities come into being, they agree that identities are largely formed by social relations. While the existentialist would argue that human beings create their characters through choices and the behaviorist would hold that people mold each other's characters through dispensing rewards and punishments, both theorists are certain that the socially significant aspects of human behavior cannot be explained by a concept of an invariant human nature. The idea that human beings are relatively plastic in relation to their characters is one component of the identity problem. The psychologist Robert Lifton has gone so far as to characterize the contemporary person in industrialized nations as "Protean man."* The modern counterparts of Proteus, the sea god who could change his shape at will, are people who put on a new self for each relationship in which they engage.

The problem of identity becomes an "identity crisis" when an individual questing for what makes him a specific person believes that the search will reveal that he has no significant character and that he is nothing but a collection of memories, consumer goods, and habitual actions which conform to the current standards of behavior in his groups. The person who is in this situation may try out different "selves," which he learns about through the mass media, literature, or people around him. The result of this strategy is a period of more or less prolonged disorganization which normally ends when the individual finds a self with which he is relatively satisfied. One of the great misfortunes of the twentieth century is that sometimes the person is never satisfied and ends by living out his existence in a state of constant experimentation.

Another way to deal with the identity crisis is to give up the quest for individuality and reconcile oneself to the condition of conforming to the requirements of available roles. This is, perhaps, what most people who have questioned the purposes of their lives finally end up doing. Certainly, it is the way of life of those who never ask "Who am I?" and accept descriptions of themselves which others give them. However, once a person has embarked on the exploration of what makes him a specific person, he is likely never to

---

*Robert Jay Lifton, "Protean Man," *Partisan Review* 35, 1 (Winter 1968): 3-27.

be fully satisfied if he identifies himself with the social roles that he performs. Social roles define the rules by which one is supposed to perform social functions. They are general standards to which everyone who performs the role is expected to adhere. Therefore, social roles never make allowance for the unique contributions of the individual. To identify oneself with the roles one performs is to feel as though one is a replaceable part in a vast social mechanism.

Others who encounter the identity crisis choose neither to seek a unique individuality nor to acquiesce to society's demands. Instead, they identify themselves with some historical task which, usually, has political implications. For example, they may choose to give their lives to fomenting a revolution, experimenting with new forms of human relationships in a utopian community, or reforming some injustice in the society. The prospect of identifying oneself with a historical task is an appealing one. For instance, many of the people involved in the space program feel that their lives have significance and meaning because they are cooperating in a noble and important endeavor. Many of those participating in revolutionary movements around the world feel the same way. However, it is probably more difficult to identify oneself with an historic mission today than it was even fifty years ago because people have become conscious that history may soon end through the explosion of nuclear weapons, horrible famines, and other threats which have become familiar topics of discussion during recent years. George Wald, a Nobel Prize-winning scientist, has gone so far as to say that much of the behavior of the currently maturing generation can be explained by the fear and the consciousness that theirs may be the last generation to exist on earth.

The problem of identity becomes important when people begin to shift their attention from what man is in general to what he is in all of his particularity. What do my race, my nation, my culture, my social class, my parents, the ways in which I gain information, the tools and technologies which I use, and my groups contribute to my personality? This many-faceted question, which became dominant in the nineteenth century, still underlies most present-day discussions of identity. The existence and importance of the query demonstrate that people still have not learned to understand the dynamics of the complex industrial societies in which they live. Concern with the problem of how much the individual can be held responsible for creating his own identity and the personalities of others follows from the recognition that a multitude of factors influence the quality of a person's life. There are two extreme responses to this problem. Some people insist that the individual's identity is determined inexorably by factors beyond his control. Others claim that the individual is free to determine his own identity in the most important respects. Most people take a "common-sense" position which includes elements of conditioning and elements of freedom. However, the existence of large numbers of "Protean men," who change their whole personalities from day to day, and automatons or "plastic people," who slavishly conform to social norms, has thrown common sense itself into question. Finally, lack of confidence in understanding the factors which make one a specific person and lack of certainty about the contribution of the individual to forming his own self often lead to the identity crisis. The person who suffers through this crisis fears that he may not have a self at all. Further, he has no standards through which he can create one. A person may emerge from an identity crisis by discovering a self-image which satisfies him, by accepting society's judgments of what he should be, or by giving his life to an historical task. Each of these strategies entails problems in a world threatened by annihilation.

The problem of identity has importance for political theorists in three ways. First, since the political theorist takes all human relations as his province of study, he will be interested in the problem of identity when other people in his society seem to be concerned with it. Second, the political theorist may notice that public problems, issues which affect entire communities of human beings, seem to be discussed and resolved partly in terms of the personal frustrations of the individuals involved in decision making. The political theorist who for this reason becomes concerned with identity is likely to take the position that private problems are often the source of public problems. He will take psychological explanations of human behavior very seriously and may even go so far as to say that public problems can be reduced to private problems. To a great extent, Plato, Harold Lasswell, and Erich Fromm, all of whom are represented in this book, approach political theory from a psychological point of view. They believe that if people could be aided in bringing their identity crises to satisfactory conclusions, many of the most intractable political problems would be resolved almost automatically. For some people, it is inviting to believe that revolutionary movements are caused by individuals who feel guilty about having wished to murder their fathers when they were five years of age. Third, other political theorists may notice that identity crises seem to be the result of social relations which stifle basic human desires or require individuals to perform contradictory actions. The theorist of this bent will hold that public problems are the source of personal frustrations. He will favor explanations of human behavior which rely on general systems of action in organizations and social norms, and he may even claim that private problems can be reduced to public problems. Jean Jacques Rousseau, David Easton, and Herbert Marcuse largely approach political theory from this systems point of view. They believe that patterns of social structure are in great part responsible for the problem of personal identity. For some people, it is enticing to believe that a successful revolution could spell the end of personal frustrations. Of course, it is possible for a political theorist to believe that private problems and public problems are interdependent. This type of theorist will give serious attention to explanations of human behavior that concentrate on the interactions between and among people. Each person will be viewed as contributing something of himself to a relationship, while the form of the relationship will, in turn, be seen as affecting the individual's character. Political theorists who are most concerned with such interactions have always been interested in the conflicts between individuals and the ways in which these conflicts influence character. Thomas Hobbes, Robert Dahl, and Albert Camus tend to approach political theory from a conflict point of view. They all believe that problems of identity emerge when we confront our fellow human beings. For some people, it is tempting to think that all of the noble rhetoric of politics is merely a veil hiding the conflicts of concrete interests.

The fact that classical and contemporary political theorists have disagreed about the nature of the problem of identity is one indication of how difficult a problem it is. Do we often feel lost and alone because of brooding desires within ourselves? Do we sometimes feel rootless and unhappy because social institutions make intolerable demands on us? Are we frequently bitter and despairing because of our disputes with the people around us? We can probably answer yes to each of these questions. That is why psychological theorists, systems theorists, and conflict theorists have always gained large followings. Unfortunately, the present state of our knowledge of man prevents us from stating with certainty which type of theory is the most accurate.

The Problem of Organized Power

It would have been convenient to have answered the questions about personal identity before posing further questions about society and politics. Most theorists have attempted to "figure out" man before they went on to discuss what men do when they are organized. However, for people in the twentieth century such a course is nearly impossible to follow. So much of what has to do with the individual seems inextricably bound up with groups. This is what led the philosopher W. H. Sheldon to call twentieth-century man a *socius*. He meant that people in this age are accustomed to thinking of themselves as inseparable from their relations to others; they are used to feeling that if they could understand their relationships to those others, they could understand themselves. Usually, however, the attempt to make an inventory and diagnosis of one's relationships fails to eventuate in self-understanding. After all, there can be no relationships without things to relate. Too often we forget about ourselves at just the times we are trying hardest to understand ourselves. This difficulty is not peculiar to social theorists, though. Whenever we attempt to defend our behavior from attack, we tend to excuse our mistakes by blaming forces beyond our control for causing them. Parents, peer groups, and power structures are especially favored whipping posts. Worst of all, we frequently find it difficult to ascribe even our successes to our own efforts. Is a success really mine, or is it a success in relation to someone else's standards? When we think of ourselves as inseparable from our relations to others, we are likely to doubt our efficacy, our competence. When we wonder whether or not we are powerless to initiate sincere actions, our thoughts may turn to the role of organized power structures in creating such uncertainty.

Just as the classical problem of human nature has been transformed into the contemporary problem of identity, the ancient problem of power has become increasingly reinterpreted as the problem of organized power structures. Before the nineteenth century, it was common to take either of two positions regarding the concept of power. Like Hobbes, one could define power as "the present means to some future apparent good." Under this definition, a person had power to the extent that he had wealth, shrewdness, a good reputation, physical strength, and arms. To be powerful meant to have the resources to gain what one desired. One who disagreed with this definition of power could substitute another which placed more emphasis on social relations. Power could then be defined as the probability that an individual would be able to get another person to do something, even against the latter's will. The more actions one could command from others, the more power one had.

It is clear that any complete definition of power would have to take both of these aspects into account. We often speak of "having the power" to perform some action. This is the sense in which Hobbes used the term. We also talk about "having power over" someone, or being able to control someone's actions. Both of these types of power have political implications. The opportunities for action within a society may either enhance or circumscribe one's ability to do what he wants. The legal, customary, and informal relations within a society may give some people the ability to command actions from others. It is probably useful to think of power as appearing in well-defined contexts. Power is the ability to perform certain specific actions or make others perform certain specific actions. For example, a police officer may have the power to arrest you, even if you are not committing a crime. He may not have the power—or the ability—to compose a symphony. Or, employing the second definition of power, a police officer may have the power to compel you to empty your pockets during a search, while he may not have the power to make you respect him.

Using the second definition of power as a starting point, political theorists often make a distinction between power and authority. Authority is the ability of one person to make others perform certain actions because they feel that he has a right to command them. A great deal of traditional political theory is concerned with the problem of the circumstances in which one should feel that someone else has the right to command him. This issue is still debated with great passion, especially when questions of civil disobedience and revolutionary activity arise. Some hold that it is right to obey an official of government only when his command is consistent with the dictates of one's conscience. Others say that we should obey the commands of public officials if they have been chosen democratically or appointed by democratically chosen authorities. Still others claim that we should obey the commands of public officials because order is preferable to anarchy. These three standpoints by no means exhaust the positions on civil disobedience.

It would be inaccurate to say that the traditional questions of power are no longer important. Almost every relationship in which we engage has an aspect of personal or interpersonal power about it. For instance, we frequently find that a supposed love affair is really a struggle between two people to change one another. Or, we note that the relationship between student and teacher is an exercise in mutual manipulation. Nevertheless, despite the pervasive effects of the drive to obtain what one desires and the struggle to make others conform with one's wishes, a new dimension of power has taken on increasing importance in the twentieth century. Much of the power which excites our concern is neither personal nor interpersonal, but *impersonal.* Increasingly, the power which affects us in our daily lives is the power of large and complex organizations such as governmental bureaucracies, corporations, universities, armies, labor unions, and hospitals. These organizations provide the settings in which the problems of power are confronted by people today. They provide both opportunities for action and limits to action in the contemporary industrialized world.

It is not surprising that a civilization which discovered the identity crisis should also be preoccupied with impersonal power. The two themes are bound up with one another. Without judging the question of whether complex organizations have created the identity crisis or whether doubts about the human self have given rise to massive bureaucracies, it is clear that the conditions intensify each other. From one point of view, it is understandably difficult to determine whether or not you have a unique self if most of your actions are carried out in accordance with the rules laid down in some organization. Even if you had some idea of what constituted your special virtues, you would likely have a difficult time expressing them. How often is it possible to act "naturally" in a college classroom, even if the professor assures you that you will not be penalized for doing so? It is not so much the individual students who impede spontaneity as it is the grading system, the fact that the chairs in which the students sit are arranged to face the instructor, and the organizational expectation that teachers are in the room to lecture and students to listen. Every organization encourages a certain measure of uniformity and, therefore, makes the problem of identity harder to solve. From another point of view, if a person is unsure of himself he may welcome the relative security which comes from identification with an organizational role. If you let them, the organizations to which you belong will provide you with the means of adjusting to any situation you encounter. By patterning their behavior in accordance with organizational norms, many people who have not resolved the problem of identity find some comfort.

In one sense, organizations, not individuals, are the significant actors in contemporary societies. They own enormous resources, employ, serve, and sometimes destroy vast numbers of people, and influence or determine public policies. Their regulations influence the activities of every one of us. Organizations are powerful because they are able to mobilize vast resources which they use to produce certain effects and exclude others. At this point, some people will raise certain objections. Are organizations not made up of people, and do not many of those people make decisions which determine the policies of their organizations? At first glance this objection would seem to carry a great deal of weight. After all, organizations do not have minds like individuals do; corporations, contrary to a popular saying, do not have souls. However, if we look closely at the people who make decisions within organizations, we find that they often have common attitudes and career patterns. To attain their positions they had to perform actions and even adopt styles of living which were organizationally desirable. It seems impossible to escape the position that power means more than the whims and desires of individuals in modern societies.

If the basis of organizational power lies in the ability to mobilize vast resources in pursuit of a task, the ways in which organizations exercise power are diverse. Perhaps the most subtle and unrecognized, and yet the most decisive, way in which organizations employ their power is in making choices to use their resources to attain certain ends rather than others. Why should classrooms be built so that rows of fixed seats face a lecture platform or a blackboard? Why should manufacturers and construction crews build automobiles and highways instead of passenger trains and tracks? Why should more money be spent to cure sick people than to prevent diseases? There are no easy answers to these questions. Some people, of course, will try to prove that it is necessary to do exactly what is being done. However, when a radio station in Chicago finds it important to report the air pollution content of the atmosphere along with the weather forecast and to warn older people to stay indoors lest they die, it is reasonable to believe that many actions are not morally necessary. Why, then, are such choices made? The contemporary critics represented in this book attempt to find general principles at work in the industrial system which account for the actual use of resources. For example, Marcuse identifies a supposed tendency of developed capitalist systems to turn imaginative culture into a commodity; Fromm talks about a similar tendency of capitalist systems to encourage consumption of economic goods rather than honest and loving human relations; and Camus speaks of a preoccupation with "bread" at the expense of "freedom." The contemporary behavioralists included here also address themselves to the problem. Lasswell concerns himself with the influence of military practices on social choices; Easton discusses the ways in which children are socialized to accept the norms of patriotism and trust of constituted authority; and Dahl shows how power becomes concentrated when people are not interested in public problems. In their own ways, the classical political theorists represented here were also aware of organized power. Plato renders a detailed description of how a dictator builds an organization which eventually enslaves him; Rousseau discusses how interest groups propagandize about the common good while pursuing their particular advantages; and Hobbes delves into the reasons why people are willing to obey officials even if they do not agree with the commands. Still, there is no universally accepted explanation of why organizations employ their resources in some ways rather than in others.

Organizations also exercise power through regulations. Everyone is familiar with the perils of red tape, but even more important are the rules, formal or tacit, which govern day-to-day behavior. Most of these regulations are not like criminal laws which state a "thou shalt not" and a penalty if one is caught disobeying. Instead, they are "if–then" rules which specify what one must do if he wants to receive any benefits from the organization. For example, if one wants a college degree, one must attain a certain minimum grade-point average; if one wants to be an insurance salesman, he must wear a jacket and tie; or (in some cases) if one wants to enter a hospital, he must have medical insurance. Examples of organizational rules could (and do) fill endless volumes. Again, some people would argue that the regulations which obtain at any given time are necessary to secure the performance of important tasks. This kind of reasoning often strains the imagination when one realizes that the regulations frequently favor the interests of certain groups at the expense of others. Further, the regulations are enforced in some cases and ignored in others. Organizations can exercise a great deal of power by applying normally disregarded rules to individuals and small groups which they view as threats.

Finally, organizations exercise power by attempting to influence governmental policy. Businesses, unions, universities, and organized interest groups are continually trying to have laws passed and administrative directives issued which will aid them in attaining particular goals and policies. Even within the government itself, agencies fight among themselves for shares of the budget and new powers. The means by which governmental policies are influenced or shaped by organizations are familiar to anyone who reads newspapers or magazines, listens to the radio, or watches television. Money is spent to activate public opinion through advertising campaigns, "spontaneous" letter-writing campaigns to sway Congressmen are initiated, "expert" testimony is given before Congressional committees and administrative agencies, and officials of all kinds are plied with favors. Much of the insignificance and political impotence which many individuals feel is the result of the resources which large organizations can muster to affect the acts of the political system. While some people argue that the organizations we belong to protect our interests better than we could ever do, there is reason to doubt this position. Organizations define our interests for us, and we may not agree with their judgments.

Today, many people believe that the growth of large-scale organizations and the mobilization of impersonal power are responsible for their failures to discover or create a satisfying self-definition. At the same time, they cannot envision a technological society which could function without such organizations. It is this dilemma which forms the background of contemporary debates about social change.

The Problem of Political Change

When a person perceives his situation as unsatisfactory, he may respond in several ways. First, he may attempt to reinterpret his condition so that the problem no longer exists. This is perhaps the most common way of dealing with frustrations. The Stoics in ancient Greece and Rome carried the process of rationalization to its ultimate conclusion. The slave-philosopher Epictetus drew a distinction between the things over which an individual has power and the things which the individual cannot control. According to Epictetus, a person could control his opinions, his desires, and his actions. He could not control his body, his property, his reputation, and his social position. In short, he has power only over his own acts. This distinction led Epictetus to an interesting conclusion—people should not worry about the things which are out of their control but should attempt to perfect their internal lives. The dissatisfied person should first look for the cause of his unhappiness. If he finds that he is troubled because of his beliefs, his wishes, or the choices he has made, he should alter them immediately. If he discovers that he is suffering because of conditions in the outside world, he should realize that he has no right to worry. There is nothing that he can do about the situation. If the person continues to worry about the world, Epictetus prescribes a simple therapy which he believes will put the mind in order. "Staightway then practice saying to every harsh appearance, 'You are an appearance, and in no manner what you appear to be.'" In other words, the last refuge for a person who is suffering in the world is to believe that the world is an illusion. Put as starkly as this, most of us would shake our heads in disbelief. How could anyone suggest that we adopt such an attitude toward life? How could anyone convince himself that the entire outside world is an illusion? Even if such a trick could be performed, how could a person justify ignoring at least half of his existence? As reasonable as these questions may seem, we nevertheless use the therapy recommended by Epictetus every day, most often unconsciously. How frequently do we rouse ourselves out of unhappiness by thinking how much worse conditions could be than they are? How often do we think that even if there are flaws in political life we are still living in the best country in the world? How many times have we assured ourselves that the decisions of our political leaders, even if we are unhappy with them, could not have been made in any other way? Epictetus was not as foolish as he first appeared. He defined, as well as anyone has since, the normal response which individuals make when they are confronted with frustration. It is far easier to believe that one's frustrations are an illusion than it is to attempt to change the conditions that are responsible for those frustrations. Particularly when one is a slave, like Epictetus, the wisest course may be to wish away one's suffering.

Many people who are concerned with the problems of identity and organized power employ the method of Epictetus. Instead of brooding about the "Who am I?" question, they identify themselves with the social roles that they are expected to perform. They become "good" students, "good" husbands, "good" fathers, and "good" junior executives. They gain a measure of security in return for suppressing their quest for individuality. Instead of worrying about their lack of power in a world of massive organizations, they accept the rewards which the organizations offer them. They enjoy whatever happiness a new car, a suburban house, or an expense account can provide. All of this does not mean that it is wrong to employ the method of Epictetus. While theorists like Marcuse, Fromm, and Camus condemn contemporary industrial societies for suppressing the most basic desires of human beings, theorists like Dahl and Hobbes believe that living in society entails such sacrifices.

Some people find themselves incapable of taking the medicine of Epictetus, especially when their identities and power over events are at stake. They believe that the problems are real, that they should be confronted, and that they should be solved, if possible. People who feel this way are likely to become interested in political and social change. In the most general sense, three ways in which social and political change may take place in the contemporary world can be defined. These three types of social change are closely related to the psychological, systems, and conflict theories which we briefly discussed earlier. First, if one believes that public problems can be reduced to private unrest, he will seek change through attempting to transform individuals in some way. While the idea of transforming individuals may appear frightening at first glance, it is really as familiar a practice as wishing away frustrations. After all, the great religions have taught that the most significant problems which human beings confront are problems of the soul. The process of authentic conversion certainly implies some transformation in the individual, as do the numerous injunctions in religious literature to imitate the acts and the internal lives of religious leaders. The clergy and other religious members of the contemporary world are often well aware of the problems of identity and organized power. They sometimes say that the loss of self which so many people experience is due to the fact that individuals have turned away from a greater self: God. They attribute the growth of tremendous and seemingly purposeless bureaucracies to a supposed inability of people to select proper goals without asking for divine guidance. They believe that desirable social change will come about if people transform their inner lives in accordance with a religious commitment.

Religious people are not the only individuals who believe that significant public problems can be reduced to private problems. Writers who adhere to a psychological theory of politics feel that social change can come about if people are aided in overcoming their internal conflicts by expert help. If political strife is really an expression of self-hatred and personal insecurity and guilt, successful efforts to help people overcome these feelings will result in a world of peace and harmony. Thus, Harold Lasswell recommends that industrialized nations set up a program of "preventive politics," in which psychiatrists will screen out of politics individuals who are likely to work out their aggressive tendencies in the public arena. Erich Fromm makes a similar proposal, which he calls "humanistic management," and Plato suggested that politics should be conducted by a "statesman" who was knowledgeable in the "science" of human nature.

Psychological theories of change are plausible enough to gain large numbers of adherents. Certain hippies felt that if people ingested enough LSD, their minds would be "expanded" to the point that they would no longer gain any satisfaction from hating. They would discover new and enlightening experiences which would make their social conflicts seem trivial. Other people believe that a massive program of "sensitivity training," in which people are allowed to express themselves honestly in a group setting, will eliminate the frustrations which supposedly cause such problems as racism. Still others believe that a system of community mental health centers will provide the opportunity for people to discover satisfying identities. However, as interesting as psychological theories of change may seem, they have problems. What are the causes of an individual's inner conflicts and frustrations? These problems might arise from the individual's participation in social roles which cause him to suppress his desires and organizations which make unmanageable demands on him. If this is the case, the individual cannot be transformed without first changing the social structures. Are all problems the result of inner conflicts and frustrations? Perhaps conflicts over scarce resources which everybody (or at least a significant group) desires are not signs of mental disease. Even if public problems can be reduced to private problems, how can frustrated people be convinced (or must they be forced) to accept programs of preventive politics or humanistic management? Questions like these lead many people to look in new directions for social change.

If one doubts that public problems can be reduced to private problems, he may adopt the position that change can only come about by altering the social structure. The most familiar theory which advocates changing the system is Marxism. Marx taught that the problem of identity arises because of the way in which capitalist industry is organized. He believed that a person could neither understand nor express his individuality if the work that he spent most of his life doing was imposed upon him by a class of people who bought his labor like one buys groceries and used his labor to produce commodities for a profit rather than for beneficial use. Marx, therefore, took the point of view that the most important private problems are public. He felt that the capitalist system of producing goods would have to be changed before people could attain satisfactory identities. He also believed that the desired change would come about through a revolution made by people who had nothing to sell but their bodies and minds. The classical problem of Marxism as a theory of change is whether or not the revolution will take place without the intervention of conscious human planning. In practice, committed Marxists have always attempted to intervene actively in the historical process. In theory, they have had many difficulties. Despite this ambiguity, Marxism has exerted a decisive influence over the systemic theories of change which have succeeded it. These later theories have usually recognized that individuals can influence the course of history through their social actions, even though the opportunities for successful action are severely limited by social roles and organizational norms. This is the position of much of the New Left and of Herbert Marcuse, whose works are represented in this book.

Systemic theories of change must deal with several problems if they are to be considered seriously. First, they must identify the general principles which characterize the social structure. Are the most significant factors in contemporary societies the gigantic private corporations, powerful organizations of all kinds, sophisticated technologies, and/or military force? Since the end of World War II, systems theorists have taken organizational power more seriously, because related bureaucratic patterns are evident in both "capitalist" America and "communist" Russia. Second, a systemic theory of change should specify the ways in which change occurs or can be made to occur. Often systemic theories describe supposed tendencies or "laws" at work in social institutions, laws which are beyond the control of individuals. For example, Marx claimed that capitalist economies tend to overproduce and are, therefore, subject to periodic depressions. Marcuse says that capitalist economies turn initiatives in imaginative culture into economic commodities. Rousseau thought that private interests tend to take over public policy for their own ends. Easton believes that one part of a social system may generate demands on another part which cannot be met. Sometimes systemic theories describe points of tension between social roles and among organizations which can be exploited by people seeking change. Third, systemic theories of change should specify the directions in which change may take place. It is in fulfilling this task that systems theorists confront their most difficult problems in the contemporary world. In a society dominated by complex organizations which perform highly specialized functions through the use of experts manipulating sophisticated technologies, the concept of a world in which these organizations would disappear or would even modify their modes of operation is hard to imagine. Some contemporary systems theorists pin their hopes on a decentralization of the bureaucracies which would take place either through peaceful or violent means. Another, related, idea would involve giving everyone affected by an organizational decision some power in determining that decision. Whether or not such plans are practicable is a vital issue for many members of the currently maturing generation.

Those who are awed by the thought of restructuring an entire society are likely to adopt a theory based on changing human relations within the extant system. Many of these people view society as a conglomeration of groups and individuals seeking fulfillment of their interests. When these interests clash, conflict results and a degree of change takes place. The conflict theorist who is interested in changing social relations often concentrates his efforts on devising the most efficient strategies for groups to employ in attaining their desires. The conflict theorist who is concerned with diminishing strife frequently works on clarifying the methods by which disputes can be resolved peacefully. In either case, such theorists examine a zone between organizational norms and individual personalities. They are apt to think that people know what they want and that the problem is to figure out how they can get it, either at the expense of, or together with, others. Conflict theorists may suggest measures of reform or conservation. They are unlikely to offer revolutionary programs because they generally take the social structure for granted. They are just as unlikely to generate plans for transforming individuals because they generally use the desires of individuals as their basis for operation. A form of conflict theory called pluralism has been used by Robert Dahl and others to describe and defend contemporary American institutions. Dahl has argued that out of the chaotic competition among groups in this society, a situation arises in which every group receives some of what it wants. The chief problem facing conflict theory in the contemporary world is obvious: efficient strategies for realizing group interests may do nothing to help people find themselves or allow people to gain a sense of dignity in a world of complex organizations.

Not surprisingly, there is no universally accepted answer to the question of how social change can be accomplished. Before this problem can be solved it will be necessary to determine what kinds of social change are desirable and what kinds are possible. The differences of opinion on both of these issues reflect underlying disagreements about the nature of identity and organized power. At the present time, and perhaps for as long as human societies exist, each person must face the responsibility of choosing whether to be a conformist, a missionary-psychologist, a revolutionary, or a reformer.

Approaches to the Study of Political Theory

Until now, we have been considering political theory from the point of view of the problems with which political theorists deal. We have pointed out that while political theorists have been known to discuss any topic from appropriate meat sauces to drinking parties, they have usually interested themselves in issues which are relevant for entire communities of human beings. In other words, they have turned their attention to the dilemmas of public life, even if they have come to believe that these dilemmas can be best explained in terms of private conflicts. Further, we have selected three problems for special mention because of their seeming importance in the contemporary world. The quest for a satisfying personal identity, the confrontation of the individual with organized power, and the debate about the ways in which social relations can be changed are all problems which excite the interest, and often the emotions, of the currently maturing generation. We have seen that these issues have also captured the attention of many political theorists.

It is reasonable to begin discussing an academic discipline by defining the problems with which it deals. If there were no questions that people wanted to ask about their public lives, it is unlikely that political theory would ever have appeared. However, there are other ways of looking at political theory than merely describing the problems which theorists discuss. Perhaps the question that has intrigued and bothered political theorists most in the twentieth century is this: How should one go about studying the issues that affect entire communities of human beings? This question can be discussed in terms either of method or of approach. In academic disciplines, a "method" refers to an orderly procedure for investigating some problem. The term is derived from the Greek word *methodos* which means "a going after, pursuit, investigation, system." Methods, then, combine two aspects which may at first seem contradictory. They are devised because of the desires of people to go after, pursue, and investigate solutions to problems that are as yet unknown. Once they are devised, methods tend to become fixed and repeatable sets of procedures for going about the task of investigation. Thus, methods are standardized and readily understood ways of exploring the unknown. In specialized and technological societies, people tend to contrive a multitude of methods adapted to specific problems. Examples of such methods are the standardized set of questions which a doctor asks you when you complain of a stomach ache and the procedures which a social scientist uses when he wants to determine which individuals should answer a questionnaire. Political theorists use methods of logical reasoning and generalization in their work. However, due to the technical and specific nature of methods, theorists who care about the ways in which public problems can be studied have debated questions of approach rather than judgments of method. Before it is possible to design a set of procedures for investigating a problem, it is necessary to determine what kinds of procedures are most appropriate.

The term "approach" is much more difficult to define than the concept of method. Simply, when we "approach" something we draw near to it. An "approach" to a building is a way of gaining access to it; a salesman's "approach" to a customer is a way of attempting to get the customer to buy some good. Thus, from ordinary usage, we can get some idea of what political theorists mean when they talk about approaches to the study of public problems. An approach is a way of drawing near to the problems of political theory. It is like a method in that it gives some direction to the actions of the investigator. However, it does not direct the investigator to perform certain well-defined procedures on the data before him. Instead, it is an attempt to supply an answer to a prior question: What aspects of all of the data about public problems are important to explore? Thus, approaches are ways of defining what information the political theorist should consider when he is discussing public problems. It is clear that when a person has some idea what information is relevant to the solution of his problem, he will at least have a chance to devise some method for manipulating that information. If he does not know what data are important, the search for a method will become absurd. One of the major problems in contemporary political theory is the lack of agreement among writers in the field about the proper approach to the subject matter. This disagreement has often led to a preoccupation with questions of how to study political theory at the expense of actually studying the public problems involved.

The Classical Approach

Writers who discussed public problems before the nineteenth century adopted, in practice, the definition of political theory that we are using in this book. They were ready to pay attention to any aspect of the lives of conscious human beings, as long as the subject affected the existence of an entire community. They were also willing to make many different kinds of pronouncements about politics. To understand what this last statement means, it is necessary to know the different ways in which one can talk about politics.

Broadly speaking, we can distinguish between statements describing what people do when they transact public affairs and what they think about public affairs, and statements prescribing what people *should* do when they transact public affairs and what they *should* think about public affairs. Under the heading of descriptive statements we can identify many subcategories. First, there are factual statements, such as "Lyndon Johnson was a President of the United States," or "Che Guevara died in Bolivia." Political theorists, who are usually interested in determining the general principles of public life, use factual statements mainly to support generalizations. Examining the work of British sociologist Morris Ginsberg we can identify several kinds of generalizations.* For instance, there are generalizations associating observed variables, such as "Businessmen tend to vote Republican." Classical political theory abounds with statements of this sort. Plato asserted that listening to love songs tended to divert a citizen's attention from the affairs of the community. Other generalizations describe how social institutions arise. An example of this kind of statement would be the assertion that states arise from a contract. Third, there are generalizations associating changes in one institution with changes in another institution. Statements linking public immorality to a decline in parental authority are examples of this mode of thought. Fourth, there are generalizations which describe cycles in public life. An example is Plato's statement that democracies eventually become dictatorships and that dictatorships eventually dissolve and new regimes supersede them. A fifth type of generalization concerns the stages of development of political institutions. An example is the familiar statement that presidential powers increase as the society becomes technologically more complex. Sixth, there are statements derived from the assumptions one makes about human behavior. As an illustration, if one assumes that human beings are greedy for scarce resources, he may state that social life without a coercive state would be a "war of all against all." Classical political theorists did not hesitate to use any of these six types of generalizations. Often they generalized from what we

---

*Morris Ginsberg, *Essays in Sociology and Social Philosophy;* Vol. 2, *Reason and Unreason in Society* (London: William Heinemann, 1956), p. 35.

today would consider insufficient evidence. Frequently, they made sweeping assumptions without giving many reasons for them. Almost always, they failed to distinguish between one type of generalization and another. Assertions derived from assumptions about human nature were phrased so that they seemed like associations between observed variables. Statements about the development of political institutions were confused with statements about their origins. Such ambiguities often grate on the contemporary critical and analytical mind.

Classical political theorists were not reluctant to make prescriptive statements. In fact, their works were usually devoted to passing judgment on actual regimes and making recommendations about the nature of the good life and how to attain it. It is this phase of classical political theory which seems to interest contemporary writers and students the most. First, many current political theorists doubt whether the terms "common good" or "right political action" have any meaning beyond characterizing situations which a person prefers. What does it mean to say that "political leaders should take the public interest into account when they make decisions"? Does it mean simply that somebody would like politicians to be less selfish, or does it mean that there is an *objective* social good which politicians have an obligation to serve? If the latter is the case, can this objective good be known in the same way that we know that an apple will fall to the earth if it drops from a tree and does not encounter intervening objects? If not, how can it be known? The same kinds of questions can be asked about such other terms as "satisfactory identity" and "desirable social change." Second, many contemporary theorists who are less skeptical about prescriptive statements believe that the classical political theorists have made moral recommendations and have described conditions of social good that are still worthy of attention today. Plato's vision of a government of "wise men" is taken seriously by many in the contemporary world, even if the wise men often turn out to be psychiatrists, social scientists, or engineers, rather than philosophically educated statesmen. Rousseau's concept of a general will which is uncorrupted by private interests forms the basis of many "Third World" political theories. The idea of an efficient society in which people have maximum freedom to pursue their own interests, which was expressed by Hobbes, exerts a profound influence in present-day Anglo-American thought.

After reading this discussion of the ways in which classical political theorists talked about public problems, one is likely to wonder whether it is sensible to speak of a classical approach to political theory at all. If an "approach" consists primarily of guidelines that direct the investigator to some kinds of data rather than to others, it appears that classical thinkers did not use any such method, that their work had little direction. They employed all types of prescriptive and descriptive statements and often confounded them with one another. Nothing human was alien to them. Thus, it is probably accurate to say that there is no well-defined classical approach. Problems of method and approach only came to the fore in the nineteenth and twentieth centuries when people became self-conscious about the differences among the various branches of knowledge. However, under the impact of modern science, writers on public problems began to question the kinds of data they used. Could the study of politics be made into a science? If scientists do not make prescriptive statements, should political theorists follow the scientific example? Must classical political theory be ignored in favor of starting afresh with rigorous methods? In response to the challenge of modern science, classical or traditional political theory has been defined as the disciplined speculation on public problems which took place before men asked such questions. Once these questions were posed, however, anyone who wanted to talk about politics discursively would feel impelled to justify doing so.

Before we discuss those contemporary approaches to political theory which embrace the idea of a science of politics and those approaches which attempt to bring the classical style up to date, it might be worthwhile to consider whether it is useful to study the classics in spite of their defects. While classical political theorists often were not concerned with technical questions of scientific method or with the analysis of sentences, they were quite interested in the substance of public problems. The conceptual distinctions they made are often used by present-day political theorists in the realms of both description and prescription. Further, the political ideals which the classicists expressed are still very much with us today in public debate. Finally, the insights of the classical theorists into the subjective modes of political life form a part of our culture which can never lose relevance as long as conscious human beings live in societies. The Hobbesian description of fear, Rousseau's delineation of the problems of education, and Plato's portrait of the tyrannical man have evoked profound moments of self-recognition for countless people ever since they were written.

The Behavioral Approach

Whenever an American political scientist speaks at length about his work, he will undoubtedly mention something about "behavioralism" or the "behavioral approach." During the quarter century since World War II, a veritable revolution in ideas has taken place in American political science. The external consequences of this revolution can be easily identified by someone with a sharp eye and a knowledge of history. Before World War II, if one had caught sight of a political scientist on campus, one would likely have witnessed him carrying a stack of law books, a sheaf of congressional or administrative reports, or a dusty classical tome. If one had looked at a professional journal of the times, one would have found learned disquisitions on Constitutional rules, sober reports on how to reform administrative agencies, and weighty essays about whether or not Rousseau had contradicted himself. Those were the days when political scientists subscribed to the "institutional" and "historical" approaches. An institutional political scientist studied the formal and legal structures of governmental organs and political parties. He might compare the rules of order in the House of Commons to the rules of order in Congress, or he might argue about the relative merits of proportional representation as opposed to single-member constituencies. The historical political scientist studied the same formal and legal structures, but also examined their similarities and differences over time. He might study the development of the presidency from Washington to Coolidge, or electoral laws in New Hampshire from 1810 to 1910. As you may imagine, political theorists had very little to do with, or say about, the institutional or historical approaches. The work which institutional and historical political scientists did was detailed, fact-oriented, and circumscribed in space and time. It frequentiy demonstrated an ignorance of what was really going on in political life and stressed the examination of written rules. What, then, were political theorists doing at the time? Mainly, they were studying the classics with an eye to determining why the great thinkers had written as they did. The theorists tried to identify the historical circumstances that led Plato to favor an aristocracy of the enlightened over democracy, Rousseau to raiɫ against progress in the arts and sciences, and Hobbes to worry so much about revolution. Those men assumed, of course, that historical circumstances were responsible for the great political theories—an assumption that many argue nearly resuɫted in the death of political theory as a serious and constructive pursuit. In a sense, they were not political theorists at all, but intellectual historians who happened to be interested in political themes.

Today, when one sees a political scientist on a campus, one will likely witness him carrying a ream of computer print-outs, a stack of questionnaires, or a glossy paperback detailing the latest empirical theory of politics. If one looked at a recent professional journal, one would find an array of statistical tables on the relationships between attitudes and voting patterns or cocoa prices and revolutions, discussions of the prerequisites for modernization in the "Third World," and disputes over whether or not systems theories can account for social change. These are external indications that the behavioral approach has been at work. The idea behind these manifestations is much more difficult to expose.

The behavioral approach originated as a reaction against institutional and historical political science. As early as 1925, C. E. Merriam, one of the first behavioralists, said: "Some day we may take another angle of approach than the formal, as other sciences do, and begin to look at political behavior as one of the essential objects of inquiry." In 1953, David Easton, a leader in the behavioral movement, wrote that American political scientists should imitate the "hypercritical Greeks" rather than those who argue, without question, that this is the best of all possible worlds. At the same time, Easton wrote: "The American political scientist is born free but is everywhere in chains, tied to a hyperfactual past. The lack of more reliable knowledge flows directly from an immoderate neglect of general theory." Merriam's statement and Easton's two remarks describe the three major principles of the behavioral approach: political science should be recast on the model of physics, chemistry, and even sociology; political scientists should be concerned with what is actually going on in political life rather than what the rules and laws would lead one to believe should be going on; and political scientists should pay more attention to systematic generalizations. To fully understand what the behavioral approach entails, it is necessary to find out what behavioralists mean by the word "science," what they think is really going on in political life, and what kinds of generalizations they think are important.

Possibly because science is so important in the contemporary world, it is a difficult phenomenon to define. Originally, the word "science" simply meant the condition of knowing rather than the states of feeling or believing. Thus, when people thought that there were objective standards of right and wrong, they could talk about a "moral science" which described these standards, and they could hold up that moral science against opinions or intuitions about right action. In modern times, however, the same relativism which turned people's attention from human nature to identity worked a change in their conception of science. Science no longer was considered knowledge of first principles or absolutes, but became an interrelated system of generalizations about a group of observed phenomena. Usually, this modern conception is what behavioralists mean by a science. Essentially, behavioralists want political scientists to orient their research toward seeking generalizations about human behavior in public affairs which can be tested by observing that behavior. Further, the behavioralists would like to see such generalizations related both to each other and to broader statements so that political science could be considered one coherent body of knowledge. If this account seems vague, it is because behavioralists differ widely on the kinds of generalizations which are important, the definition of public affairs or politics, the appropriate methods of observation, and the bases on which generalizations should be compared. However, they do agree that political scientists should concern themselves with investigating and elaborating descriptive generalizations rather than with formulating prescriptive statements or making factual judgments. They also agree that the descriptive generalizations should be about actual human activities rather than about systems of legal rules or formal administrative procedures.

We can make these points in another way by discussing how behavioralists define their work vis-à-vis the tasks of other, related scholars. Frequently, behavioralists say that moral philosophers should be concerned with making prescriptive statements about human behavior, historians should be concerned with making factual judgments about that behavior, and legal scholars should be concerned with identifying the general characteristics of systems of rules. The political scientist is then left with the task of making and relating descriptive generalizations about human behavior. By no means, however, do all of the scholars concerned agree with the behavioralist's *prescriptive* statement about what they should do.

Despite the behavioralist's concern with purging his work of prescriptive statements, the behavioral revolution did have a moral aspect. Many behavioralists felt that it was wrong (in addition to being "unscientific") for the institutionalists and historicists to study rules while ignoring the power struggles of the real world. Harold Lasswell was particularly influential in directing the attention of political scientists to the study of organized power and its effects on the individual. David Easton devised the definition of politics as "the authoritative allocation of values." He meant that political scientists should study how public goods are actually distributed, rather than how they are supposed to be distributed according to laws and constitutions. Robert Dahl became concerned with investigating how the governments that we call democratic actually work, rather than how they are supposed to work according to textbooks in prescriptive theory. Many behavioralists will say that the investigation and relation of descriptive generalizations about public affairs is a moral activity because such generalizations will provide the information necessary to make intelligent moral decisions.

When we examine the descriptive generalizations that behavioralists make, we find that they vary as much as those in the classics. There are associations of observed variables, statements derived from assumptions about human behavior, and generalizations about the stages of development of political institutions. We find fewer statements about the origins of political institutions, cycles in political life, and generalizations associating changes in one institution with changes in another. Behavioralists often say that the latter kinds of generalizations cannot yet be confidently made because political science is still young.

Clearly, behavioralism is an approach, as we defined the term. It is an attempt to answer the question: Which of the many aspects of public problems are important to explore? The answer is that political scientists should investigate actual human behavior in public life with a view toward making descriptive generalizations about it, and that political theorists should relate these generalizations to one another and suggest new generalizations for further testing. While the idea of a behavioral science of politics has appealed to many political scientists, there are others who do not want to renounce the task of making prescriptive statements, or moral judgments, about public life. They are as diverse as the classicists were, but they are united in sharing a critical attitude toward much of contemporary life.

The Neo-Classical and Critical Approach

In classical political theory we can identify three distinct, but related, enterprises: description, prescription, and criticism. Descriptions are factual or general statements which provide information about what is actually going on in public life, or what the theorist believes is going on. Prescriptions are pronouncements about what should go on in public life, or what the theorist believes should go on. Critical judgments are statements that compare descriptions of public life with prescriptions. They are evaluations of how actual societies measure up to some ideal of a good society. Every critical judgment, thus, contains at least an implicit reference to some state of affairs that is considered desirable. Critical judgments also contain reference to what the critic thinks are the important aspects of what actually exists. Critical judgments need not conclude that the actual state of affairs is bad. If the critic believes that existing public affairs are being conducted in accordance with his principles of right action, he will defend, become an "apologist" for, political reality. What is necessary before criticism can take place is not dissatisfaction, but an ideal of a good society and some information about public life as it is being conducted. Once these prerequisites have been met, critical judgments become almost inevitable. The ideal frees the critic from slavish acceptance of his world as the best of all possible worlds, and it impels him to compare what is to what he thinks ought to be. The existence of criticism is, then, a sign of personal freedom. Without standards of judgment that are independent of the requirements of his social roles, the individual would become lost in a faceless mass. Many contemporary political theorists believe that a loss of such standards has taken place and that the individual is being herded into an ovine flock.

Whether or not this is the case, criticism in general can only be condemned rationally if a person holds neither moral standards nor ideals. And even such a denunciation would betray a moral judgment. Of course, particular critical judgments can provoke reasonable disagreement, either because one does not affirm the implied ideal or because one believes that the description of reality is mistaken. Critical judgments are often associated with practical judgments, which describe measures that the critic believes should be instituted to bring existing reality more into line with the ideal. These measures may range from reform proposals to revolutionary programs. It is obvious that two people may share the same critical judgments about public life and disagree a great deal on practical judgments. Not everybody who deplores private business corporations is a communist, and not everyone who bemoans the "decline" of religion is a conservative.

We may say that we find the classical political theorists interesting today because of their prescriptive statements. Classical thinkers described ideals of the good public life, as well as models of what they believed was the "best possible" public life. Their prescriptions are still very much alive in contemporary political controversy and theory. Clearly, we find the behavioralists, and other political scientists who are concerned with making descriptive generalizations, interesting also because of what they tell us about public life as it is conducted. Those political scientists and political theorists who have resisted behavioralism have tended to concentrate on making critical and practical judgments. They have shown how politics in the contemporary world measures up to a wide variety of social ideals drawn from both classical and modern political theory. They are the writers who have been perhaps most important in defining the problems of identity, organized power, and political change. We find the critics interesting because they aid us in making our own moral judgments, even if they cannot judge for us. In a very significant sense, whether a critic is an apologist, a reformist, or a revolutionary, he contributes to our freedom.

Like the classical theorist, the critic talks about public life in a variety of ways. Even if he does not devise his own prescriptive statements, but adopts them from another political theorist, he must provide good reasons for his choices. In other words, he must be something of a moral philosopher. Even if he does not investigate actual political systems completely, but reviews research reports and journalistic essays, he must justify his regarding of some descriptive generalizations as more important than others. He must be knowledgeable about the scientific approach to the study of public life. Finally, he must, like a judge, determine which standards should be applied to a given description.

The contemporary critics represented in this book each have a social ideal by which they judge existing conditions. Fromm enunciates a vision of a society in which people are no longer ashamed to love one another, and he attempts to show that present industrial societies substitute material consumption and mechanism for love and vitality. Marcuse sees a society in which people can develop creative imagination, and he tries to demonstrate that contemporary industrial societies transform high culture into industry. Camus compares a world of self-determining individuals to a world of bureaucratized automatons. Each of these men is concerned with the tasks of description, prescription, and comparison.

It might appear that the critics differ not at all from the classical thinkers. This is partially true. However, each of the critics has had to confront the challenge of modern science and its emphasis on descriptive statements. The growth of science in general and behavioral political science in particular has exerted the beneficial effect of impelling most modern political theorists to become conscious of the kinds of statements that they make. Whether or not this self-conscious position toward the use of language has resulted in better political theory is debatable. Some political theorists speak about language more than they talk of public life, and this situation itself has led to a great deal of criticism. More important than this debate and the frequent heated exchanges between behavioralists and critics, however, is the fact that both the behavioral and critical approaches flourish and the judgment is that neither of them is likely to disappear in the near future.

A Word About Theory

Thus far, we have discussed the kinds of problems that political theorists treat and the types of approaches that they use to investigate these problems. In the rest of this book, we shall see how the problems of identity, power, and change are dealt with by classical thinkers, behavioralists, and contemporary critics. We shall also see how these problems are treated in terms of psychological, systems, and conflict theories. We have already made brief mention of these three theories, but we have not yet discussed what a theory is. Clarification of this term is necessary before the differing analyses of identity, power, and change can be fully understood.

As was the case with "science," the term "theory" used to have a much less restricted meaning than it does at present. Originally, it simply meant the results of thinking or contemplation. Today, political theorists use the word "theory" in the same way that it is normally employed in modern science. In short, theory most often refers to the fundamental principles by which a set of descriptive generalizations can be related to one another, or to the bases on which a set of prescriptive statements can be justified. Thus, we can talk about descriptive and prescriptive theories. The psychological, systems, and conflict theories discussed here are examples of descriptive theories. They are attempts to relate descriptive generalizations about observed occurrences in public life to even more general statements about the nature of personality, social structure, and human interaction, respectively. For example, a psychological theorist may relate the emergence of revolutionary movements to an increase in the number of people who feel that their lives have been wasted; a systems theorist may relate the emergence of the same revolutionary movements to an increase in the number of unemployed people; while a conflict theorist may relate the emergence of these revolutionary movements to a decline in the bargaining power of certain groups in a society.

Most of the writers represented in this book are also prescriptive theorists. Descriptive theorists, depending upon whether they favor psychological, systems, or conflict theory, tend to define what ought to be in terms of some idea of the healthy personality, an harmonious and well-ordered set of social institutions, and/or an idea of social peace with maximum freedom of action for human beings. Thus, the descriptive and prescriptive theories of a given writer tend to stress the same aspects of public life. Such coherence, however, is not logically necessary. Descriptive psychological theorists, for example, may develop prescriptive theories stressing social peace.

The definition of theory presented here is not the only one used by political theorists. Some writers define a theory as a logically connected set of propositions of increasing generality which explain a body of observed data. Such theorists are using theories in physics and chemistry as their models for a political theory. Unfortunately, logically coherent and empirically verified political theories are matters for the future, if they are ever developed. At present, most political theories are sets of general principles to which descriptive generalizations are related, often in a very loose fashion, or they are general statements about the nature of the right and the good. If we keep this modest point of view in mind, we will be less likely to be disappointed in the works of the writers who appear in this book.

1

Psychological Theories

Since a political theory is supposed to specify a pattern of relationships between a number of observations and generalizations about public life, one of the major problems involved in constructing such a theory is that of deciding upon what principles the relationships should be based. Throughout the history of political theory, a large number of integrating principles have been suggested by various writers, and some of these principles have become so influential that they form part of our common-sense wisdom about politics and public affairs. For example, Marx suggested that much of political behavior could be understood in terms of the ways in which productive goods are owned, while St. Augustine attempted to demonstrate that political activities could be made meaningful by being considered the outcome of an interplay between material greed and religious commitment. Other possible "fundamental principles" quickly occur to any person who takes an interest in public affairs and tries to sort out the frequently confusing statements of officials, politicians, journalists, and friends. Many believe that public affairs are fundamentally a matter of conflicts among racial groups or between the rich and the poor, the depraved and the righteous, nationalists and internationalists, the silent majority and the vocal minority, the independent innovators and the conforming herd, the free souls and the organization men, the young and the old, or the military establishment and civilians. The person who told you yesterday that all problems would be solved if the vocal minority would shut up, today probably claims at the top of his lungs that government bureaucrats are leading the country down the road to ruin. If political theorists have any minimum social task to perform, it is to make some sense out of all of the "absolute principles" that people proclaim from day to day in the public arena.

One way to reduce the multitude of principles supposedly at work in public life to some manageable order is to devise a smaller number of general categories under which these principles can be classified. Political theorists have always attempted such tasks of classification, and the division of this book into psychological, systems, and conflict theories is an effort of this sort. Whether or not one believes that human beings are basically greedy and self-centered, or thinks that they are precious, spontaneous, vital, and loving organisms, he nevertheless finds some basis for affirming that the roots of public life can be discovered in the personality. Whether or not one cherishes the free enterprise system or favors some kind of socialist organization of society, he still encounters reasons to believe that public affairs can best be explained by investigating the dynamics of a social system far more powerful than the particular individuals composing it. Whether or not one thinks that public problems are the result of the hot and cold wars between racial groups or the struggle for power between individuals, he has to consider describing the essence of politics as conflict. The views of psychological, systems, and conflict theorists are persuasive, and each theory helps us organize and understand a large number of the more crude "fundamental principles" of public debate. In fact, the three theories are so persuasive that it is difficult, if not impossible, to determine which one is the most basic. Generally, political theorists commit themselves primarily to one or another of these three views. However, such a commitment is not logically necessary. Some writers attempt to understand public life in terms of "infra-human" principles, or factors which precede what we normally think of as human activities. These writers explain politics by making reference to genetic inheritance, biological instincts, geography, climate, and other such factors. Other theorists try to understand public life in terms of "super-human" principles, or factors which supersede what we usually mean by human activities. Such writers explain politics by making reference to the "will of God," the operation of "fate," the activities of the "world spirit," and other like conceptions. Further, there are "eclectic" political theorists who attempt to combine a variety of principles into their pattern of thought. In this book, we are concerned with political theorists who try to understand public affairs through the development of principles on the human level. These theorists are interested in thinking, feeling, and willing human beings, their relationships, and their works. We are also concerned with writers who are committed rather than eclectic. Of course, in the writings of any significant political theorist there will be elements of the psychological, systems, and conflict points of view. Any emphasis of one of the theoretical perspectives to the exclusion of the other two would result in a bizarre and distorted product of the human mind. However, the most significant political theorists have also usually believed that their particular theoretical commitment was of decisive importance in understanding the others.

Psychological, systems, and conflict theories all have their origins in classical political thought. Indeed, the psychological, systems, and conflict theories of behavioralists and contemporary critics are really commentaries on and refinements of the three classical themes. Three brief quotations from the classical literature in the field will help describe the essentials of each of them. In *The Republic,* Plato described the basic elements of psychological theory. "Do you see, then, that there must be as many types of human character as there are forms of government? Constitutions cannot come out of sticks and stones; they must result from the preponderance of certain characters which draw the rest of the community in their wake. So if there are five forms of government, there must be five kinds of mental constitution among individuals." In other words, Plato said that one can understand what goes on in public life by understanding the personalities of the people involved in it. Further, if we know something about the public life of a community, we can infer the kinds of people who live in that community. That public life is analogous to private life, or even an expression of private life, that the "state is the individual writ large," is the basic proposition of psychological theories of politics.

The fundamental theme of systems theory was expressed by Rousseau in a famous passage in his *Social Contract.* "Man is born free, and everywhere he is in chains. Many a man believes himself to be the master of others who is, no less than they, a slave." Thus, Rousseau believed that the significant aspects of social life are the result of forces beyond any single individual's control. Public life is not analogous to private life; in fact, public life may even condition what goes on in people's heads.

Hobbes expressed the fundamental principle of conflict theory in an equally famous passage in his *Leviathan.* "Hereby it is manifest that, during the time men live without a common power to keep them all in awe, they are in that condition which is called war, and such a war as is of every man against every man. For war consists not in battle only, or the act of fighting, but in a tract of time wherein the will to contend by battle is sufficiently known. . . ." In other words, according to Hobbes, the basic fact of politics is the relationship of conflict between men rather than the expression of individual personalities in public or the domination of human beings by a social system. Social systems are brought into play to alleviate human conflicts, and the desires of individual persons are the raw materials for conflict relations.

The basic unit of psychological theories of public life is what Erich Fromm has called "social character." Fromm believes that the human being is characterized by needs to assimilate things (for example, food) and to socialize with people. These needs existed prior to society, but the forms in which they are satisfied or thwarted depend upon the social structure. "Man in this concept is seen as characterized by his passionate strivings towards objects—men and nature—and his need of relating himself to the world." Social character is formed as a result of the ways in which societies channel the two needs of men. Thus, it is the character structure common to a group of people which is molded *"by any given society so as to be useful for the functioning of that particular society."* The major factor in the formation of social character is, for Fromm, *"the practice of life as it is constituted by the mode of production and the resulting social stratification."* Fromm sees social character as the decisive link between the social structure and the ideas and ideals that characterize a society. Social structures, or ways of organizing human effort, help produce the social character, but the social character also creates ideals which represent its fullest expression. These ideals, in turn, change the social character and may, eventually, change the social structure itself. It is clear that Fromm is not a psychological theorist in the sense that he reduces all public activity to private activity. He begins by specifying two needs which human beings, as individuals, have; he goes on to say that these needs are satisfied or thwarted within social systems; and he ends by stating that the needs and the ways in which they are directed create a social character. Fromm remarks that the average person must want to do what he has to do if he is to function in a socially acceptable way. Social character represents the personal justification for doing what society demands.

Harold Lasswell's concept of "character" is much the same as Fromm's idea of social character. For Lasswell, character means *"the self-system of the person, together with the degree of support, opposition or nonsupport received from the unconscious parts of the personality."* Character is the product of the treatment which a person receives within the family during his early years. Since family relations vary between cultures, the content of character varies similarly. For example, if a child's desires are frustrated often enough during his first few years of life, he will come to expect very little from others and will be unwilling to freely cooperate with others in collective endeavors. As an adult, however, he may not even be aware of his low expectations and inability to cooperate. His "self-system," or idea of himself, may, indeed, include the ideas that others are generous and that it is good to help others out. Nevertheless, while he has forgotten or repressed his early frustrations, they are still active in his personality, preventing him from exercising authentic trust or giving voluntary aid. Lasswell believes that the level of frustration which individuals experience in childhood is a major factor in determining whether or not democratic politics can arise in a society. Suspicious and self-centered people, he feels, cannot tolerate the risks and ambiguities of a democracy. Lasswell, like Fromm, considers character to be a necessary link between ideals and social structures. However, while Fromm thinks that the way in which production is organized is of major importance in determining social character, Lasswell believes that the institution of the family is decisive in conditioning character. These differences are insignificant when similarities between the concepts of social character and character are considered.

Plato, of course, was the first theorist to emphasize the importance of character as a concept through which public life could be made meaningful. Like Lasswell and Fromm, he believed that there was a preponderance of "democratic men" in democracies, "oligarchic men" in oligarchies, and so on down the list of possible forms of government. He also held that the structure of government influenced the content of social character, and that social character, in turn, intensified the significant aspects of the regime. For Plato, the determining factor in shaping social character was more general than the mode of production or the relationships within the family. Plato thought that the kinds of values which the community sought and the way in which these values were distributed to individuals were of decisive importance in conditioning social character. For example, a community committed to the values of military honor and conquest would be characterized by men of quick spirit and daring who would also be subject to the temptations of wine, women, and song. In other words, a military state would be truly a community of soldiers. A community devoted to business and trading would be characterized by selfish and wasteful men who would ignore the needs of the society upon which they depended for their affluence.

There is an ambiguity within psychological theories which you may already have noticed. While the basic unit of these theories is social character, social character itself is not independent of systems of social relations. Psychological theorists have always had the problem of figuring out how much the individual contributes to his personality and how much the society contributes. A further problem has been deciding how much individual initiatives can influence the operation of social systems. Frequently, psychological theorists sound like systems theorists, especially when they say that social character is "molded" by one or another institution. However, they remain different from other theorists in their concern with the idea of character, which is primarily a psychological concept, or a distinction within the realm of personality. Whatever its origins, social character belongs to individuals. They may conform to its standards or rebel against it in a variety of ways, but they must in some way come to terms with it because it is part of them. Social character is essentially that part of your personality which you gain from living with others. Some think that it forms the whole of the personality, others believe that it is merely a facade, and still others think that it is controlling in some contexts and inoperative in others.

Social character should not be confused with identity, which refers to the characteristics which make one a specific person. Identity includes both the similarities and differences between one individual and others. It is bound up with the feeling that one knows who he is as a definite person. Identity also refers to those aspects of the personality which are most significant for the individual. If the person is most concerned with being a good Christian or Jew, for example, his identity will be concentrated in that role, and the fact that he may shine shoes for a living will not be of great significance. Social character, on the other hand, refers to that part of the personality which an individual has in common with the other members of his group. One's social character may form a part of one's identity, in some cases it may become indistinguishable from one's identity (as in the case of a compulsive conformist), or it may be actively repudiated by the individual in search of self-definition. If a variety of social characters are available in a community, the individual may have an opportunity to choose among them. In any case, the concept of social character developed by the psychological theorists is of great importance in clarifying the problem of identity as we discussed it earlier. One of the primary reasons why the "identity crisis" has become a theme of contemporary civilization is the fact that many people are finding their social characters unsatisfactory. They do not want to be *homo consumens* or *homo mechanicus,* as Fromm calls the man devoted to consuming material goods and the man devoted to worshiping the power of technology respectively. Most people would rather have the open, confident, flexible, and dynamic self which Lasswell calls "democratic," than the suspicious, uncertain, rigid, and stagnant self which their parents, teachers, employers, and friends seem to want to force upon them. They would prefer the rational persuasion which Plato advocates for solving social problems over the force and fraud of Plato's tyrannical man and the power-hungry people they see around them. It seems that when one's social character satisfies him he may not even realize that it has a social aspect. It will be so comfortable that he thinks of it as his own. It is when people become disturbed with their social characters that they begin to define the term and understand that they might be different from what their social roles require. They begin to distinguish between their precious, and often only possible, identities, and the social characters which disgust them. They believe that this distinction is profound and, perhaps, the most basic distinction that can be made in human life. They contrast identity and social character as irreconcilable opposites. None of the psychological theorists believe that such an opposition is desirable or possible. The theorists would say that the individual can develop his unique qualities fully only after he has gained a satisfying social character. Thus, it should not be so much a matter of abolishing social roles as a task of developing social roles which people consider significant and worthy of them. Why people have become so dissatisfied with their social characters is one of the major questions which contemporary psychological theorists discuss—and which a classicist like Plato can also treat in a relevant manner.

PLATO

Plato's writings represent the classical approach to a psychological theory of public affairs. Plato was born in Athens in 427 B.C., a time when that city-state was about to undergo a long period of social disorganization and political change. He was brought up in an aristocratic environment, and as he grew up he witnessed the eclipse of the values which he had been taught to revere. It is often the case that political theories arise when the assumptions about public life that people take for granted are challenged in the realm of doctrine or in the sphere of action. A person who discovers that the individuals around him do not share his point of view, or that political affairs are being conducted to secure values to which he is not committed, may respond to the new information in several ways. He may change his commitments and align himself with the new patterns of thought and action. Young people today often suggest that their elders should follow this course. However, almost everybody is aware of the many difficulties involved in attempting to change a way of life that has become almost habitual. Further, the person may pretend that the world has not really changed. This is perhaps the most common response, and it is one that is fraught with tragedy. Third, the person may continue to adhere to his former commitments, but in a conscious and critical manner. He will say that the essential principles of the old way of life are still viable, but that their application to particular circumstances must be altered. Finally, the individual may work out a novel commitment which is fully aligned neither with the movements of change nor with the life of the past. This is probably the most difficult response, but it is the one that people in search of an identity most prefer. Essentially, Plato responded to the decline of Athenian aristocracy by adhering to the principles of his upbringing but drastically altering their application to the point that his doctrine could be considered novel.

Plato believed that a good society must be governed by an aristocracy. However, he thought that the older aristocracies of birth, military prowess, and wealth could not be rationally defended. He came to the conclusion that only an aristocracy of wisdom, i.e., rule by a group of people trained and competent in the "science" of statecraft, had the moral right to administer the affairs of an entire community. Thus, for Plato, the good of a community could be known by those who had the native capacity and the proper training to understand it. He did not make a sharp distinction between prescriptive and descriptive statements. The principles of Plato's science were psychological, in that the rulers would work directly with individuals, rather than through the mediation of social structures. The aristocracy would be composed of engineers of the soul. "This, then, is the end, let us declare, of the web of the statesman's activity, the direct interweaving of the characters of restrained and courageous men. . . ." Contemporary supporters of a government of scientific experts owe a great deal to Plato's early venture. They, too, believe that the social good can be known descriptively and that a good society can be brought about only if psychological conditioning or therapy is substituted for force.

Identity*

Do you know, I said, that governments vary as the dispositions of men vary, and that there must be as many of the one as there are of the other? Or do you suppose that States spring from "oak and rock," and not from the human natures which are in them, and as it were, turn the scale and draw other things after them?

By no means, he said, they can spring from no other source.

Then if the constitutions of States are five, the dispositions of individual minds will also be five?

Certainly.

Must we not then infer that the individual is wise in the same way and in virtue of the same quality which makes the State wise!

Certainly.

Also that the State is brave in the same way and by the same quality as an individual is brave, and that there is the same correspondence in regard to the other virtues?

Assuredly.

Therefore the individual will be acknowledged by us to be just in the same way in which the State has been found just?

That follows of course.

We cannot but remember that the justice of the State consisted in each of the three classes doing the work of its own class?

I do not think we have forgotten, he said.

*Pages 33-45 from *The Dialogues of Plato,* trans. Benjamin Jowett, 4th ed., 1953, vol. 2. Reprinted by permission of the Clarendon Press, Oxford, pp. 296-300, 332-333, 409, 430-440. Material from *The Statesman,* on pages 45-51, reprinted by permission of the publishers and *The Loeb Classical Library* from Plato, *The Statesman,* trans. H.N. Fowler (Cambridge, Mass.: Harvard University Press), pp. 175-195.

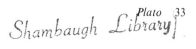

We must now record in our memory that the individual in whom the several components of his nature do their own work will be just, and will do his own work?

Yes, he said, we must record that important fact.

First, it is proper for the rational principle, which is wise, and has the care of the whole soul, to rule, and for the spirit to be the subject and ally?

Certainly.

And, as we were saying, the blending of music and gymnastic will bring them into accord, nerving and sustaining the reason with noble words and lessons, and moderating and soothing and civilizing the wildness of passion by harmony and rhythm?

Quite true, he said.

And these two, thus nurtured and educated, and having learned truly to know their own functions, will rule over the concupiscent, which in each of us is the largest part of the soul and by nature most insatiable of gain; over this they will keep guard, lest, waxing great and strong with the full-ness of bodily pleasures, as they are termed, the concupiscent soul, no longer confined to her own sphere, should attempt to enslave and rule those who are not her natural-born subjects, and overturn the whole life of man?

Very true, he said.

Both together will they not be the best defenders of the whole soul and the whole body against attacks from without; the one counselling, and the other going out to fight as the leader directs, and courageously executing his commands and counsels?

True.

Likewise it is by reference to spirit that an individual man is deemed courageous, because his spirit retains in pleasure and in pain the com-mands of reason about what he ought or ought not to fear?

Right, he replied.

And we call him wise on account of that little part which rules, and which proclaims these commands; the part in which is situated the knowl-edge of what is for the interest of each of the three parts and of the whole?

Assuredly.

And would you not say that he is temperate who has these same ele-ments in friendly harmony, in whom the one ruling principle of reason, and the two subject ones of spirit and desire, are equally agreed that rea-son ought to rule, and do not rebel?

Certainly, he said, that is a precise account of temperance whether in the State or individual.

And, finally, I said, a man will be just in that way and by that quality which we have often mentioned.

That is very certain.

And is justice dimmer in the individual, and is her form different, or is she the same which we found her to be in the State?

There is no difference in my opinion, he said.

Because, if any doubt is still lingering in our minds, a few commonplace instances will satisfy us of the truth of what I am saying.

What sort of instances do you mean?

If the case is put to us, must we not admit that the just State, or the man of similar nature who has been trained in the principles of such a State, will be less likely than the unjust to make away with a deposit of gold or silver? Would any one deny this?

No one, he replied.

Will such a man ever be involved in sacrilege or theft, or treachery either to his friends or to his country?

Never.

Neither will he ever, for any reason, break faith where there have been oaths or agreements?

Impossible.

No one will be less likely to commit adultery, neglect his father and mother, or fail in his religious duties?

No one.

And the reason for all this is that each part of him is doing its own business, whether in ruling or being ruled?

Exactly so.

Are you satisfied then that the quality which makes such men and such states is justice, or do you hope to discover some other?

Not I, indeed.

Then our dream has been realized, and the suspicion which we expressed that, at the beginning of our work of construction, some divine power must have conducted us to a primary form of justice, has now been verified?

Yes, certainly.

And the division of labor which required the carpenter and the shoemaker and the rest of them to devote himself to the work for which he is naturally fitted, and to do nothing else, was a shadow of justice, and for that reason it was of use?

Clearly.

And in reality justice was such as we were describing, being concerned however, not with a man's external affairs, but with an inner relationship in which he himself is more truly concerned; for the just man does not permit the several elements within him to interfere with one another, or any of them to do the work of others—he sets in order his own inner life, and is his own master and his own law, and at peace with himself; and when he has bound together the three principles within him, which may be compared to the higher, lower, and middle notes of the scale, and any that are intermediate between them—when he has bound all these together, and is no longer many, but has become one entirely temperate and perfectly adjusted nature, then he proceeds to act, if he has to act, whether in a matter of property, or in the treatment of the body, or in some affair of politics or private business; always thinking and calling that which preserves and cooperates with this harmonious condition, just and good action, and the knowledge which presides over it, wisdom, and that which at any time impairs this condition, he will call unjust action, and the opinion which presides over it ignorance.

You have said that exact truth, Socrates.

Very good; and if we were to affirm that we had discovered the just man and the just State, and the nature of justice in each of them, we should not be far from the truth?

Most certainly not.

May we say so, then?

Let us say so.

And now, I said, injustice has to be considered.

Clearly.

Must not injustice be a strife which arises among the same three principles—a meddlesomeness, and interference, and rising up of a part of the soul against the whole, an assertion of unlawful authority, which is made by a rebellious subject against a true prince, of whom he is the natural vassal—what is all this confusion and delusion but injustice and intemperance and cowardice and ignorance, and, in short, every form of vice?

Exactly so.

And if the nature of justice and injustice is known, then the meaning of acting unjustly and being unjust, or again of acting justly, is now also perfectly clear?

How so? he said.

Why, I said, they are like disease and health; being in the soul just what disease and health are in the body.

How so? he said.

Why, I said, that which is healthy causes health, and that which is unhealthy causes disease.

Yes.

And just actions cause justice, and unjust actions cause injustice?

That is certain.

And the creation of health is the institution of a natural order and government of one by another in the parts of the body; and the creation of disease is the production of a state of things at variance with this natural order?

True.

And is not the creation of justice the institution of a natural order and government of one by another in the parts of the soul, and the creation of injustice the production of a state of things at variance with the natural order?

Exactly so, he said.

Then virtue is the health and beauty and well-being of the soul, and vice the disease and weakness and deformity of the same?

True.

And how are virtue and vice acquired—is it not by good and evil practices?

Assuredly.

The time has come, then, to answer the final question of the comparative advantage of justice and injustice: Which is the more profitable, to be just and act justly and honorably, whether one's character is or is not known, or to be unjust and act unjustly, if one is unpunished, that is to say unreformed?

In my judgment, Socrates, the question has now become ridiculous. We know that, when the bodily constitution is gone, life is no longer endurable, though pampered with all kinds of meats and drinks, and having all wealth and all power; and shall we be told that when the natural health of our vital principle is undermined and corrupted, life is still worth having to a man, if only he be allowed to do whatever he likes, except to take steps to acquire justice and virtue and escape from injustice and vice; assuming them both to be such as we have described!

Yes, I said, the question is, as you say, ridiculous . . . . .

Power

Last of all comes the most beautiful of all, man and State alike, tyranny and the tyrant; these we have now to consider.

Quite true, he said.

Say then, my friend, what do we find the character of tyranny to be?—that it has a democratic origin is evident.

Clearly.

And does not tyranny spring from democracy in the same manner, so to speak, as democracy from oligarchy?

How?

The good which oligarchy proposed to itself and the object for which it was established was wealth—am I not right?

Yes.

Thus, the insatiable desire of wealth and the neglect of all other things for the sake of money-getting was also the ruin of oligarchy?

True.

And democracy also is brought to dissolution by an insatiable desire for that which she designates as good?

What do you suppose that to be?

Freedom, I replied; which, as they tell you in a democracy, is the glory of the State—and that therefore in a democracy alone will the freeman of nature deign to dwell.

Yes; the saying is in everybody's mouth.

To return, then, to the question I was going to ask: is it true that the insatiable desire of this good, and the neglect of other things, introduces change in this constitution also, and occasions a demand for tyranny?

How so?

When a democracy which has begun to thirst for freedom has evil cup-bearers presiding over the feast, and has drunk too deeply of the strong wine of freedom, then, unless her rulers are very amenable and give a plentiful draught, she calls them to account and punishes them, and says that they are cursed oligarchs.

Yes, he replied, a very common occurrence.

Yes, I said; and men who obey their rulers are insultingly termed by her slaves who hug their chains and men of naught; she would have subjects who are like rulers, and rulers who are like subjects: these are men after her own heart, whom she praises and honors both in private and public. Now, in such a State, can there be anything to stop the progress of liberty?

Certainly not.

By degrees the anarchy must find a way into private houses, and end by getting among the animals and infecting them?

How do you mean?

I mean that the father grows accustomed to descend to the level of his sons and to fear them, and the son is on a level with his father; he shows no respect or reverence for either of his parents, such being his notion of freedom. And the metic is equal with the citizen and the citizen with the metic, and the stranger is quite as good as either.

Yes, he said, that is the way.

And these are not the only evils, I said—there are several lesser ones: In such a state of society the master fears and flatters his scholars, and the scholars despise their masters and their tutors also; young and old are all alike; and the young man is on a level with the old, and is ready to compete with him in word or deed; and old men condescend to the young and are full of pleasantry and gaiety; they are loath to be thought morose and authoritative, and therefore they adopt the manners of the young.

Quite true, he said.

But the last extreme of popular liberty is when the slave bought with money, whether male or female, is just as free as his or her purchaser; nor must I forget to tell of the liberty and equality of the two sexes in relation to each other.

Why not, as Aeschylus says, utter the word which rises to our lips?

That is what I am doing, I replied; and I must add that no one who does not know would believe how much greater is the liberty which the animals who are under the dominion of man have in a democracy than in any other State: for truly, the she-dogs, as the proverb says, are as good as their she-mistresses, and the horses and asses have a way of marching along with all the rights and dignities of freemen; and they will run at any body who comes in their way if he does not leave the road clear for them: and all things are just ready to burst with liberty.

When I am on my way to the country, he said, I often experience what you describe. You and I have dreamed the same thing.

And above all, I said, and as the result of all, see how sensitive the citizens become; they chafe impatiently at the least touch of authority, and at length, as you know, they cease to care even for the laws, written or unwritten; they will have no master over them at all.

Yes, he said, I know it too well.

Such, my friend, I said, is the fair and glorious beginning out of which springs tyranny.

Glorious indeed, he said. But what is the next step?

The ruin of oligarchy is the ruin of democracy; the same disease magnified and intensified by liberty overmasters democracy—the truth being that the excessive increase of anything often causes a reaction in the opposite direction; and this is the case not only in the seasons and in vegetable and animal life, but above all in forms of government.

True.

The excess of liberty, whether in States or individuals, seems only to pass into excess of slavery.

Yes, the natural order.

And so it is from democracy, and from no other source, that tyranny naturally arises, and the harshest and most complete form of tyranny and slavery out of the most extreme form of liberty?

As we might expect, he said.

That, however, was not, as I believe, your question—you rather desired to know what is the disorder which is generated alike in oligarchy and democracy, and is the ruin of both?

Just so, he said.

Well, I said, I meant to refer to the class of idle spendthrifts, of whom the more courageous are the leaders and the more timid the followers, the same whom we compare to drones, some stingless, and others having stings.

A very just comparison.

These two classes create disturbance in every city in which they are generated, being what phlegm and bile are to the body. And the good physician and lawgiver of the State ought, like the wise beemaster, to keep them at a distance and prevent, if possible, their ever coming in; and if they have anyhow found a way in, then he should have them and their cells cut out as speedily as possible.

Yes, by all means, he said.

Then, in order that we may obtain a more distinct view of our subject, let us imagine democracy to be divided, as indeed it is, into three classes; for in the first place freedom creates rather more drones in the democratic than there were in the oligarchical State.

That is true.

And in the democracy they are certainly more aggressive.

How so?

Because in the oligarchical State they are disqualified and driven from office, and therefore they cannot train or gather strength; whereas in a democracy they are almost the entire ruling power, and while the keener sort speak and act, the rest keep buzzing about the bema and do not suffer a word to be said on the other side; hence in democracies almost everything is managed by the drones.

Very true, he said.

Then there is another class which is always being severed from the mass.

What is that?

Those who are most orderly by nature—a class, which in a nation of traders is sure to be the richest.

Naturally so.

They are the most squeezable persons and yield the largest amount of honey to the drones.

Why, yes, he said, there is little to be squeezed out of people who have little.

And this is called the wealthy class, and is the food of the drones.

That is pretty much the case, he said.

The people are a third class, consisting of those who work with their own hands; they are not politicians, and have not much to live upon. This, when assembled, is the largest and most powerful class in a democracy.

True, he said; but then the multitude is seldom willing to congregate unless they get a little honey.

But then they do share, I said, in so far as their leaders can deprive the rich of their estates and distribute them among the people; at the same time taking care to reserve the larger part for themselves.

Why, yes, he said, to that extent the people do share.

And the persons whose property is taken from them are compelled to defend themselves by speech before the people and by action as they best can?

What else can they do?

And then, although they may have no desire of change, the others charge them with plotting against the people and being friends of oligarchy?

True.

And the end is that when they see the people, not of their own accord, but through ignorance and because they are deceived by informers, seeking to do them wrong, then at last they are forced to become oligarchs in reality; they do not wish to be, but the sting of the drones torments them and breeds revolution in them.

That is exactly the truth.

Then come impeachments and judgments and trials of one another.

True.

The people have always some champion whom they are wont to set over them and nurse into greatness.

Yes, that is their way.

So much then is clear, that whenever tyranny appears, the protectorship of the people is the root from which it springs.

Yes, that is quite clear.

How then does a protector begin to change into a tyrant? Clearly when he begins to do what the man is said to do in the tale of the Arcadian temple of Lycaean Zeus.

What tale?

The tale is that he who has tasted the entrails of a single human victim minced up with the entrails of other victims is destined to become a wolf. Did you never hear it?

O yes.

And the protector of the people is like him; having a mob entirely at his disposal, he is not restrained from shedding the blood of kinsmen; by the favorite method of false accusation he brings them into court and murders them, making the life of man to disappear, and with unholy tongue and lips tasting the blood of his fellow citizens; some he kills and others he banishes, at the same time hinting at the abolition of debts and partition of lands: and after this, what will be his destiny? Must he not either perish at the hands of his enemies, or from being a man become a wolf — that is, a tyrant?

Inevitably.

This, I said, is he who forms a party against the owners of property.

The same.

After a while he is driven out, but comes back, in spite of his enemies, a tyrant full grown.

That is clear.

And if they are unable to expel him, or to get him condemned to death by a public accusation, they conspire to assassinate him secretly.

Yes, he said, that is their usual way.

Then comes the famous request for a bodyguard, which is the device of all those who have got thus far in their tyrannical career — "Let not the people's friend," as they say, "be lost to them."

Exactly.

The people readily assent; probably because all their fears are for him — they have none for themselves.

Very true.

And when a man who is wealthy and is also accused of being an enemy of the people sees this, then, my friend, as the oracle said to Croesus,

By pebbly Hermus' shore he flees and rests not, and is not ashamed to be a coward.[1]

And quite right too, said he, for if he were, he would never be ashamed again.

But if he is caught he dies.

Of course.

And he, the protector of whom we spoke, is to be seen, not "larding the plain" with his bulk, but himself the overthrower of many, standing up in the chariot of State with the reins in his hand, no longer protector, but tyrant absolute.

No doubt, he said.

And now let us consider the happiness of the man, and also of the State in which a creature like him is generated.

Yes, he said, let us consider that.

At first, in the early days of his power, he is full of smiles, and he salutes every one whom he meets; — he to be called a tyrant, who is making promises in public and also in private! releasing men from their debts, and distributing land to the people and his followers, and professing to be so gracious and kind to every one!

Of course, he said.

But when he has disposed of foreign enemies by conquest or treaty, and there is nothing to fear from them, then he is always stirring up some war or other, in order that the people may require a leader.

To be sure.

Has he not also another object, which is that they may be impoverished by payment of taxes, and thus compelled to devote themselves to their daily wants and therefore less likely to conspire against him?

Clearly.

And if any of them are suspected by him of having such notions of freedom as may make them rebellious to his authority, he will have a good pretext for destroying them by placing them at the mercy of the enemy; and for all these reasons the tyrant must be always getting up a war.

He must.

Now he begins to grow unpopular.

A necessary result.

Then some of those who joined in setting him up, and who are in power, speak their minds to him and to one another, and the more courageous of them cast in his teeth what is being done.

---

[1] Herod. i. 55.

Yes, that may be expected.

And the tyrant, if he means to rule, must get rid of them all; he cannot stop while he has a friend or an enemy who is good for anything.

He cannot.

And therefore he must look about him and see who is valiant, who is high-minded, who is wise, who is wealthy; happy man, he must be the enemy of them all, and must plot their destruction whether he will or no, until he has made a purgation of the State.

Yes, he said, and a rare purgation.

Yes, I said, not the sort of purgation which the physicians make of the body; for they take away the worse and leave the better part, but he does the reverse.

If he is to rule, I suppose that he cannot help himself.

What a blessed alternative, I said: — to be compelled to dwell only with the many bad and to be by them hated, or not to live at all!

Yes, that is the alternative.

And the more detestable such actions make him to the citizens the more satellites and the greater devotion in them will he require?

Certainly.

And who are the devoted band, and where will he procure them?

They will flock to him, he said, of their own accord, if he pays them.

By the dog! I said, you seem to foresee a new invasion of drones, of every sort and from every land.

Yes, he said, and I am right.

But whom will he enlist on the spot? Will he not be ready —

To do what?

To rob the citizens of their slaves, and set them free and enroll them in his bodyguard?

To be sure, he said; and he will be able to trust them best of all.

What a blessed creature, I said, must this tyrant be, if he has put to death the others and has these for his trusted friends.

Why, yes, he said; these are really the kind of men he employs.

Yes, I said, and these new citizens whom he has called into existence admire him and are his companions, while the good hate and avoid him.

Of course.

So it is not without reason that tragedy is reputed a wise thing and Euripides a great tragedian.

Why so?

Why, because he is the author of the pregnant saying,

Tyrants are wise by living with the wise;

and he clearly meant to say that they are the wise whom the tyrant makes his companions.

Yes, he said, and he also praises tyranny as godlike; and many other things of the same kind are said by him and by the other poets.

And therefore, I said, the tragic poets being wise men will forgive us and any others who live after our manner if we do not receive them into our State, because they are the eulogists of tyranny.

Yes, he said, those who have the wit will doubtless forgive us.

But they will continue to go to other cities and attract mobs, and hire voices fair and loud and persuasive, and draw the cities over to tyrannies and democracies.

Very true.

Moreover, they are paid for this and receive honor—the greatest honor, as might be expected, from tyrants, and the next greatest from democracies; but the higher they ascend our constitution hill, the more their reputation fails, and seems unable from shortness of breath to proceed further.

True.

But we are wandering from the subject: let us therefore return and inquire how the tyrant will maintain that fair and numerous and various and ever changing army of his.

Evidently, he said, if there are sacred treasures in the city, he will confiscate and spend them; and in so far as the fortunes of his victims may suffice, he will be able to diminish the taxes which he would otherwise have to impose upon the people.

And when these fail?

Why, clearly, he said, then he and his boon companions, whether male or female, will be maintained out of his father's estate.

You mean to say that the people, from whom he has derived his being, will maintain him and his companions?

Yes, he said; they will be obliged to do so.

But what if the people fly into a passion, and aver that a grown-up son ought not to be supported by his father, but that the father should be supported by the son! The father did not bring him into being, or settle him in life, in order that when his son became a man he should himself be the servant of his own servants and should support him and his rabble of slaves and companions; but that his son should protect him, and that by his help he might be emancipated from the government of the rich and aristocratic, as they are termed. And so he bids him and his companions depart, just as any other father might drive out of the house a riotous son and his undesirable associates.

By heaven, he said, then the parent will discover what a monster he has been fostering in his bosom; and, when he wants to drive him out, he will find that he is weak and his son strong.

Why, you do not mean to say that the tyrant will use violence? What! beat his father if he opposes him?

Yes, he will, having first disarmed him.

Then he is a parricide, and a cruel guardian of an aged parent; and this is real tyranny, about which there can be no longer a mistake: as the saying is, the people who would escape the smoke which is the slavery of freemen, has fallen into the fire which is the tyranny of slaves. And instead of that abundant and ill-timed liberty, it puts on the harshest and bitterest form of slavery, that is, slavery to slaves.

That, he said, is indeed what happens.

Very well; and may we not rightly say that we have sufficiently discussed the manner of the transition from democracy to tyranny? and the nature of tyranny when it has come into being.

Yes, quite enough, he said . . . .

Change

I said: Until philosophers are kings in their cities, or the kings and princes of this world have the spirit and power of philosophy, and political greatness and wisdom meet in one, and those commoner natures who pursue either to the exclusion of the other are compelled to stand aside, cities will never have rest from their evils,—no, nor the human race, as I believe,—and then only will this our ideal State have a possibility of life and behold the light of day. Such was the thought, my dear Glaucon, which I would fain have uttered if it had not seemed too extravagant; for to be convinced that in no other State can there be happiness private or public is indeed a hard thing. . . .

STRANGER. It has, apparently, become necessary, after all, to explain a difficult matter.

YOUNG SOCRATES. But certainly the explanation must be made.

STRANGER. It is difficult, for the assertion that one part of virtue is in a way at variance with another sort of virtue may very easily be assailed by those who appeal to popular opinion in contentious arguments.

YOUNG SOCRATES. I do not understand.

STRANGER. I will say it again in another way. I suppose you believe that courage is one part of virtue.

YOUNG SOCRATES. Certainly.

STRANGER. And, of course, that self-restraint is different from courage, but is also a part of virtue of which courage is a part.

YOUNG SOCRATES. Yes.

STRANGER. Now I must venture to utter a strange doctrine about them.

YOUNG SOCRATES. What is it?

STRANGER. That, in a way, they are in a condition of great hostility and opposition to each other in many beings.

YOUNG SOCRATES. What do you mean?

STRANGER. Something quite unusual; for, you know, all the parts of virtue are usually said to be friendly to one another.

YOUNG SOCRATES. Yes.

STRANGER. Now shall we pay careful attention and see whether this is so simple, or, quite the contrary, there is in some respects a variance between them and their kin?

YOUNG SOCRATES. Yes; please tell how we shall investigate the question.

STRANGER. Among all the parts we must look for those which we call excellent but place in two opposite classes.

YOUNG SOCRATES. Say more clearly what you mean.

STRANGER. Acuteness and quickness, whether in body or soul or vocal utterance, whether they are real or exist in such likenesses as music and graphic art produce in imitation of them—have you never yourself praised one of them or heard them praised by others?

YOUNG SOCRATES. Yes, of course.

STRANGER. And do you remember in what way they praise them as occasion offers?

YOUNG SOCRATES. Not in the least.

STRANGER. I wonder if I can express to you in words what I have in mind.

YOUNG SOCRATES. Why not?

STRANGER. You seem to think that is an easy thing to do. However, let us consider the matter as it appears in the opposite classes. For example, when we admire, as we frequently do in many actions, quickness and energy and acuteness of mind or body or even of voice, we express our praise of them by one word, courage.

YOUNG SOCRATES. How so?

STRANGER. We say acute and courageous in the first instance, also quick and courageous, and energetic and courageous; and when we apply this word as a common term applicable to all persons and actions of this class, we praise them.

YOUNG SOCRATES. Yes, we do.

STRANGER. But do we not also praise the gentle type of movement in many actions?

YOUNG SOCRATES. We do, decidedly.

STRANGER. And in doing so, do we not say the opposite of what we said about the other class?

YOUNG SOCRATES. How is that?

STRANGER. We are always saying "How quiet!" and "How restrained!" when we are admiring the workings of the mind, and again we speak of actions as slow and gentle, of the voice as smooth and deep, and of every rhythmic motion and of music in general as having appropriate slowness; and we apply to them all the term which signifies, not courage, but decorum.

YOUNG SOCRATES. Very true.

STRANGER. And again, on the other hand, when these two classes seem to us out of place, we change our attitude and blame them each in turn; then we use the terms in the opposite sense.

YOUNG SOCRATES. How is that?

STRANGER. Why, whatsoever is sharper than the occasion warrants, or seems to be too quick or too hard, is called violent or mad, and whatever is too heavy or slow or gentle, is called cowardly and sluggish; and almost always we find that the restraint of one class of qualities and the courage of the opposite class, like two parties arrayed in hostility to each other, do not mix with each other in the actions that are concerned with such qualities. Moreover, if we pursue the inquiry, we shall see that the men who have these qualities in their souls are at variance with one another.

YOUNG SOCRATES. In what do you mean that they are at variance?

STRANGER. In all those points which we just mentioned, and probably in many others. For men who are akin to each class, I imagine, praise some qualities as their own and find fault with those of their opposites as alien to themselves, and thus great enmity arises between them on many grounds.

YOUNG SOCRATES. Yes, that is likely to be the case.

STRANGER. Now this opposition of these two classes is mere child's play; but when it affects the most important matters it becomes a most detestable disease in the state.

YOUNG SOCRATES. What matters does it affect?

STRANGER. The whole course of life, in all probability. For those who are especially decorous are ready to live always a quiet and retired life and to mind their own business; this is the manner of their intercourse with everyone at home, and they are equally ready at all times to keep peace in some way or other with foreign states. And because of this desire of theirs, which is often inopportune and excessive, when they have their own way they quite unconsciously become unwarlike, and they make the young men unwarlike also; they are at the mercy of aggressors; and thus in a few years they and their children and the whole state often pass by imperceptible degrees from freedom to slavery.

YOUNG SOCRATES. That is a hard and terrible experience.

STRANGER. But how about those who incline toward courage? Do they not constantly urge their countries to war, because of their excessive desire for a warlike life? Do they not involve them in hostilities with many powerful opponents and either utterly destroy their native lands or enslave and subject them to their foes?

YOUNG SOCRATES. Yes, that is true, too.

STRANGER. Then in these examples how can we deny that these two classes are always filled with the greatest hostility and opposition to one another?

YOUNG SOCRATES. We certainly cannot deny it.

STRANGER. Have we not, then, found just what we had in view in the beginning, that important parts of virtue are by nature at variance with one another and also that the persons who possess them exhibit the same opposition?

YOUNG SOCRATES. Yes, I suppose that is true.

STRANGER. Let us then take up another question.

YOUNG SOCRATES. What question?

STRANGER. Whether any constructive science voluntarily composes any, even the most worthless, of its works out of good and bad materials, or every science invariably rejects the bad, so far as possible, taking only the materials which are good and fitting, out of which, whether they be like or unlike, it gathers all elements together and produces one form or value.

YOUNG SOCRATES. The latter, of course.

STRANGER. Then neither will the true natural art of statecraft ever voluntarily compose a state of good and bad men; but obviously it will first test them in play, and after the test will entrust them in turn to those who are able to teach and help them to attain the end in view; it will itself give orders and exercise supervision, just as the art of weaving constantly commands and supervises the carders and others who prepare the materials for its web, directing each person to do the tasks which it thinks are requisite for its fabric.

YOUNG SOCRATES. Certainly.

STRANGER. In the same way I think the kingly art, keeping for itself the function of supervision, will not allow the duly appointed teachers and foster fathers to give any training, unless they can thereby produce characters suitable to the constitution it is creating, but in these things only it exhorts them to give instruction. And those men who have no capacity for courage and self-restraint and the other qualities which tend toward virtue, but by the force of an evil nature are carried away into godlessness, violence, and injustice, it removes by inflicting upon them the punishments of death and exile and deprivation of the most important civic rights.

YOUNG SOCRATES. That is about what people say, at any rate.

STRANGER. And those in turn who wallow in ignorance and craven humility it places under the yoke of slavery.

YOUNG SOCRATES. Quite right.

STRANGER. As for the rest of the people, those whose natures are capable, if they get education, of being made into something fine and noble and of uniting with each other as art requires, the kingly art takes those natures which tend more toward courage, considering that their character is sturdier, like the warp in weaving, and those which incline toward decorum, for these, to continue the simile, are spun thick and soft like the threads of the woof, and tries to combine these natures of opposite tendencies and weave them together in the following manner.

YOUNG SOCRATES. In what manner?

STRANGER. First it binds the eternal part of their souls with a divine bond, to which that part is akin, and after the divine it binds the animal part of them with human bonds.

YOUNG SOCRATES. Again I ask what do you mean?

STRANGER. I mean that really true and assured opinion about honor, justice, goodness and their opposites is divine, and when it arises in men's souls, it arises in a godlike race.

YOUNG SOCRATES. That would be fitting at any rate.

STRANGER. Do we not know, then, that the statesman and good lawgiver is the only one to whom the power properly belongs, by the inspiration of the kingly art, to implant this true opinion in those who have rightly received education, those of whom we were just now speaking?

YOUNG SOCRATES. Well, probably.

STRANGER. And let us never, Socrates, call him who has not such power by the names we are now examining.

YOUNG SOCRATES. Quite right.

STRANGER. Now is not a courageous soul, when it lays hold upon such truth, made gentle, and would it not then be most ready to partake of justice? And without it, does it not incline more toward brutality?

YOUNG SOCRATES. Yes, of course.

STRANGER. And again if the decorous nature partakes of these opinions, does it not become truly self-restrained and wise, so far as the state is concerned, and if it lacks participation in such qualities, does it not very justly receive the shameful epithet of simpleton?

YOUNG SOCRATES. Certainly.

STRANGER. Then can we say that such interweaving and binding together of the bad with the bad or of the good with the bad ever becomes enduring, or that any science would ever seriously make use of it in uniting such persons?

YOUNG SOCRATES. Of course not.

STRANGER. But we may say that in those only who were of noble nature from their birth and have been nurtured as befits such natures it is implanted by the laws, and for them this is the medicine prescribed by science, and, as we said before, this bond which unites unlike and divergent parts of virtue is more divine.

YOUNG SOCRATES. Very true.

STRANGER. The remaining bonds, moreover, being human, are not very difficult to devise or, after one has devised them, to create, when once this divine bond exists.

YOUNG SOCRATES. How so? And what are the bonds?

STRANGER. Those made between states concerning intermarriages and the sharing of children by adoption, and those relating to portionings and marriages within the state. For most people make such bonds without proper regard to the procreation of children.

YOUNG SOCRATES. How is that?

STRANGER. The pursuit of wealth or power in connection with matrimony—but why should anyone ever take the trouble to blame it, as though it were worth arguing about?

YOUNG SOCRATES. There is no reason for doing so.

STRANGER. We have better cause, however, to speak our minds about those whose chief care is the family, in case their conduct is not what it should be.

YOUNG SOCRATES. Yes; very likely.

STRANGER. The fact is, they act on no right theory at all; they seek their ease for the moment; welcoming gladly those who are like themselves, and finding those who are unlike them unendurable, they give the greatest weight to their feeling of dislike.

YOUNG SOCRATES. How so?

STRANGER. The decorous people seek for characters like their own; so far as they can they marry wives of that sort and in turn give their daughters in marriage to men of that sort; and the courageous do the same, eagerly seeking natures of their own kind, whereas both classes ought to do quite the opposite.

YOUNG SOCRATES. How so, and why?

STRANGER. Because in the nature of things courage, if propagated through many generations with no admixture of a self-restrained nature, though at first it is strong and flourishing, in the end blossoms forth in utter madness.

YOUNG SOCRATES. That is likely.

STRANGER. But the soul, on the other hand, that is too full of modesty and contains no alloy of courage or boldness, after many generations of the same kind becomes too sluggish and finally is utterly crippled.

YOUNG SOCRATES. That also is likely to happen.

STRANGER. It was these bonds, then, that I said there was no difficulty in creating, provided that both classes have one and the same opinion about the honorable and the good. For indeed the whole business of the kingly weaving is comprised in this and this alone—in never allowing the self-restrained characters to be separated from the courageous, but in weaving them together by common beliefs and honors and dishonors and opinions and interchanges of pledges, thus making of them a smooth and, as we say, well-woven fabric, and then entrusting to them in common forever the offices of the state.

YOUNG SOCRATES. How is that to be done?

STRANGER. When one official is needed, by choosing a president who possesses both qualities; and when a board is desired, by combining men of each class. For the characters of self-restrained officials are exceedingly careful and just and conservative, but they lack keenness and a certain quick and active boldness.

YOUNG SOCRATES. That also seems, at least, to be true.

STRANGER. The courageous natures, on the other hand, are deficient in justice and caution in comparison with the former, but excel in boldness of action; and unless both these qualities are present it is impossible for a state to be entirely prosperous in public and private matters.

YOUNG SOCRATES. Yes, certainly.

STRANGER. This, then, is the end, let us declare, of the web of the statesman's activity, the direct interweaving of the characters of restrained and courageous men, when the kingly science has drawn them together by friendship and community of sentiment into a common life, and having perfected the most glorious and the best of all textures, clothes with it all the inhabitants of the state, both slaves and freemen, holds them together by this fabric, and omitting nothing which ought to belong to a happy state, rules and watches over them.

YOUNG SOCRATES. You have given us, Stranger, a most complete and admirable treatment of the king and the statesman. . . .

HAROLD LASSWELL

Harold Lasswell is one of the pioneers in the exploration of the behavioral approach to the study of public affairs. Like Plato, he was born at a time when his country and the world were about to experience significant changes. While Donnellson, Illinois, in 1902 was not Athens in 427 B.C. and small-town Protestant America was not aristocratic Greece, the sensitive American of Lasswell's generation witnessed just as shocking disruptions in society as the sensitive Athenian of Plato's time. Unlike Plato, however, Lasswell responded to the changes around him by becoming a moving spirit in furthering many of them. As was the case with many other intelligent and morally aware members of his generation, Lasswell became preoccupied with the problem of modern warfare, its causes, and its possible prevention. He found a clue to the causes of war in the literature of Freudian psychoanalysis and was the first political theorist to render a disciplined application of Freud's theories to the realm of public affairs. Lasswell was able to boldly depart from the institutional and historical approaches and investigate psychoanalytic theory because of his graduate education at the University of Chicago in the 1920's. At that time, under the guidance of C. E. Merriam, political scientists at the University of Chicago were developing the behavioral approach that was later to revolutionize political science.

Lasswell's contributions to American political science go far beyond his work in Freudian theory. It is not too much to say that he pioneered in almost every aspect of the behavioral movement. He has been active in exploring the relations between political science and law, fostering the analysis of propaganda, examining the theory of power, and studying ruling elites and the discipline of international relations. As political science becomes more specialized it is unlikely that many wide-ranging minds like Lasswell's will appear in the discipline. Through all of his work, Lasswell has maintained an interest in the peaceful resolution of conflicts through the application of modern psychological techniques.

Like Plato, Lasswell believes that a good society can only come about through the replacement of force by science. While Plato discussed a science of statesmanship, however, Lasswell talks about a "politics of prevention." The first principle of this politics of prevention is that "political movements derive their vitality from the displacement of private affects upon public

Shambaugh Library

objects." In other words, Lasswell says that people use public life as an arena in which they can work out their private frustrations. In most cases, the people involved do not even realize that they are doing this. They believe that their motives are pure and that they are supporting policies because they are in the public interest. However, others, particularly psychiatrists, can understand that their actions are based on such things as the fact that their mothers deprived them of gratifications at an early age. The only way to eliminate destructive conflict, Lasswell believes, is to give psychologists the power to insure that public affairs are conducted by men relatively free of frustrations. Lasswell's writings are characteristic of the psychological theories of politics. He clearly believes that the problems of whole communities can be traced to problems of the personality.

Identity*

The Democratic Community

Since we are concerned with the significance of democratic character for the democratic community, our principal frame of reference is the community. Our conception of character, and our judgment of the impact of character upon democracy, will depend upon the empirical study of how the democratic community is solidified, undermined, or, on the contrary, brought into being, on the basis of character.

Let us therefore begin by clarifying the characteristics of the democratic community, which is the form of society which it is our purpose to achieve on the widest possible scale in both space and time. A democratic community is one in which human dignity is realized in theory and fact. It is characterized by wide rather than narrow participation in the shaping and sharing of values. By the term "value" we refer to a category of "preferred events." The social process we conceive to be comprehensible as "*man* striving for *values* through *institutions* upon *resources*." For the statement of goal values, and also for descriptive purposes, it is convenient to operate with a short list of value categories. At present the following eight terms appear to provide a workable list: *power, respect, affection, rectitude, well-being, wealth, skill, enlightenment*. Sometimes it is useful to subdivide this set of values according to the degree to which attitudes are important, or are supplemented by relatively impersonal standards. When the attitudes are prominent, we speak of *deference* values, and put in this category power, respect, affection, and rectitude. When attitudes are supplemented by comparatively impersonal stan-

*Pages 59-65 reprinted with permission of The Macmillan Company from *The Political Writings of Harold D. Lasswell* by Harold Lasswell. Copyright © 1951 by The Free Press, a Corporation, Glencoe, Illinois. Pages 52-58, 65-70 reprinted from *The Analysis of Political Behavior: An Empirical Approach,* by Harold Lasswell, copyright © 1948, by permission of Archon Books and Routledge & Kegan Paul Ltd.

dards, we speak of *welfare* values, and include well-being, wealth, skill, and enlightenment.

Consider briefly the deference values. A power relationship is distinguishable by the prevailing expectation (or application) of violence, or of some other extreme deprivation of value used in support of a choice. No overt use of physical instrumentalities is essential, and it is this aspect of the relationship that justifies the inclusion of power among the deference values. It is obvious that respect is peculiarly bound up with the quality of the attitudes prevailing in an interpersonal relationship. Respect can be indicated by symbolic expressions concerning the total position of the "self" in relation to the "other." Affection, of course, is understood in terms of feelings and of the accompanying estimates of "self" and "other." By rectitude we understand the sense of responsibility for sustaining a given order of human relationships. Thus rectitude sustains democracy when there is a sense of responsibility which is interpreted in reference to patterns consistent with, and sustaining, the democratic commonwealth.

We consider well-being to be one of the welfare values, since somatic considerations occupy an important part in the evaluation of a given set of relations in terms of health or disease. Wealth often involves claims to the services of such tangible resources as land, buildings, and other facilities. Skill so frequently involves some level of proficiency in the handling of resources that we think of the acquisition and exercise of skill as among the welfare values. The content of the communications which are made in connection with enlightenment are often amenable to relatively impersonal tests for truth or falsity, comprehensiveness or restrictedness.

Equipped with some such list of categories, we are in a position to consider any community according to the old formula: *Who gets what (values) when and how?*[1] If we think of democracy as general shaping and sharing, despotisms are at the other end of the scale, characterized by the concentration of values in relatively few hands . . . .

Character and Personality

When we speak of character we are referring to a part, not the whole, of personality. The comprehensive term for the enduring traits of an individual which are manifested in interpersonal relationships is "personality."

---

[1] In my *Politics* (1936) which is herewith reprinted I spoke of safety, income, and deference as "representative" values. Safety can be treated as equivalent to well-being, income to wealth, and deference, if desired, to the subdivided list comprising power, respect, affection, rectitude. This list is still to be taken as "representative" rather than "definitive."

Hence we are speaking of personality when we mention the aptitudes, skills (and knowledges) of an individual. We also refer to personality when alluding to the strength and direction of basic drives, such as the sexual. The personality also includes the automatic and unconscious restrictions and compulsions which modify the expression of basic drives. Such patterns can be made more explicit by considering the "mechanisms" upon which chief reliance is put in mediating among the drives, and between drives and the conscious processes of perception, imagination, recall, and the like. The unconscious restrictions and compulsions can be viewed negatively, in terms of the "defenses" which have been evolved by the individual in the course of his experience with other people. Viewed positively, we consider the "ego ideals" which have been elaborated in the course of the same experience. The traditional psychoanalytic categories have divided the personality into the tripartite sectors of the "ego, the superego and the id." These are roughly equivalent to what we have just been calling the "basic impulses"; the "unconscious and automatic restrictions, compulsions and mechanisms" (viewed negatively and positively as defenses and ego ideals); and the "conscious processes."

In the study of interpersonal relations it is useful to examine the ego for the purpose of discovering "the self-system."[2] "The self-system, in turn comprises three main sets of patterns: identifications, demands, expectations."[3] When we refer to ourselves in the privacy of meditation, we are aware of such subjective events as feeling a strong sense of "I" or "me" or "we." The primary symbols are the "I," "me," and "Harold Lasswell"; and they are linked with such secondary symbols as "family, friends, neighbors, nation," and the like. The "others" who are included in the "I-me-we system" are part of the identifications belonging to the self-system as a whole. The "others" who are not so included are not part of the self.

We experience ourselves directly as loving and hating, liking and disliking, inciting and moderating many of the features of the self and of the "not-self." Such patterns of preference and determination may be called the "demand" system of the self. The demands can be conveniently classified according to the categories of value which were introduced above, including both the deference and welfare values. Moreover, the demand-system includes demands "by the self upon the self" and "upon others." And the demands may be linked with the various identification components of the self-system. Thus the part of the identification-system related

---

[2] As Harry Stack Sullivan called it in his later articles.

[3] The classification of the "identifications, demands, and expectations" follows my usage in earlier publications. The fundamental distinctions were developed within the general frame of thinking made current by several scholars, notably George Herbert Mead, whose contributions are today receiving such active recognition in the textbooks of social psychology.

to the "political party" may include demands for power as evidenced by success in winning elections and modifying policies. The identification-system pertaining to the family or the fraternity may be concerned with different values, or with different interpretations of these values.

In some ways it is simplest to introduce the "expectation-system" as the residual category comprising all of the subjective events not included among the identifications and demands. In general, it is a question of the assumptions entertained about past, present, and future, irrespective of likes and dislikes, or of the drawing of the boundaries of the self. Therefore the expectations embrace all of the "fact assumptions" and "projections" (future-pictures) of the individual. The "expectation sys-tem," in turn, can be relatively specialized in subpatterns which are close-ly linked with identification and demand subsystems. Thus all that per-tains to power may be closely integrated with the demand for power on behalf of the party or the nation or some other entity.

We are now in a position to introduce the term "character" for the purpose of conferring upon it a meaning which absorbs many of the con-ceptions which are current in much professional and lay usage. *By char-acter we mean the self-system of the person, together with the degree of support, opposition, or nonsupport received from the unconscious parts of the personality.* When we say that a man is of steadfast character it is implied that he has sufficient command of the resources of the whole personality to maintain the self-system despite environing conditions which may be adverse. If we say that some one is "characterless," we are im-plying that he cannot be counted upon to perform a consistent role in human relations, whether where difficulties are to be overcome or merely from one comparable situation to another. The implication is that inner energies are in such severe conflict that vacillation or weakness continually occurs; or that a level of functioning was never achieved in which con-sistent responses were integrated. However, the idea of "character" is not that of rigidity and repetitiveness. On the contrary, the preservation of the system as a whole depends upon suppleness in adapting to circumstances that might shatter a less versatile pattern. Pliability must be kept within the limits of the larger contours, so that the pattern "snaps back" when testing conditions are removed . . . .

The Self-System in Democratic Character: The Open Ego

We may now proceed to formulate our conception of democratic character, an enterprise that falls in two grand divisions, the first of which has to do with the self-system, the second with the energy-system. The initial step in characterizing the self-system is to select the system of identifications which appears to be consonant with democratic character. It is, of course, to be understood that the present sketch is designed to serve as an aid to empirical inquiry, and that the "theoretical model" of the democratic character will undoubtedly undergo extensive modification as scientific work in this area gains in scope and depth.

Let us take as the outstanding characteristic of democratic character, in reference to identifications, *the maintenance of an open as against a closed ego*. By this expression our intention is to convey the idea that the democratic attitude toward other human beings is warm rather than frigid, inclusive and expanding rather than exclusive and constricting. We are speaking of an underlying personality structure which is capable of "friendship," as Aristotle put it, and which is unalienated from humanity. Such a person transcends most of the cultural categories that divide human beings from one another, and senses the common humanity across class and even caste lines within the culture, and in the world beyond the local culture. In the extreme case we have "saints" who have undergone the deprivations of the concentration camp without losing the serenity of outlook that reaches out hopefully and tolerantly toward other human beings.

The conception of the open ego is something other than the capacity to enter into an intense and all-embracing sentimental bond with another person. Often such passionate attachments represent a socialization of fears and hostilities directed against other human beings. It operates as a preventive of the degree of detachment which enables the individual to sense the feelings and viewpoints of others in the life of an entire group, such as appears to be characteristic of those persons who are well-equipped to function in a democratic manner.[4]

It is apparent that the prototypes of many later experiences are undergone in the early years of life, and especially in early infancy. So far as we can tell the "primary ego" evolved during the early weeks of life is a fusion of experiences which are not capable of being sorted into a sharply delimited "out there" and "me." Experiences connected with nursing (the intake of food and body contact) are divisible into those which are gratifying (the indulgences) and nongratifying (the deprivations). Harry Stack Sullivan has suggested that the first or gratifying experiences become structured around the image of the "good mother," and that the second or nongratifying experiences are attributed to the "bad mother," even though the boundaries of the ego are lacking in focus. Soon the limits of the "me" and the "not me" gain in precision, and this in turn redefines the possibilities for symbolizing and localizing the recurring patterns of indul-

---

[4] Helen Hall Jennings; *A Study of Personality in Inter-Personal Relations,* Second Edition, New York, Longmans, Green and Co., 1950. "The universal characteristic of the leaders in this study may be a 'logical' carrying out of their larger insight into the needs of persons generally and at least partially a reflection of greater emotional maturity on their part that appears to characterize the average member," p. 201. This is a report of an investigation conducted by sociometric techniques of the 400 individuals in the New York State Training School for Girls.

gence and deprivation. When there is a "me," there is also a stream of characterizations emanating from the environment in terms of "good" and "naughty," which are usually integrated with a variety of comforts and discomforts on the physical level. The recurring sources of gratification become stably symbolized as "my mother," "my body," and the like, and the identification-system begins to include and exclude according to the prevailing stratifications of the social system into which the infant is becoming integrated.[5]

There is reason to believe that in some cultures the possibility of developing an outgoing democratic character is excluded at an early period. The prevailing patterns of child care appear to induce early despair that profound gratifications can emanate from other human beings; yet they prevent this despair from putting a stop to all externalized activity. Indulgences are wrested from the hostile, reluctant universe by a variety of sly maneuvers.[6]

The Self-System in Democratic Character: Values Multiple and Shared

Our characterization of the democratic community has provided a frame in which the demand-system of the democratic character can be rather clearly set forth. Let us speak of the democratic character as *multi-valued, rather than single-valued, and as disposed to share rather than to hoard or to monopolize.* In particular, little significance is attached to the exercise of power as a scope value.

The characteristics of democratic character have often been cast into relief by the study of individuals who are infatuated with the pursuit of one value to such a point that the integrity of the common life is imperiled thereby. This is perhaps most obvious in studies that have been made of the *homo politicus,* the man who, when compared with others similarly situated in culture and class, relies with relish upon the "pursuit of power by the use of power." Since we understand that power relationships have, or are assumed by the participants to possess, the element of severe deprivation, it is apparent that the human being who is fascinated by power is out of harmony with our basic concept of human dignity.[7]

---

[5] See especially, "The Meaning of Anxiety in Psychiatry and Life," 11 *Psychiatry* (1948) pp. 1ff.

[6] Ruth Benedict and Margaret Mead have been the most energetic explorers of the impact of child-rearing practices upon the other features of culture. I refer here to the interpretation of the Hobbesan life of Dobu.

[7] In the Salmon Lectures at the N. Y. Academy of Medicine the present writer developed some hypotheses concerning the power-centered man which were first outlined in the *Psychopathology and Politics,* which is herewith reprinted. See *Power and Personality,* New York, Norton, 1948.

The psychiatrist feels at home in the study of ardent seekers after power in the arena of politics because the physician recognizes the extreme ego-centricity and sly ruthlessness of some of the paranoid patients with whom he has come in contact in the clinic. To the power-centered person all human beings and all contacts with others are opportunities for imposing his will, or for enlisting the other person in some manner that contributes to the imposition of his own will in some future situation. Hence he imposes a wall of insulation and isolation between himself and others, with the result that a growing sense of alienation from mankind becomes one of the recurring complaints of those who attain power, or only aspire with all the intensity of their being to acquire it . . . .

The Self-System of the Democratic Character: Confidence in Human Potentialities

When we turn from the demand-structure of the democratic character to the consideration of the pattern of expectation we note at once that it is essential to have *deep confidence in the benevolent potentialities of man*. This affirmative trust is very different from the apathetic endurance of life in the manner of the apathetic orphan.[8]

Unless there is some early basis for trust in the benevolence of the surrounding world, we can hardly expect that the individual will develop predispositions capable of carrying him through adverse experiences. This is the deep significance of the "good mother" image in contributing to the formation of a perspective that fosters inclusive identifications with other people. It has become amply apparent in the course of research on the infant that the expectation of benevolence is a factor enabling the infant to put forth the energy to live. . . .[9,10]

---

[8]Even though this response may enable the individual to survive under such drastically adverse conditions as a concentration camp in later life. See Ralph R. Greenson, "The Psychology of Apathy,"*Psychoanalytic Quarterly XVIII*(1949), pp. 290-302.

[9]Consult Margarethe Ribble, "The Significance of Infantile Sucking for the Psychic Development of the Individual," and "Disorganizing Factors of Infant Personality," reprinted in *Contemporary Psychopathology: A Source Book,* edited by S. S. Tomkins, Cambridge, Harvard University Press, 1947, pp. 1-15.

[10]The importance of recognizing the *potential* benevolence of human beings is emphasized, for example, in analyses of democracy by C. E. Merriam, T. V. Smith, A. D. Lindsay, R. M. MacIver, James Bryce, Hugo Krabbe, Hans Kelsen, and many others.

Power

What is important for our purposes is to envisage the possible emergence of the military state under present technical conditions. There are no examples of the military state combined with modern technology. During emergencies the great powers have given enormous scope to military authority, but temporary acquisitions of authority lack the elements of comparative permanence and acceptance that complete the garrison state. Military dictators in states marginal to the creative centres of Western civilization are not integrated with modern technology; they merely use some of its specific elements.

The military men who dominate a modern technical society will be very different from the officers of history and tradition. It is probable that the specialists on violence will include in their training a large degree of expertness in many of the skills that we have traditionally accepted as part of modern civilian management.

The distinctive frame of reference in a fighting society is fighting effectiveness. All social change is translated into battle potential. Now there can be no realistic calculation of fighting effectiveness without knowledge of the technical and psychological characteristics of modern production processes. The function of management in such a society is already known to us; it includes the exercise of skill in supervising technical operations, in administrative organization, in personnel management, in public relations. These skills are needed to translate the complicated operations of modern life into every relevant frame of reference—the frame of fighting effectiveness as well as of pecuniary profit.

This leads to the seeming paradox that, as modern states are militarized, specialists on violence are more preoccupied with the skills and attitudes judged characteristic of nonviolence. We anticipate the merging of skills, starting from the traditional accoutrements of the professional soldier, moving toward the manager and promoter of large-scale civilian enterprise.

In the garrison state, at least in its introductory phases, problems of morale are destined to weigh heavily on the mind of management. It is easy to throw sand in the gears of the modern assembly line; hence, there must be a deep and general sense of participation in the total enterprise of the state if collective effort is to be sustained. When we call attention to the importance of the "human factor" in modern production, we sometimes fail to notice that it springs from the multiplicity of special environments that have been created by modern technology. Thousands of technical operations have sprung into existence where a few hundred were found before. To complicate the material environment in this way is to multiply the foci of attention of those who live in our society. Diversified foci of attention breed differences in outlook, preference, and loyalty. The labyrinth of specialized "material" environments generates profound ideological divergencies that cannot be abolished, though they can be mitigated, by the methods now available to leaders in our society. As long as modern technology prevails, society is honeycombed with cells of separate experience, of individuality, of partial freedom. Concerted action under such conditions depends upon skillfully guiding the minds of men; hence the enormous importance of symbolic manipulation in modern society.

The importance of the morale factor is emphasized by the universal fear which it is possible to maintain in large populations through modern instruments of warfare. The growth of aerial warfare in particular has tended to abolish the distinction between civilian and military functions. It is no longer possible to affirm that those who enter the military service take the physical risk while those who remain at home stay safe and contribute to the equipment and the comfort of the courageous heroes at the front. Indeed, in some periods of modern warfare, casualties among civilians may outnumber the casualties of the armed forces. With the socialization of danger as a permanent characteristic of modern violence the nation becomes one unified technical enterprise. Those who direct the violence operations are compelled to consider the entire gamut of problems that arise in living together under modern conditions.

There will be an energetic struggle to incorporate young and old into the destiny and mission of the state. It is probable that one form of this symbolic adjustment will be the abolition of "the unemployed." This stigmatizing symbol will be obsolete in the garrison state. It insults the dignity of millions, for it implies uselessness. This is so, whether the "unemployed" are given a "dole" or put on "relief" projects. Always there is the damaging stigma of superfluity. No doubt the garrison state will be distinguished by the psychological abolition of unemployment—"psychological" because this is chiefly a matter of redefining symbols.

In the garrison state there must be work—and the duty to work—for all. Since all work becomes public work, all who do not accept employment flout military discipline. For those who do not fit within the structure of the state there is but one alternative—to obey or die. Compulsion, therefore, is to be expected as a potent instrument for internal control of the garrison state.

The use of coercion can have an important effect upon many more people than it reaches directly; this is the propaganda component of any "propaganda of the deed." The spectacle of compulsory labor gangs in prisons or concentration camps is a negative means of conserving morale—negative since it arouses fear and guilt. Compulsory labor groups are suitable popular scapegoats in a military state. The duty to obey, to serve the state, to work—these are cardinal virtues in the garrison state. Unceasing emphasis upon duty is certain to arouse opposing tendencies within the personality structure of all who live under a garrison regime. Everyone must struggle to hold in check any tendencies, conscious or uncon-scious, to defy authority, to violate the code of work, to flout the inces-sant demand for sacrifice in the collective interest. From the earliest years youth will be trained to subdue—to disavow, to struggle against—any specific opposition to the ruling code of collective exactions.

The conscience imposes feelings of guilt and anxiety upon the individual whenever his impulses are aroused, ever so slightly, to break the code. When the coercive threat that sanctions the code of the military state is internalized in the consciences of youth, the spectacle of labor gangs is profoundly disturbing. A characteristic response is self-righteousness—quick justification of coercive punishment, tacit acceptance of the inference that all who are subject to coercion are guilty of antisocial conduct. To main-tain suspended judgment, to absolve others in particular instances, is to give at least partial toleration to counter-mores tendencies within the self. Hence, the quick substitute responses—the self-righteous attitude, the de-flection of attention. Indeed, a characteristic psychic pattern of the military state is the "startle pattern," which is carried over to the internal as well as to the external threat of danger. This startle pattern is overcome and stylized as alert, prompt, commanding adjustment to reality. This is ex-pressed in the authoritative manner that dominates military style—in ges-ture, intonation, and idiom.

The chief targets of compulsory labor service will be unskilled manual workers, together with counter-elite elements who have come under sus-picion. The position of the unskilled in our society has been deteriorating, since the machine society has less and less use for unskilled manual labor. The coming of the machine was a skill revolution, a broadening of the role of the skilled and semi-skilled components of society.[11] As the value of labor declines in production, it also declines in warfare; hence, it will be treated with less consideration. (When unskilled workers are relied upon as fighters, they must, of course share the ideological exultation of the community as a whole and receive a steady flow of respect from the so-cial environment.) Still another factor darkens the forecast for the bottom layers of the population in the future garrison state. If recent advances in pharmacology continue, as we may anticipate, physical means of con-trolling response can replace symbolic methods. This refers to the use of drugs not only for temporary orgies of energy on the part of front-line fighters but in order to deaden the critical function of all who are not held in esteem by the ruling elite.

For the immediate future, however, ruling elite must continue to put

---

[11] See Sogge, T. M., "Industrial Classes in the United States," *Journal of the American Statistical Association,* June, 1933; and Clark, Colin, "National Income and Outlay," in Pigou, A. C., *Socialism versus Capitalism* (London, 1937), pp. 12-22. Sogge's paper is a continuation of an earlier investigation by Alvin H. Hansen.

their chief reliance upon propaganda as an instrument of morale. But the manipulation of symbols, even in conjunction with coercive instruments of violence, is not sufficient to accomplish all the purposes of a ruling group. We have already spoken of the socialization of danger, and this will bring about some equalitarian adjustments in the distribution of income for the purpose of conserving the will to fight and to produce.

In addition to the adjustment of symbols, goods, and violence, the political elite of the garrison state will find it necessary to make certain adaptations in the fundamental practices of the state. Decisions will be more dictatorial than democratic, and institutional practices long connected with modern democracy will disappear. Instead of elections to office or referenda on issues there will be government by plebiscite. Elections foster the formation and expression of public opinion, while plebiscites encourage only unanimous demonstrations of collective sentiment. Rival political parties will be suppressed, either by the monopolization of legality in one political party (more properly called a political "order") or by the abolition of all political parties. The ruling group will exercise a monopoly of opinion in public, thus abolishing the free communication of fact and interpretation. Legislatures will be done away with, and if a numerous consultative body is permitted at all it will operate as an assembly; that is, it will meet for a very short time each year and will be expected to ratify the decisions of the central leadership after speeches that are chiefly ceremonial in nature. Plebiscites and assemblies thus become part of the ceremonializing process in the military state.

As legislatures and elections go out of use, the practice of petition will play a more prominent role. Lawmaking will be in the hands of the supreme authority and his council; and, as long as the state survives, this agency will exert effective control.

What part of the social structure would be drawn upon in recruiting the political rulers of the garrison state? As we have seen, the process will not be by general election but by self-perpetuation through co-option. The foremost positions will be open to the officers' corps, and the problem is to predict from what part of the social structure the officers will be recruited. Morale considerations justify a broad base of recruitment for ability rather than social standing. Although fighting effectiveness is a relatively impersonal test that favors ability over inherited status, the turnover in ruling families from generation to generation will probably be low. Any recurring crisis, however, will strengthen the tendency to favor ability. It seems clear that recruitment will be much more for bias and obedience than for objectivity and originality. Yet, as we shall presently see, modern machine society has introduced new factors in the military state—factors tending to strengthen objectivity and originality.

In the garrison state all organized social activity will be governmentalized; hence, the role of independent associations will disappear, with the exception of secret societies (specifically, there will be no organized economic, religious, or cultural life outside of the duly constituted agencies of government). Government will be highly centralized, though devolution may be practiced in order to mitigate "bureaucratism." Not only will the administrative structure be centralized, but at every level it will tend to integrate authority in a few hands.

We have sketched some of the methods at the disposal of the ruling elites of the garrison state—the management of propaganda, violence, goods, practices. Let us consider the picture from a slightly different standpoint. How will various kinds of influence be distributed in the state? Power will be highly concentrated, as in any dictatorial regime. We have already suggested that there will be a strong tendency toward equalizing the distribution of safety throughout the community (that is, negative safety, the socialization of threat in modern war). In the interest of morale there will be some moderation of huge differences in individual income, flattening the pyramid at the top, bulging it out in the upper-middle and middle zones. In the garrison state the respect pyramid will probably resemble the income pyramid. So great is the multiplicity of functions in modern processes of production that a simple scheme of military rank is flagrantly out of harmony with the facts. Summarizing, the distribution of safety will be most uniform throughout the community, distribution of power will show the largest inequalities. The patterns of income and respect will fall between these two. The lower strata of the community will be composed of those subject to compulsory labor, tending to constitute a permanent pariah caste.

What about the capacity of the garrison state to produce a large volume of material values? The elites of the garrison state, like the elites of recent business states, will confront the problem of holding in check the stupendous productive potentialities of modern science and engineering. We know that the ruling elites of the modern business state have not known how to control productive capacity; they have been unwilling to adopt necessary measures for the purpose of steadying the tempo of economic development. The rulers of the garrison state will be able to regularize the rate of production, since they will be free from many of the conventions that have stood in the way of adopting measures suitable to this purpose in the business state. The business elite has been unwilling to revise institutional practices to the extent necessary to maintain a continually rising flow of investment. The institutional structure of the business state has called for flexible adjustment between governmental and private channels of activity and for strict measures to maintain price flexibility. Wherever the business elite has not supported such necessary arrangements, the business state itself has begun to disintegrate.

Although the rulers of the garrison state will be free to regularize the rate of production, they will most assuredly prevent full utilization of modern productive capacity for nonmilitary consumption purposes. The elite of the garrison state will have a professional interest in multiplying gadgets specialized to acts of violence. The rulers of the garrison state will depend upon war scares as a means of maintaining popular willingness to forego immediate consumption. War scares that fail to culminate in violence eventually lose their value; this is the point at which ruling classes will feel that blood-letting is needed in order to preserve those virtues of sturdy acquiescence in the regime which they so much admire and from which they so greatly benefit. We may be sure that if ever there is a rise in the production of nonmilitary consumption goods, despite the amount of energy directed toward the production of military equipment, the ruling class will feel itself endangered by the growing "frivolousness" of the community.[12]

We need to consider the degree to which the volume of values produced in a garrison state will be affected by the tendency toward rigidity. Many factors in the garrison state justify the expectation that tendencies toward repetitiousness and ceremonialization will be prominent. To some extent this is a function of bureaucracy and dictatorship. But to some extent it springs also from the preoccupation of the military state with danger. Even where military operations are greatly respected, the fighter must steel himself against deep-lying tendencies to retreat from death and mutilation. One of the most rudimentary and potent means of relieving fear is some repetitive operation—some reiteration of the old and well established. Hence the reliance on drill as a means of disciplining men to endure personal danger without giving in to fear of death. The tendency to repeat, as a means of diminishing timidity, is powerfully reinforced by successful repetition, since the individual is greatly attached to whatever has proved effective in maintaining self-control in previous trials. Even those who deny the fear of death to themselves may reveal the depth of their unconscious fear by their interest in ritual and ceremony. This is one of the subtlest ways by which the individual can keep his mind distracted from the discovery of his own timidity. It does not occur to the ceremonialist that in the spider web of ceremony he has found a moral equivalent of war—an unacknowledged substitute for personal danger.

The tendency to ceremonialize rather than to fight will be particularly prominent among the most influential elements in a garrison state. Those standing at the top of the military pyramid will doubtless occupy high positions in the income pyramid. During times of actual warfare it may be necessary to make concessions in the direction of moderating gross-income differences in the interest of preserving general morale. The pros-

---

[12]The perpetuation of the garrison state will be favoured by some of the psychological consequences of self-indulgence. When people who have been disciplined against self-indulgence increase their enjoyments, they often suffer from twinges of conscience. Such self-imposed anxieties signify that the conscience is ever vigilant to enforce the orthodox code of human conduct. Hence, drifts away from the established order of disciplined acquiescence in the proclaimed values of the garrison state will be self-correcting. The guilt generated by self-indulgence can be relieved through the orgiastic reinstatement of the established mores of disciplined sacrifice.

pect of such concessions may be expected to operate as a deterrent factor against war. A countervailing tendency, of course, is the threat to sluggish and well-established members of the upper crust from ambitious members of the lower officers' corps. This threat arises, too, when there are murmurs of disaffection with the established order of things on the part of broader components of the society.

It seems probable that the garrison state of the future will be far less rigid than the military states of antiquity. As long as modern technical society endures, there will be an enormous body of specialists whose focus of attention is entirely given over to the discovery of novel ways of utilizing nature. Above all, these are physical scientists and engineers. They are able to demonstrate by rather impersonal procedures the efficiency of many of their suggestions for the improvement of fighting effectiveness. We therefore anticipate further exploration of the technical potentialities of modern civilization within the general framework of the garrison state . . . .

Change

Generalizing broadly, political methods have involved the manipulation of symbols, goods, and violence, as in propaganda, bribery, and assassination. It is common to act on the assumption that they are to be applied in the settlement of conflicting demands, and not in the obviation of conflict. In so far as they rest upon a philosophy, they identify the problem of politics with the problem of coping with differences which are sharply drawn.

The identification of the field of politics with the field of battle, whether the theater be the frontier or the forum, has produced an unfortunate warp in the minds of those who manage affairs, or those who simply think about the management of affairs. The contribution of politics has been thought to be in the elaboration of the methods by which conflicts are resolved. This has produced a vast diversion of energy toward the study of the formal etiquette of government. In some vague way, the problem of politics is the advancement of the good life, but this is at once assumed to depend upon the modification of the mechanisms of government. Democratic theorists in particular have hastily assumed that social harmony depends upon discussion, and that discussion depends upon the formal consultation of all those affected by social policies.

The time has come to abandon the assumption that the problem of politics is the problem of promoting discussion among all the interests concerned in a given problem. Discussion frequently complicates social difficulties, for the discussion by far-flung interests arouses a psychology of conflict which produces obstructive, fictitious, and irrelevant values.

The problem of politics is less to solve conflicts than to prevent them; less to serve as a safety valve for social protest than to apply social energy to the abolition of recurrent sources of strain in society.

This redefinition of the problem of politics may be called the idea of preventive politics. The politics of prevention draws attention squarely to the central problem of reducing the level of stain and maladaptation in society. In some measure it will proceed by encouraging discussion among all those who are affected by social policy, but this will be no iron-clad rule. In some measure it will proceed by improving the machinery of settling disputes, but this will be subordinated to a comprehensive program, and no longer treated as an especially desirable mode of handling the situation.

The recognition that people are poor judges of their own interest is often supposed to lead to the conclusion that a dictator is essential. But no student of individual psychology can fail to share the conviction of Kempf that "Society is *not* safe . . . when it is forced to follow the dictations of one individual, of one autonomic apparatus, no matter how splendidly and altruistically it may be conditioned." Our thinking has too long been misled by the threadbare terminology of democracy versus dictatorship, of democracy versus aristocracy. Our problem is to be ruled by the truth about the conditions of harmonious human relations, and the discovery of the truth is an object of specialized research; it is no monopoly of people as people, or of the ruler as ruler. As our devices of accurate ascertainment are invented and spread, they are explained and applied by many individuals inside the social order. Knowledge of this kind is a slow and laborious accumulation.

The politics of prevention does not depend upon a series of changes in the organization of government. It depends upon a reorientation in the minds of those who think about society around the central problems: What are the principal factors which modify the tension level of the community? What is the specific relevance of a proposed line of action to the temporary and permanent modification of the tension level?

The politics of prevention will insist upon a rigorous audit of the human consequences of prevailing political practices. How does politics affect politicians? One way to consider the human value of social action is to see what that form of social action does to the actors. When a judge has been on the bench thirty years, what manner of man has he become? When an agitator has been agitating for thirty years, what has happened to him? How do different kinds of political administrators compare with doctors, musicians, and scientists? Such a set of inquiries would presuppose that we were able to ascertain the traits with which the various individuals began to practice their role in society. Were we able to show what certain lines of human endeavor did to the same reactive type, we would lay the foundation for a profound change in society's esteem for various occupations.

Any audit of the human significance of politics would have to press far beyond the narrow circle of professional politicians. Crises like wars, revolutions, and elections enter the lives of people in far-reaching ways. The effect of crises on mental attitude is an important and uncertain field. Thus it is reported that during the rebellion of 1745-1746 in Scotland there was little hysteria (in the technical pathological sense). The same was true of the French Revolution and of the Irish Rebellion. Rush reported in his book *On the Influence of the American Revolution on the Human Body* that many hysterical women were "restored to perfect health by the events of the time." Havelock Ellis, who cites these instances, comments that "in such cases the emotional tension is given an opportunity for explosion in new and impersonal channels, and the chain of morbid personal emotions is broken."[13]

The physical consequences of political symbolism may be made the topic of investigation from this point of view:

> When the affect can not acquire what it needs, uncomfortable tensions or anxiety (fear) are felt, and the use of the symbol or fetish, relieving this anxiety, has a marked physiological value in that it prevents the adrenal, thyroid, circulatory, hepatic, and pulmonic compensatory strivings from becoming excessive.[14]

Political programs will continually demand reconsideration in the light of the factors which current research discloses as bearing upon the tension level. Franz Alexander recently drew attention to the strains produced in modern civilization by the growing sphere of purposive action. He summed up the facts in the process of civilized development in the following way: "Human expressions of instinct are subject to a continual tendency to rationalization, that is, they develop more and more from playful, uncoordinated, purely pleasure efforts into purposive actions." The "discomfort of civilization" of which Freud recently wrote in the *Unbehagen der Kultur* is characteristic of the rationalized cultures with which we are acquainted. Life is poor in libidinal gratifications of the primitive kind which the peasant, who is in close touch with elementary things, is in a position to enjoy.[15] Modern life furnishes irrational outlets in the moving picture and in sensational crime news. But it may be that other means of relieving the strain of modern living can be invented which will have fewer drawbacks.

Preventive politics will search for the definite assessment, then, of cultural patterns in terms of their human consequences. Some of these human

---

[13] *Studies in the Psychology of Sex,* I, 231.

[14] Kempf, *Psychopathology,* p. 704.

[15] Franz Alexander, "Mental Hygiene and Criminology," *First International Congress on Mental Hygiene.*

results will be deplored as "pathological," while others will be welcomed as "healthy." One complicating factor is that valuable contributions to culture are often made by men who are in other respects pathological. Many pathological persons are constrained by their personal difficulties to displace more or less successfully upon remote problems, and to achieve valuable contributions to knowledge and social policy.[16] Of course the notion of the pathological is itself full of ambiguities. The individual who is subject to epileptic seizures may be considered in one culture not a subnormal and diseased person, but a supernormal person. Indeed, it may be said that society depends upon a certain amount of pathology, in the sense that society does not encourage the free criticism of social life, but establishes taboos upon reflective thinking about its own presuppositions. If the individual is pathological to the extent that he is unable to contemplate any fact with equanimity, and to elaborate impulse through the processes of thought, it is obvious that society does much to nurture disease. This leads to the apparent paradox that successful social adjustment consists in contracting the current diseases. If "health" merely means a statistical report upon the "average," the scrutiny of the individual ceases to carry much meaning for the modification of social patterns. But if "health" means something more than "average," the intensive study of individuals gives us a vantage ground for the reevaluation of the human consequences of cultural patterns, and the criticism of these patterns.[17]

If the politics of prevention spreads in society, a different type of education will become necessary for those who administer society or think about it. This education will start from the proposition that it takes longer to train a good social scientist than it takes to train a good physical scientist.[18] The social administrator and social scientist must be brought into direct contact with his material in its most varied manifestations. He must mix with rich and poor, with savage and civilized, with sick and well, with old and young. His contacts must be primary and not exclusively secondary. He must have an opportunity for prolonged self-scrutiny by the best-developed methods of personality study, and he must laboriously achieve a capacity to deal objectively with himself and with all others in human society.

This complicated experience is necessary since our scale of values is less the outcome of our dialectical than of our other experiences in life. Values change more by the unconscious redefinition of meaning than by rational

---

[16] For an appreciation of the role of the pathological person in society see Wilhelm Lange-Eichbaum, *Genie-Irrsinn, and Ruhm,* and Karl Birnbaum, *Grundzüge der Kulturpsychopathologie.*

[17] Something like this is no doubt the thought in Trigant Burrow's very obscure book on *The Social Basis of Consciousness.*

[18] This point was forcibly made by Beardsley Ruml in his speech at the dedication of the Social Science Research Building at the University of Chicago. See *The New Social Science,* edited by Leonard D. White, pp. 99–111.

analysis. Every contact and every procedure which discloses new facts has its repercussions upon the matrix of partially verbalized experience, which is the seeding ground of conscious ideas.

One peculiarity of the problem of the social scientist is that he must establish personal contact with his material. The physical scientist who works in a laboratory spends more time adjusting his machinery than in making his observations, and the social scientist who works in the field must spend more time establishing contacts than in noting and reporting observations. What the instrumentation technique is to the physicist, the cultivation of favorable human points of vantage is for most social scientists. This means that the student of society, as well as the manager of social relations, must acquire the technique of social intercourse in unusual degree, unless he is to suffer from serious handicaps, and his training must be directed with this in mind.

The experience of the administrator-investigator must include some definite familiarity with all the elements which bear importantly upon the traits and interests of the individual. This means that he must have the most relevant material brought to his attention from the fields of psychology, psychopathology, physiology, medicine, and social science. Since our institutions of higher learning are poorly organized at the present time to handle this program, thorough curricular reconstructions will be indispensable.[19]

What has been said in this chapter may be passed in brief review. Political movements derive their vitality from the displacement of private affects upon public objects. Political crises are complicated by the concurrent reactivation of specific primitive motives which were organized in the early experience of the individuals concerned. Political symbols are particularly adapted to serve as targets for displaced affect because of their ambiguity of reference, in relation to individual experience, and because of their general circulation. Although the dynamic of politics is the tension level of individuals, all tension does not produce political acts. Nor do all emotional bonds lead to political action. Political acts depend upon the symbolization of the discontent of the individual in terms of a more inclusive self which champions a set of demands of social action.

Political demands are of limited relevance to the changes which will produce permanent reductions in the tension level of society. The political methods of coercion, exhortation, and discussion assume that the role of politics is to solve conflicts when they have happened. The ideal of a politics of prevention is to obviate conflict by the definite reduction of the tension level of society by effective methods, of which discussion will be but one. The preventive point of view insists upon a continuing audit of

---

[19] I have suggested that those who write human biography should be included among those who require this comprehensive training. See "The Scientific Study of Human Biography," *Scientific Monthly,* January 1930.

the human consequences of social acts, and especially of political acts. The achievement of the ideal of preventive politics depends less upon changes in social organization than upon improving the methods and the education of social administrators and social scientists.

The preventive politics of the future will be intimately allied to general medicine, psychopathology, physiological psychology, and related disciplines. Its practitioners will gradually win respect in society among puzzled people who feel their responsibilities and who respect objective findings. A comprehensive functional conception of political life will state problems of investigation, and keep receptive the minds of those who reflect at length upon the state.

ERICH FROMM

Like Lasswell, Erich Fromm was born at the beginning of the twentieth century. The changes he has experienced in his lifetime have been particularly catastrophic because his origins are in Germany. Fromm became a psychiatrist and lectured for a time at the Psychoanalytic Institute in his native Frankfurt. However, when the Nazis gained power in Germany, he was forced, as were so many other German scholars, to find refuge in the United States. The Nazis were particularly averse to psychiatry because it had first been given systematic elaboration as a science by Sigmund Freud, who was Jewish. Thus, the Nazis believed that psychoanalytic theory was a weapon that Jews would use to brainwash and morally disarm the German people and other "Aryans." It was through the application of such reasoning in public policy that Germany and Austria, which had been the world centers of psychoanalysis, lost their supremacy in this field to the United States.

Fromm responded to the challenges of his generation in much the same way that Lasswell did. Just as Lasswell, the political scientist, has attempted to assimilate the insights of psychiatry into the analysis of public problems, Fromm, the psychoanalyst, has tried to show how his discipline can contribute to the improvement of sociological and political theory. However, while Lasswell has worked by means of the behavioral approach, Fromm has adopted a critical analysis based on Marxist thought. Fromm's interests have also been wide-ranging. He has written about social movements, religion, love, revolution, and social reform. He, too, has exhibited a comprehensive mind, which is not common in an age of specialization.

Fromm's idea of a good society is much less aristocratic than those advocated by Plato and Lasswell. In fact, Fromm has captured the attention of many of the thinkers of the New Left because of his preference for a highly decentralized society in which ordinary people have power over their conditions of work and leisure. He calls his plan "humanistic management" and contrasts it to the method of bureaucracy in which power flows downward. "The basic principle of the humanistic management method is that, in spite of the bigness of the enterprises, centralized planning, and cybernation, the individual participant asserts himself toward the managers, circumstances, and machines, and ceases to be a powerless particle which has no active part in the process. Only by such affirmation of his will can the energies of the individual be liberated and his mental balance be restored." Fromm believes that mental health depends less on the efforts of a wise elite to emphasize some character traits in the population at the expense of others (as in Plato), or on the efforts of an elite or psychologists to rid people of frustrations (as in Lasswell), than on the restructuring of social institutions so that people will be and feel responsible for their actions. Thus, Fromm is not a pure psychological theorist who believes that public problems are essentially private problems. Instead, he has concentrated on the psychological effects of organized power. It is his diagnosis of organized power as the cause of personal despair that has given his writings their contemporary force. Humanistic management would make use of experts, but it would also greatly expand the sphere of personal decision.

Identity*

. . . .The concept of the social character answers important questions which were not dealt with adequately in Marxist theory.

(1) Why is it that a society succeeds in gaining the allegiance of most of its members, even when they suffer under the system and even if their reason tells them that their allegiance to it is harmful to them? Why has their *real* interest as human beings not outweighed their *fictitious* interests produced by all kinds of ideological influences and brainwashing? Why has consciousness of their class situation and of the advantages of socialism not been as effective as Marx believed it would be? The answer to this question lies in the phenomenon of the social character. Once a society has succeeded in molding the character structure of the average person in such a way that he likes to do that which he has to do, he is satisfied with the very conditions that society imposes upon him. As one of Ibsen's characters once said: He can do anything he wants to do because he wants only what he can do. Needless to say, a social character which is, for instance, satisfied with submission is a crippled character. But crippled or not, it serves the purpose of a society requiring submissive men for its proper functioning.

(2) The concept of the social character also serves to explain the link between the material basis of a society and the "ideological superstructure." Marx has often been interpreted as implying that the ideological superstructure was *nothing but* the reflection of the economic basis. This interpretation is not correct; but the fact is that in Marx's theory the

nature of the relation between basis and superstructure was not sufficiently explained. A dynamic psychological theory can show that society produces the social character, and that the social character tends to produce and to hold onto ideas and ideologies which fit it and are nourished by it. However, it is not only the economic basis which creates a certain social character which, in turn, creates certain ideas. The ideas, once created, also influence the social character and, indirectly, the social economic structure. What I emphasize here is *that the social character is the intermediary between the socioeconomic structure and the ideas and ideals prevalent in a society*. It is the intermediary in both directions, from the economic basis to the ideas and from the ideas to the economic basis. The following scheme expresses this concept:

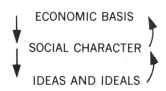

ECONOMIC BASIS

SOCIAL CHARACTER

IDEAS AND IDEALS

(3) The concept of social character can explain how human energy is used by a society, like any other raw material for the needs and purposes of that society. Man, in fact, is one of the most pliable natural forces; he can be made to serve almost any purpose; he can be made to hate or to cooperate, to submit or to stand up, to enjoy suffering or happiness.

(4) While all this is true, it is also true that man can solve the problem of his existence only by the full unfolding of his human powers. The more crippled a society makes man the sicker he becomes, even though consciously he may be satisfied with his lot. But unconsciously he is dissatisfied, and this very dissatisfaction is the element which inclines him eventually to change the social forms that cripple him. If he cannot do this, his particular kind of pathogenic society will die out. Social change and revolution are caused not only by new productive forces which conflict with older forms of social organization, but also by the conflict between inhuman social conditions and unalterable human needs. One can do almost anything to man, yet only almost. The history of man's fight for freedom is the most telling manifestation of this principle.

(5) The concept of social character is not only a theoretical one lending itself to general speculation; it is useful and important for empirical studies which aim at finding out what the incidence of various kinds of "social character" is in a given society or social class. Assuming that one defines the "peasant character" as individualistic, hoarding, stubborn, with little satisfaction in cooperation, little sense of time and punctuality, this syndrome of traits is by no means a summation of various traits, but a structure, charged with energy; this structure will show intensive resistance by

either violence or silent obstructionism if attempts are made to change it; even economic advantages will not easily produce any effects. The syndrome owes its existence to the common mode of production which has been characteristic of peasant life for thousands of years. The same holds true for a declining lower middle class, whether it is that which brought Hitler to power, or the poor whites in the South of the United States. The lack of any kind of positive cultural stimulation, the resentment against their situation, which is one of being left behind by the forward-moving currents of their society, the hate toward those who destroyed the images which once gave them pride, have created a character syndrome which is made up of love of death (necrophilia), intense and malignant fixation to blood and soil, and intense group narcissism (the latter expressed in intense nationalism and racism). One last example: the character structure of the industrial worker contains punctuality, discipline, capacity for teamwork; this is the syndrome which forms the minimum for the efficient functioning of an industrial worker. (Other differences—like dependence-independence; interest-indifference; activity-passivity—are at this point ignored, although they are of utmost importance for the character structure of the worker now and in the future.)

(6) The most important application of the concept of the social character lies in distinguishing the future social character of a socialist society as visualized by Marx from the social character of nineteenth-century capitalism, with its central desire for possession of property and wealth, and from the social character of the twentieth century (capitalist or communist), which is becoming ever more prevalent in the highly industrialized societies: the character of *homo consumens*.

Homo consumens is the man whose main goal is not primarily to *own* things, but to *consume* more and more, and thus to compensate for his inner vacuity, passivity, loneliness, and anxiety. In a society characterized by giant enterprises, giant industrial, governmental, and labor bureaucracies, the individual, who has no control over his circumstances of work, feels impotent, lonely, bored, and anxious. At the same time, the need for profit of the big consumer industries, through the medium of advertising, transforms him into a voracious man, an eternal suckling who wants to consume more and more, and for whom everything becomes an article of consumption: cigarettes, liquor, sex, movies, television, travel, and even education, books, and lectures. New artificial needs are created, and man's tastes are manipulated. (The character of *homo consumens* in its more extreme forms is a well-known psychopathological phenomenon. It is to be found in many cases of depressed or anxious persons who escape into overeating, overbuying, or alcoholism to compensate for the hidden depression and anxiety.) The greed for consumption (an extreme form of what Freud called the "oral-receptive character") is becoming the dominant psychic force in present-day industrialized society. *Homo consumens* is under the illusion of happiness, while unconsciously he suffers from his boredom and passivity. The more power he has over machines the more powerless he becomes as a human being; the more he consumes the more he becomes a slave to the ever-increasing needs which the industrial system creates and manipulates. He mistakes thrill and excitement for joy and happiness, and material comfort for aliveness; satisfied greed becomes the meaning of life, the striving for it a new religion. The freedom to consume becomes the essence of human freedom.

This spirit of consumption is precisely the opposite of the spirit of a socialist society as Marx visualized it. He clearly saw the danger inherent in capitalism. His aim was a society in which man *is* much, not in which he *has* or *uses* much. He wanted to liberate man from the chains of his material greed, so that he could become fully awake, alive, and sensitive, and not be the slave of his greed. "The production of too many useful things," he wrote, "results in the creation of too many useless people." He wanted to abolish extreme poverty, because it prevents man from becoming fully human; but he also wanted to prevent extreme wealth, in which the individual becomes the prisoner of his greed. His aim was not the *maximum* but the *optimum* of consumption, the satisfaction of those genuine human needs which serve as a means to a fuller and richer life.

It is one of the historical ironies that the spirit of capitalism, the satisfaction of material greed, is conquering the communist and socialist countries which, with their planned economy, would have the means to curb it. This process has its own logic: the material success of capitalism was immensely impressive to those poorer countries in Europe in which communism had been victorious, and the victory of socialism became identified with successful competition with capitalism *within* the spirit of capitalism. Socialism is in danger of deteriorating into a system which can accomplish the industrialization of poorer countries more quickly than capitalism, rather than of becoming a society in which the development of man, and not that of economic production, is the main goal. This development has been furthered by the fact that Soviet communism, in accepting a crude version of Marx's "materialism," lost contact, as did the capitalist countries, with the humanist spiritual tradition of which Marx was one of the greatest representatives.

It is true that the socialist countries have still not solved the problem of satisfying the *legitimate* material needs of their populations (and even in the United States 40 percent of the population is not "affluent"). But it is of the utmost importance that socialist economists, philosophers, and psychologists be aware of the danger that the goal of *optimal* consumption can easily change to that of *maximal* consumption. The task for the socialist theoreticians is to study the nature of human needs; to find criteria for the distinction between *genuine* human needs, the satisfaction of which makes man more alive and sensitive, and *synthetic* needs created by capitalism, which tend to weaken man, to make him more passive and bored, a slave to his greed for things.

What I am stressing here is not that production as such should be restricted; but that once the optimal needs of individual consumption are fulfilled, it should be channeled into more production of the means for social consumption such as schools, libraries, theaters, parks, hospitals, public transportation, etc. The ever-increasing individual consumption in the highly industrialized countries suggests that competition, greed, and envy are engendered not only by private property, but also by unlimited private consumption. Socialist theoreticians must not lose sight of the fact that the aim of a humanist socialism is to build an industrial society whose mode of production shall serve the fullest development of the total man, and not the creation of *homo consumens;* that socialist society is an industrial society fit for human beings to live in and to develop . . . .

. . . In a bureaucratically organized and centralized industrialism, tastes are manipulated so that people consume maximally and in predictable and profitable directions. Their intelligence and character become standardized by the ever increasing role of tests which select the mediocre and unadventurous in preference to the original and daring. Indeed, the bureaucratic-industrial civilization which has been victorious in Europe and North America has created a new type of man; he can be described as the *organization man,* as the *automaton man,* and as *homo consumens.* He is, in addition, *homo mechanicus;* by this I mean a gadget man, deeply attracted by all that is mechanical, and inclined against that which is alive. It is true that man's biological and physiological equipment provides him with such strong sexual impulses that even *homo mechanicus* still has sexual desires and looks for women. But there is no doubt that the gadget man's interest in women is diminishing. A New Yorker cartoon pointed to this very amusingly; a salesgirl trying to sell a certain brand of perfume to a young female customer recommends it by remarking: "It smells like a new sports car." Indeed, any observer of male behavior today will confirm that this cartoon is more than a clever joke. There are apparently a great number of men who are more interested in sports cars, television and radio sets, space travel, and any number of gadgets than they are in women, love, nature, food; who are more stimulated by the manipulation of nonorganic, mechanical things than by life. It is not even too farfetched to assume that *homo mechanicus* is more proud of and fascinated by devices which can kill millions of people across a distance of several thousand miles within minutes, than he is frightened of and depressed by the possibility of such mass destruction. *Homo mechanicus* still enjoys sex and drink. But all these pleasures are sought within the frame of reference of the mechanical and unalive. He expects that there must be a button which, if pushed, will bring happiness, love, pleasure. (Many go to a psychoanalyst under the illusion that he can teach them where to find the button.) He looks at women as one would at a car: he knows the right buttons to push, he enjoys his power to make her "race" and he remains the cold, watching observer. *Homo mechanicus* becomes more and more interested in the manipulation of machines rather than in participation in and response to life. Hence he becomes indifferent to life, fascinated by the mechanical, and eventually attracted by death and total destruction.

Consider the role that killing plays in our amusements. The movies, the comic strips, the newspapers are full of excitement because they are full of reports of destruction, sadism, brutality. Millions of people live humdrum but comfortable existences—and nothing excites them more than to see or read of killings, whether it is murder or a fatal accident in an automobile race. Is this not an indication of how deep this fascination with death has already become? Or think of expressions such as being "thrilled to death" or "dying to" do this or that, or the expression "it kills me." Consider the indifference to life which is manifested in our rate of automobile accidents.

Briefly then, intellectualization, quantification, abstractification, bureaucratization, and reification—the very characteristics of modern industrial society, when applied to people rather than to things, are not the principles of life but those of mechanics. People living in such a system become indifferent to life and even attracted to death. They are not aware of this. They take the thrills of excitement for the joys of life and live under the illusion that they are very much alive when they have many things to own and to use. The lack of protest against nuclear war, the discussions of our "atomologists" of the balance sheet of total or half-total destruction, shows how far we have already gone into the "valley of the shadow of death."

These features of a necrophilous orientation exist in all modern industrial societies, regardless of their respective political structures. What Soviet state-capitalism has in common in this respect with corporate capitalism is more important than the features in which the systems differ. Both systems have in common the bureaucratic-mechanical approach, and both are preparing for total destruction.

The affinity between the necrophilous contempt for life and the admiration for speed and all that is mechanical has become apparent only in the last decades. Yet as early as in 1909 it was seen and succinctly expressed by Marinetti in his *Initial Manifesto of Futurism:*

1. We shall sing the love of danger, the habit of energy and boldness.

2. The essential elements of our poetry shall be courage, daring and rebellion.

3. Literature has hitherto glorified thoughtful immobility, ecstasy and sleep; we shall extol aggressive movement, feverish insomnia, the double quick step, the somersault, the box on the ear, the fisticuff.

4. We declare that the world's splendor has been enriched by a new beauty; the beauty of speed. A racing motor car, its frame adorned with great pipes, like snakes with explosive breath . . . a roaring motorcar, which looks as though running on a shrapnel is more beautiful than the *Victory of Samothrace.*

5. We shall sing of the man at the steering wheel, whose ideal stem transfixes the Earth, rushing over the circuit of her orbit.

6. The poet must give himself with frenzy, with splendor and with lavishness, in order to increase the enthusiastic fervor of the primordial elements.

7. There is no more beauty except in strife. No masterpiece without aggressiveness. Poetry must be a violent onslaught upon the unknown forces, to command them to bow before man.

8. We stand upon the extreme promontory of the centuries! ... Why should we look behind us, when we have to break in the mysterious portals of the Impossible? Time and Space died yesterday. Already we live in the absolute, since we have already created speed, eternal and ever-present.

9. We wish to glorify war—the only health giver of the world—militarism, patriotism, the destructive arm of the Anarchist, the beautiful Ideas that kill, the contempt for woman.

10. We wish to destroy the museums, the libraries, to fight against moralism, feminism, and all opportunistic and utilitarian meannesses.

11. We shall sing of the great crowds in the excitement of labor, pleasure and rebellion; of the multi-colored and polyphonic surf of revolutions in modern capital cities; of the nocturnal vibration of arsenals and workshops beneath their violent electric moons; of the greedy stations swallowing smoking snakes; of factories suspended from the clouds by their strings of smoke; of bridges leaping like gymnasts over the diabolical cutlery of sunbathed rivers; of adventurous liners scenting the horizon; of broad-chested locomotives prancing on the rails, like huge steel horses bridled with long tubes; and of the gliding flight of aeroplanes, the sound of whose screw is like the flapping of flags and the applause of an enthusiastic crowd.[1]

It is interesting to compare Marinetti's necrophilous interpretation of technique and industry with the deeply biophilous interpretation to be found in Walt Whitman's poems. At the end of his poem "Crossing Brooklyn Ferry" he says:

> Thrive, cities—bring your freight, bring your shows, ample and sufficient rivers,
> Expand, being than which none else is perhaps more spiritual,
> Keep your places, objects than which none else is more lasting.
> You have waited, you always wait, you dumb, beautiful ministers,
> We receive you with free sense at last, and are insatiate henceforward,
> Not you any more shall be able to foil us, or withhold yourselves from us,
> We use you, and do not cast you aside—we plant you permanently within us,
> We fathom you not—we love you—there is perfection in you also,

---

[1] Joshua C. Taylor, *Futurism,* Doubleday Co., 1909, p. 124.

You furnish your parts toward eternity,
Great or small, you furnish your parts toward the soul.

Or at the end of the "Song of the Open Road":

> Camerado, I give you my hand!
> I give you my love more precious than money,
> I give you myself before preaching or law;
> Will you give me yourself? Will you come travel with me?
> Shall we stick by each other as long as we live?

Whitman could not have expressed his opposition to necrophilia better than in this line: "To pass on (oh living, always living!) and leave the corpses behind."

If we compare Marinetti's attitude toward industry with that of Walt Whitman, it becomes clear that industrial production as such is not necessarily contrary to the principles of life. The question is whether the principles of life are subordinated to those of mechanization, or whether the principles of life are the dominant ones. Obviously, so far the industrialized world has not found an answer to the question which is posed here. How is it possible to create a humanist industrialism as against the bureaucratic industrialism which rules our lives today? . . .

Power

The first Industrial Revolution is being followed by the second Industrial Revolution, the beginning of which we witness at the present time. It is characterized by the fact not only that *living energy* has been replaced by mechanical energy, but that *human thought* is being replaced by the thinking of machines. Cybernetics and automation ("cybernation") make it possible to build machines that function much more precisely and much more quickly than the human brain for the purpose of answering important technical and organizational questions. Cybernation is creating the possibility of a new kind of economic and social organization. A relatively small number of mammoth enterprises has become the center of the economic machine and will rule it completely in the not-too-distant future. The enterprise, although legally the property of hundreds of thousands of stockholders, is managed (and for all practical purposes managed independently of the legal owners) by a self-perpetuating bureaucracy. The alliance between private business and government is becoming so close that the two components of this alliance become ever less distinguishable. The majority of the population in America is well fed, well housed, and well amused, and the sector of "underdeveloped" Americans who still live under substandard conditions will probably join the majority in the foreseeable future. We continue to profess individualism, freedom, and faith in God, but our professions are wearing thin when compared with the reality of the organization man's obsessional conformity guided by the principle of hedonistic materialism.

If society could stand still—which it can do as little as an individual—things might not be as ominous as they are. But we are headed in the direction of a new kind of society and a new kind of human life, of which we now see only the beginning and which is rapidly accelerating.

The Vision of the Dehumanized Society of A.D. 2000

What is the kind of society and the kind of man we might find in the year 2000, provided nuclear war has not destroyed the human race before then?

If people knew the likely course which American society will take, many if not most of them would be so horrified that they might take adequate measures to permit changing the course. If people are not aware of the direction in which they are going, they will awaken when it is too late and when their fate has been irrevocably sealed. Unfortunately, the vast majority are not aware of where they are going. They are not aware that the new society toward which they are moving is as radically different from Greek and Roman, medieval and traditional industrial societies as the agricultural society was from that of the food gatherers and hunters. Most people still think in the concepts of the society of the first Industrial Revolution. They see that we have more and better machines than man had fifty years ago and mark this down as progress. They believe that lack of direct political oppression is a manifestation of the achievement of personal freedom. Their vision of the year 2000 is that it will be the full realization of the aspirations of man since the end of the Middle Ages, and they do not see that the year 2000 may be not the fulfillment and happy culmination of a period in which man struggled for freedom and happiness, but the beginning of a period in which man ceases to be human and becomes transformed into an unthinking and unfeeling machine.

It is interesting to note that the dangers of the new dehumanized society were already clearly recognized by intuitive minds in the nineteenth century, and it adds to the impressiveness of their vision that they were people of opposite political camps.[2]

A conservative like Disraeli and a socialist like Marx were practically of

---

[2] Cf. the statements by Burckhardt, Proudhon, Baudelaire, Thoreau, Marx, Tolstoy quoted in *The Same Society,* pp. 184 ff.

the same opinion concerning the danger to man that would arise from the uncontrolled growth of production and consumption. They both saw how man would become weakened by enslavement to the machine and his own ever-increasing cupidity. Disraeli thought the solution could be found by containing the power of the new bourgeoisie; Marx believed that a highly industrialized society could be transformed into a humane one, in which man and not material goods were the goal of all social efforts.[3] One of the most brilliant progressive thinkers of the last century, John Stuart Mill, saw the problem with all clarity:

> I confess I am not charmed with the ideal of life held out by those who think that the normal state of human beings is that of struggling to get on; that the trampling, crushing, elbowing, and treading on each other's heels, which form the existing type of social life, are the most desirable lot of human kind, or anything but the disagreeable symptoms of one of the phases of industrial progress. . . . Most fitting, indeed, is it, that while riches are power, and to grow as rich as possible the universal object of ambition, the path to its attainment should be open to all, without favor or partiality. But the best state for human nature is that in which, while no one is poor, no one desires to be richer, nor has any reason to fear being thrust back by the efforts of others to push themselves forward.[4]

It seems that great minds a hundred years ago saw what would happen today or tomorrow, while we to whom it is happening blind ourselves in order not to be disturbed in our daily routine. It seems that liberals and conservatives are equally blind in this respect. There are only few writers of vision who have clearly seen the monster to which we are giving birth. It is not Hobbes' *Leviathan,* but a Moloch, the all-destructive idol, to which human life is to be sacrificed. This Moloch has been described most imaginatively by Orwell and Aldous Huxley, by a number of science-fiction writers who show more perspicacity than most professional sociologists and psychologists.

I have already quoted Brzezinski's description of the technetronic society, and only want to quote the following addition: "The largely humanist-oriented, occasionally ideologically minded intellectual dissenter . . . is rapidly being displaced either by experts and specialists . . . or by the generalists-integrators, who become in effect house-ideologues for those in power, providing overall intellectual integration for disparate actions."[5]

A profound and brilliant picture of the new society has been given recently by one of the most outstanding humanists of our age, Lewis Mumford.[6] Future historians, if there are any, will consider his work to be one

---

[3] Cf. Erich Fromm, *Marx's Concept of Man* (New York: Ungar, 1961).

[4] *Principles of Political Economy* (London: Longmans, 1929; 1st edition, 1848).

[5] "The Technetronic Society," p. 19.

[6] Lewis Mumford, *The Myth of the Machine.*

of the prophetic warnings of our time. Mumford gives new depth and perspective to the future by analyzing its roots in the past. The central phenomenon which connects past and future, as he sees it, he calls the "megamachine."

The "megamachine" is the totally organized and homogenized social system in which society as such functions like a machine and men like its parts. This kind of organization by total coordination, by "the constant increase of order, power, predictability, and above all control," achieved almost miraculous technical results in early megamachines like the Egyptian and Mesopotamian societies, and it will find its fullest expression, with the help of modern technology, in the future of the technological society.

Mumford's concept of the megamachine helps to make clear certain recent phenomena. The first time the megamachine was used on a large scale in modern times was, it seems to me, in the Stalinist system of in-dustrialization, and after that, in the system used by Chinese Communism. While Lenin and Trotsky still hoped that the Revolution would eventually lead to the mastery of society by the individual, as Marx had visualized, Stalin betrayed whatever was left of these hopes and sealed the betrayal by the physical extinction of all those in whom the hope might not have completely disappeared. Stalin could build his megamachine on the nucleus of a well-developed industrial sector, even though one far below those of countries like England or the United States. The communist leaders in China were confronted with a different situation. They had no industrial nucleus to speak of. Their only capital was the physical energy and the passions and thoughts of 700 million people. They decided that by means of the complete coordination of this human material they could create the equivalent of the original accumulation of capital necessary to achieve a technical development which in a relatively short time would reach the level of that of the West. This total coordination had to be achieved by a mixture of force, personality cult, and indoctrination which is in con-trast to the freedom and individualism Marx had foreseen as the essential elements of a socialist society. One must not forget, however, that the ideals of the overcoming of private egotism and of maximal consumption have remained elements in the Chinese system, at least thus far, although blended with totalitarianism, nationalism, and thought control, thus vitiat-ing the humanist vision of Marx.

The insight into this radical break between the first phase of industrial-ization and the second Industrial Revolution, in which society itself be-comes a vast machine, of which man is a living particle, is obscured by certain important differences between the megamachine of Egypt and that of the twentieth century. First of all, the labor of the live parts of the Egyptian machine was forced labor. The naked threat of death or starva-tion forced the Egyptian worker to carry out his task. Today, in the twentieth century, the worker in the most developed industrial countries, such as the United States, has a comfortable life—one which would have seemed like a life of undreamed-of luxury to his ancestor working a hundred years ago. He has, and in this point lies one of the errors of Marx, participated in the economic progress of capitalist society, profited from it, and, indeed, has a great deal more to lose than his chains.

The bureaucracy which directs the work is very different from the bureaucratic elite of the old megamachine. Its life is guided more or less by the same middle-class virtues that are valid for the worker; although its members are better paid than the worker, the difference in consumption is one of quantity rather than quality. Employers and workers smoke the same cigarettes and they ride in cars that look the same even though the better cars run more smoothly than the cheaper ones. They watch the same movies and the same television shows, and their wives use the same refrigerators.[7]

The managerial elite are also different from those of old in another respect: they are just as much appendages of the machine as those whom they command. They are just as alienated, or perhaps more so, just as anxious, or perhaps more so, as the worker in one of their factories. They are bored, like everyone else, and use the same antidotes against boredom. They are not as the elites were of old—a culture-creating group. Although they spend a good deal of their money to further science and art, as a class they are as much consumers of this "cultural welfare" as its recipients. The culture-creating group lives on the fringes. They are creative scientists and artists, but it seems that, thus far, the most beautiful blossom of twentieth-century society grows on the tree of science, and not on the tree of art.

The Present Technological Society

Its Principles

The technetronic society may be the system of the future, but it is not yet here; it can develop from what is already here, and it probably will, unless a sufficient number of people see the danger and redirect our course. In order to do so, it is necessary to understand in greater detail the operation of the present technological system and the effect it has on man.

What are the guiding principles of this system as it is today?

It is programed by two principles that direct the efforts and thoughts of everyone working in it: The first principle is the maxim that something *ought* to be done because it is technically *possible* to do it. If it is possible to build nuclear weapons, they must be built even if they might destroy us all. If it is possible to travel to the moon or to the planets, it must be

---

[7] The fact that the underdeveloped sector of the population does not take part in this new style of life has been mentioned above.

done, even if at the expense of many unfulfilled needs here on earth. This principle means the negation of all values which the humanist tradition has developed. This tradition said that something should be done because it is needed for man, for his growth, joy, and reason, because it is beautiful, good, or true. Once the principle is accepted that something ought to be done because it is technically possible to do it, all other values are dethroned, and technological development becomes the foundation of ethics.[8]

The second principle is that of *maximal efficiency and output.* The requirement of maximal efficiency, leads as a consequence to the requirement of minimal individuality. The social machine works more efficiently, so it is believed, if individuals are cut down to purely quantifiable units whose personalities can be expressed on punched cards. These units can be administered more easily by bureaucratic rules because they do not make trouble or create friction. In order to reach this result, men must be deindividualized and taught to find their identity in the corporation rather than in themselves. . . .

Change

What Is the Nature of "Humanistic Management" and Its Methods?

The basic principle of the humanistic management method is that, in spite of the bigness of the enterprises, centralized planning, and cybernation, the individual participant asserts himself toward the managers, circumstances, and machines, and ceases to be a powerless particle which has no active part in the process. Only by such affirmation of his will can the energies of the individual be liberated and his mental balance be restored.

The same principle of humanistic management can also be expressed in this way: While in alienated bureaucracy all power flows from above downward, in humanistic management there is a two-way street; the "subjects"[9] of the decision made above respond according to their own will and concerns; their response not only reaches the top decision makers but forces them to respond in turn. The "subjects" of decision making have a

---

[8] While revising this manuscript I read a paper by Hasan Ozbekhan, "The Triumph of Technology: 'Can' Implies 'Ought.' " This paper, adapted from an invited presentation at MIT and published in mimeographed form by System Development Corporation, Santa Monica, California, was sent to me by the courtesy of Mr. George Weinwurm. As the title indicates, Ozbekhan expresses the same concept as the one I present in the text. His is a brilliant presentation of the problem from the standpoint of an outstanding specialist in the field of management science, and I find it a very encouraging fact that the same idea appears in the work of authors in fields as different as his and mine. I quote a sentence that shows the identity of his concept and the one presented in the text: "Thus, feasibility, which is a strategic concept, becomes elevated into a normative concept with the result that whatever technological reality indicates we *can* do is taken as implying that we *must* do it" (p.7).

[9] In the following, I shall call those subject to control by bureaucracy "subjects."

right to challenge the decision makers. Such a challenge would first of all require a rule that if a sufficient number of "subjects" demanded that the corresponding bureaucracy (on whatever level) answer questions, explain its procedures, the decision makers would respond to the demand.

At this point, so many objections to the foregoing suggestions will have accumulated in the mind of the reader that I had better discuss them right here if I do not want to lose the reader's attention for what follows in this chapter. I deal first with the management of enterprises.

The first objection probably is that the type of active participation of the "subjects" would be incompatible with efficient centralized management and planning. This objection is plausible (a) provided one does not have any compelling reason to think that the present method of alienated bureaucracy is pathogenic; (b) if one thinks only of the tried and proven methods and shies away from imaginative new solutions; (c) if one insists that even if one could find new methods, the principle of maximal efficiency must never be given up even for a time. If, on the other hand, one follows the considerations offered in this book and recognizes the grave danger for the total system of our society inherent in our bureaucratic methods, these objections are not as compelling as they are to those who are satisfied with the operation of our present system.

More specifically, if one recognizes the difficulties and does not start out with the conviction that they are unsurmountable, one will begin to examine the problems concretely and in detail. Here, too, one may arrive at the conclusion that the dichotomy between maximal centralization and complete decentralization presents an unnecessary polarization, that one can deal with the concept of *optimal* centralization and *optimal* grass-roots participation. Optimal centralization would be the degree of centralization which is necessary for effective large-scale organization and planning; optimal participation would be the participation which does not make centralized management impossible, yet permits the participants the optimum of responsible participation. This formulation is obviously rather general and not sufficient as a basis for taking immediate steps. If a problem of such magnitude emerges in the application of scientific knowledge to technique, the engineer is not discouraged; he recognizes the necessity of research which will result in the solution of the problem. But as soon as we deal with human problems, such difficulties tend to discourage most people or they flatly state that "it cannot be done."

We have, indeed, an unbounded imagination and initiative for solving technical problems, but a most restricted imagination when we deal with human problems. Why is this so? An obvious answer is that we do not have the knowledge in the field of the science of man that we have in the natural sciences and in technique. But this answer is not convincing; why don't we have the necessary knowledge? Or, and this is even more to the point, why don't we apply the knowledge we do have? Nothing can be *proved* without further study, but I am convinced that to find a practical solution for the integration of optimal centralization and optimal decentralization will be less difficult than to find technical solutions for space travel. The real answer why this kind of research is not done lies in the fact that, considering our present priorities, our interest in finding humanely more acceptable solutions to our social organization is only feeble. Nevertheless, while emphasizing the need for research, we must not forget that there has already been a good deal of experimentation and discussion about these problems going on in the last decades. Both in the field of industrial psychology and management science, one finds a number of valuable theoretical discussions and experiments.

Another objection, often combined with the previous one, says that as long as there is an effective control of decision making on the political level, there is no need for active participation in a corporation, since it will be properly supervised by the legislative and executive branches of the government. This objection does not take into account the fact that today government and the corporations are already so interwoven that it is difficult to say who controls whom—furthermore, that government decisions themselves are not under effective control by the citizens. But even if there existed a satisfactory active participation of the citizens in the political process, as it is suggested here, the corporation itself must become responsive to the will, not only of the participants, but of the public at large inasmuch as it is affected by the decisions of the corporation. If such direct control over the corporation does not exist, it will be very difficult for the government to exercise power over the private sector of the system.

Another objection will point out that the double responsibility in decision making which is proposed here will be a source of endless friction between the top and the "subjects" and will be ineffective for this psychological reason. Talking about the problem in an abstract sense, we may easily find it formidable, but once such changes are accepted, the resulting conflicts will be far less sharp and insoluble than they are if one looks at the picture in an abstract way. After all, the managers have an interest in performing, and so have the participants in an enterprise. As soon as the bureaucrat becomes "vulnerable," that is to say, begins to respond to desires and claims from those subject to him, both sides will become more interested in the problems than in preserving their positions either as authority or challenger. That this is possible has been shown at a number of universities in the United States and abroad where once the participation of students was accepted, there was little friction between administration and students. This has been demonstrated in the Yugoslav system of the self-management of the workers and in the experience of the many cooperative movements all over the world.

If the bureaucratic mode were changed from an alienated to a humanistic one, it would necessarily lead to a change in the type of manager who is successful. The defensive type of personality who clings to his bureaucratic image and who is afraid of being vulnerable and of confronting persons directly and openly would be at a disadvantage. On the other hand, the imaginative, nonfrightened, responsive person would be successful if the method of management were changed. These considerations show how erroneous it is to speak of certain methods of management which cannot be changed because the managers "would not be willing or capable of changing them." What is left out here is the fact that new methods would constitute a selective principle of managers. This does not mean that most present managers would be replaced by the new type of manager. No doubt there are many who under the present system cannot utilize their responsive capacities and who will be able to do so once the system gives them a chance.

Among the objections to the idea of active participation of the individual in the enterprises in which he works, perhaps the most popular one is the statement that, in view of increasing cybernation, the working time of the individual will be so short and the time devoted to leisure so long that the activation of the individual will no longer need to take place in his work situation, but will be sufficiently accomplished during his leisure time. This idea, I believe, is based on an erroneous concept of human existence and of work. Man, even under the most favorable technological conditions, has to take the responsibility of producing food, clothing, housing, and all other material necessities. This means he has to work. Even if most physical labor is taken over by the machines, man has still to take part in the process of the exchange between himself and nature; only if man were a disembodied being or an angel with no physical needs, would work completely disappear. Man, being in need of assimilating nature, of organizing and directing the process of material production, of distribution, of social organization, of responses to natural catastrophes, can never sit back and let things take care of themselves. Work in a technological society may not be a "curse" any more, but that paradisaical state in which man does not have to take care of his material needs is a technological fantasy. Or will the solution be, as Brzezinski predicts, that only the elite will have the privilege of working while the majority is busy with consumption? Indeed, that could be a solution to the problem, but it would reduce the majority to the status of slaves, in the paradoxical sense that they would become irresponsible and useless parasites, while the freeman alone would have the right to live a full life, which includes work. *If man is passive in the process of production and organization, he will also be passive during his leisure time.* If he abdicates responsibility and participation in the process of sustaining life, he will acquire the passive role in all other spheres of life and be dependent on those who take care of him. We already see this happening today. Man has more leisure time than before, but most people show this passiveness in the leisure which is forced upon them by the method of alien-ated bureaucratism. Leisure time is mostly of the spectator or consumption type; rarely is it an expression of activeness.

One example may clarify the point I am trying to make, that of taking care of one's health. It seems quite feasible that many functions of the art of medicine can be taken over by the computer, like diagnosis, treat-ment, prescription, etc. But it appears doubtful that the capacity for high-ly individualized observation, which the outstanding physician has, can be replaced by the computer, e.g., observation of the expression in a person's eye or face, a capacity impossible to quantify and to translate into pro-gramming language. Outstanding achievements in medicine will be lost in a completely automatized system.[10] But beyond this, the individual will be so completely conditioned to submit to machines that he will lose the capacity to take care of his health in an active, responsible way. He will run to the "health service" whenever he has a physical problem, and he will lose the ability to observe his own physical processes, to discern changes, and to consider remedies for himself, even simple ones of keeping a diet or doing the right kind of exercise.

If man should be relieved of the task of being responsible for the func-tioning of the productive and administrative system, he would become a being of complete helplessness, lack of self-confidence, and dependence on the machine and its specialists; he would not only be incapable of making active use of his leisure time, he would also face a catastrophe whenever the smooth functioning of the system was threatened.

In this respect one more point, and a very important one, must be mentioned. Even if machines could take care of all work, of all planning, of all organizational decisions, and even of all health problems, they can-not take care of the problems arising between man and man. In this sphere of interpersonal relations, human judgment, response, responsibility, and decision the machine cannot replace human functioning. There are those, like Marcuse, who think that in a cybernated and "nonrepressive" society that is completely satisfied materially there would be no more human conflicts like those expressed in the Greek or Shakespearean drama or the great novels. I can understand that completely alienated people can see the future of human existence in this way, but I am afraid they express more about their own emotional limitations than about future possibilities. The assumption that the problems, conflicts, and tragedies between man and man will disappear if there are no materially unfulfilled needs is a childish daydream.

Active participation in the affairs of the country as a whole and of

---

[10] Just as the computer chess player is better than the average chess player but not as good as the chess master, or as the computer can be programed to compose music à la Mozart or Beethoven without ever reaching the qualities of a Mozart or Beethoven composition.

states and communities, as well as of large enterprises, would require the formation of face-to-face groups, within which the process of information exchange, debate, and decision making would be conducted. Before discussing the structure of such groups, in all kinds of centralized enterprises and political decision making, respectively, let us have a look at the characteristics such face-to-face groups should have.

The first is that the *number* of participating people must be restricted in such a way that the discussion remains direct and does not allow the rhetoric or the manipulating influence of demagogues to become effective. If people meet regularly and know each other, they begin to feel whom they can trust and whom they cannot, who is constructive and who is not, and in the process of their own participation, their own sense of responsibility and self-confidence grows.

Second, objective and relevant *information* which is the basis for everyone's having an approximately clear and accurate picture of the basic issues must be given to each group. . . .

A Movement

The conclusion seems unavoidable that the ideas of activation, responsibility, participation—that is, of the humanization of technological society—can find full expression only in a *movement* which is not bureaucratic, not connected with the political machines, and which is the result of active and imaginative efforts by those who share the same aims. Such a movement itself, in its organization and method, would be expressive of the aim to which it is devoted: to educate its members for the new kind of society in the process of striving for it.

In the following, I will try to describe three different forms of this movement.

The first step would be the formation of a National Council which could be called the "Voice of American Conscience." I think of a group of, say, fifty Americans whose integrity and capability are unquestioned. While they might have different religious and political convictions, they would share the humanist aims which are the basis for the humanization of technological society. They would deliberate and issue statements which, because of the weight of those who issued them, would be newsworthy, and because of the truth and rationality of their contents would win attention from at least a large sector of the American public. Such Councils could also be formed in a local level, dealing with the general questions but specifically with the practical questions relevant for the city or state which they represented. One could imagine that there might be a whole organization of Councils of the Voice of American Conscience, with a nationally representative group and many local groups following basically the same aims. . . .

It is essential that the Groups not be based on particular formulations of concepts which one member has to accept in order to participate. What matters is the practice of life, the total attitude, the goal, and not a specific conceptualization. All this does not mean that the Groups should be inarticulate, that they should not discuss or even argue over concepts, but that what unites them is the attitude and action of every member and not a conceptual slogan to which he subscribes. The Group should, of course, have a general aim—which has been expressed before as the general aim of the movement. But they may very well differ considerably among themselves as to methods. I could imagine one Group which was in favor of civil disobedience and another which did not favor civil disobedience. Each individual would have a chance to join that particular Group whose attitude was most congenial to his own and yet be part of a larger movement which could even permit itself to have diversity as considerable as that between civil disobedience and its opposite.

As to the question of the relation between the Voice of the American Conscience, the Clubs, and the Groups, I would suggest that there be no formal bureaucratic relation, except perhaps that the Clubs and the Groups could draw on resources presented by a common office of information, and/or by a publication serving both Clubs and Groups. It seems also possible that individual members of the Groups would choose to work in the Clubs as their special project.

This whole outline of the movement is meant to be a very tentative proposal of how to begin. Maybe better ones will be made in debating these proposals. In fact, there are a large number of voluntary, purposeful communal groups already existing, from whose experience a great deal can be learned. There is an ever-increasing tendency in the direction of individual initiative in group activity in all classes of the population, from student communities to farmers' organizations, like the National Farmers' Organization. There are purposeful agricultural communities, many of which are functioning successfully on the economic and the human plane, and there are many forms of community living in cities. Spontaneous formation of purposeful groups has, in fact, deep roots in the American tradition. There is no lack of example and of data which would be helpful in building this movement.

The movement is conceived as an important element in the transformation of society which would allow the individual to find ways for immediate participation and action, and give an answer to his question: What can I do? It will allow the individual to emerge from his chronic isolation.

We are in the very midst of the crisis of modern man. We do not have too much time left. If we do not begin now, it will probably be too late. But there is hope—because there is a real possibility that man can reassert himself, and that he can make the technological society human. "It is not up to us to complete the task, but we have no right to abstain from it."[11]

---

[11] Mischna, *Pirke Aboth.*

2

Systems Theories

Few terms in the lexicon of political theorists have been abused as much as the word "system." Frequently one hears political scientists talking about systems analysis, systems theory, the political system, the American system, or just "the system." It would be a mistake to think that "system" was being used the same way in each case. In fact, if one asked a political scientist what he meant by a specific use of the term, there is a good chance that he would admit to being confused. In everyday language, which also contains many forms of the word "system," ambiguities and minor confusions do not create inordinate difficulties. We can usually sort out what a person means by quickly investigating the context of his remarks. However, in the discourse of political theory, as in any specialized branch of human thinking, terminological problems are much more serious. One must be sure of the way in which a political theorist is using his key terms before one can even begin to understand his line of argument. This does not mean that each word in the vocabulary of political theory must have only one usage. There would be no way to enforce such a demand in an environment of relative academic freedom. Moreover, even if such enforcement could be made to work, an array of rigid definitions would be likely to stifle the progressive development of thought. Rather, terminological problems are best avoided when the writer or speaker specifies his definitions at the beginning of the discussion and holds to the same usage throughout his argument. Even this recommendation, however, frequently goes unheeded. Like other human beings, political theorists have been known to seek a margin of advantage over both their opponents in the discipline and their audiences. One way of gaining a distinct advantage in theoretical activity is to keep the usage of one's terms vague. This allows the theorist to shift his meanings when it is convenient to do so. Of course, such tactics do nothing to improve the quality of political theory. At best they are unconscious errors, and at worst they are outright attempts at fraud.

In our discussion of systems theory, we will at least try to define the terms we use. This in itself will be no easy task because of the wide variety of meanings that are currently attached to the word "system" alone. We may begin by looking at some of these meanings. The word "system" is derived from the Greek term "synistanai," which means a placing together. All of the current usages have in common at least the notion of some things being brought together and perhaps related to one another. In general, then, the meanings of "system" vary according to what is being brought together and the way in which the things in question are related to one another. In ordinary language, we talk of a "system" for winning at card games or succeeding at a task. Here we are bringing together a set of practical rules and relating them as steps on the way to a goal. In political theory, "system" is not used in this manner. Instead, political theorists talk about approaches and methods. We also talk about systems of thought, such as the system of Newtonian physics or the system of Euclidean geometry. Here a group of generalizations or assumptions and theorems about a given subject are being brought together and related either logically or in some looser way. Again, political theorists usually do not use "system" in this sense. Instead, they normally speak of theories of politics. Finally, in day-to-day language, we may talk about systems of objects in the world. For example, we make reference to systems of government, biological systems like the respiratory system, and transportation systems. Here we are bringing together certain objects and relating them, usually, by trying to show some interdependence between them. While some meaning of this sort is often implied when political theorists use the word "system," there are still many difficulties. First, what elements are brought together to form a political system? Second, how are these elements interdependent?

How a political theorist answers the above questions depends upon his approach to the study of public affairs. When institutionalists employ the term "system," they normally mean bringing together the body of laws and regulations produced by a government and relating them to a body of written or unwritten constitutional rules which specify how those laws and regulations are supposed to be produced. When behavioralists use the term "system," they are primarily speaking of bringing together a set of public activities and relating them to the roles of the various actors. They then frequently attempt to show that these roles are interdependent. The entire network of public roles may be considered a "political system." When contemporary critics use the term "system," they also mean the bringing together of a set of public activities. However, they often relate those activities to a general principle which they believe is at work in a given society or group of societies. For example, Marxists view the "capitalist system" as a set of activities which can be understood by relating them to the principle of privately owned industries composed of firms whose owners organize production to maximize profits. There is a fourth use of the term "system" in political theory which is employed in a highly specialized current of thought called "systems theory." Here "system" refers to a set of interrelated variables, as distinguished from an environment, which has a tendency to maintain itself under the impact of environmental disturbances. When we discuss systems theories of politics in this book, we are not referring to this last usage, even though David Easton, who is represented here, does utilize such a definition.

Do the institutionalists, the behavioralists, and the contemporary critics have anything in common when they use the word "system"? At first glance it would not seem so, for they bring together different objects and relate them in different ways. Appearances, however, may be misleading. Whatever political theorists who use the word "system" may bring together, they do *not* bring together complete human beings. This does not mean that a group of human beings who interact with one another cannot be considered a system. Instead, it means that political theorists do not normally use the term "system" to characterize such a group. The political system, in other words, rarely refers to all of the human beings who live under a government and all of their thoughts, feelings, actions, and interactions. Thus, to systems theorists the primary element in the political system is not the individual person. This marks the major difference between systems theories of public life and the psychological theories of public affairs—which do make the individual person the important unit of analysis.

Systems theories of public life always encounter the barrier of common sense. It is difficult for people to believe that political activity is not best understood by studying human beings as whole entities. If complete persons are not the elements of political systems, what elements are more worthy of consideration? We have already noted that institutional political scientists study laws, constitutions, and regulations rather than human beings. However, we also remarked that classical, behavioral, and critical thinkers have not looked with favor on this approach. They have felt that there was more to public life than what is reflected in dusty archives. Yet many classicists, behavioralists, and critics have adopted systems theories of public life. How is this possible?

Political theorists who have adopted a systems point of view have usually brought together only some human activities and have related them to roles or general principles of social organization. Implicit in their work has been the definition of "political system" used in this book. We refer to a political system as a bringing together of the public activities in a community and the relating of these activities to public roles or general principles of social organization. Public activities are those activities which directly or indirectly affect the entire community, and public roles are sets of rights and duties which have reference to that community. In other words, public affairs are "systematized" or form a "system" when they display some identifiable pattern. It is useless to talk about a political system when there is no such pattern. This does not mean that the actors in the political system that we are observing are conscious of the pattern. It is the theorist who observes the pattern.

The behavioral political theorists tend to relate public activities to specific roles and then relate the roles to one another. Thus, in order to understand the behavioral approach to systems theory, it is necessary to grasp the concept of "role." Roles are associated with the positions that a person occupies in a society. They can be viewed as the rights and duties which are generally recognized as being attached to a person who occupies a position or as the behavior that is expected of a person who occupies a position. Everyone is familiar with the practice of role playing, even if some people cannot supply a rigorous definition of "role." College students usually realize that they are expected to refrain from causing disruptions in the middle of a class, while students in elementary and high school are often less sure about proper behavior in this respect. The same person who disturbed his elementary-school teachers by having ruler fights and passing love notes will often, on reaching college, remain silent through dull lectures and break out in a sweat when he has to pay a visit to a professor's office. What accounts for this behavioral change? Is it conceivable that the person has undergone a revolution in his entire personality structure during the lapse of a few years? Systems theorists would raise serious doubts about the existence of such rapid and comprehensive changes in personality. Instead, they would point out that disruptive classroom behavior frequently wins a person respect in high school while it yields scorn in college. Further, they would show that elementary- and high-school teachers expect disturbances as part of a day's work, while college professors will not tolerate such problems. In short, the role of the elementary- or high-school student is not the same as the role of the college student. Even if the official rights and duties attached to both roles are similar, the informal expectations are often worlds apart. Thus, a systems theory of education would describe the roles of students, teachers, administrators, and, perhaps, janitors, without ever mentioning complete human beings. Only that segment of human activity related to happenings in and around the school would be included in such a systems theory.

System theories of politics devised by behavioralists analyze public roles, or roles that have reference to the affairs of an entire community of human beings. Many of these roles are familiar to all of us. For example, there is the role of the voter, the role of the candidate for public office, the role of the bureaucrat, the role of the legislator, the role of the elected executive, and the role of the judge. Both legal rights and duties and informal expectations are attached to all of these roles. When they place all public roles in some sort of relationship to one another, many behavioral theorists believe that they can discern an overall pattern of public activity which they call the "political system." David Easton is one of the leading advocates of this position. Easton claims that a political system is constituted by those human acts which have reference to "the authoritative allocation of values" for a society. These acts can be organized into roles that are in turn organized into the pattern of activity which he calls the political system. He states clearly that public roles do not exhaust human activity, and that there are other roles within the family system, the economic system, the educational system, and so on.

The concept of role is frequently a source of anxiety for people. They wonder whether their full humanity is exhausted by the sum of their roles. They wonder if their seemingly unique identities result merely from the fact that no one else plays all of the same roles that they do. They become preoccupied with the fear that they are no more than products of a social system far greater than any individual human being. While there are dangers that individuals will be reduced to the condition of mere social functionaries in a highly organized technological society, there is no reason to jump to the conclusion that people are simply personifications of the sums of their roles. Certainly, the pressures to conform to role expectations are strong. If roles embody rights, duties, and expectations, the person who does not exercise his rights, discharge his duties, and fulfill the expectations of a significant number of others will be subject to penalties. For example, the student who disrupts a class in college may be dismissed from that class, dropped from school altogether, or politely told to pay a visit to the resident psychologist. However, every person in a highly organized technological society has a variety of roles to play. Some conflict with one another and others demand conflicting actions. While such role conflicts are often a source of profound discomfort, they are also a gateway to freedom. A person may emphasize one of his roles over another, one part of a given role over another part, or even, in rare cases, invent a new role. Thus, if the behavioral approach to systems theory does not take the complete human being as the basic unit of the political system, neither does such an approach make the complete human being into a marionette.

Contemporary social critics who adopt a systems point of view are even more concerned with human beings than the behavioralists. In general, the critics do not sharply distinguish political activity from other modes of human activity; they prefer to examine the entire range of social acts. Like the behavioralists, they claim that these actions can be described in terms of a meaningful pattern. However, they believe that this pattern is less dependent upon a network of role expectations than it is upon some general principle of social organization. To understand what is meant by a "general principle of social organization," it would be helpful to consider the work of Herbert Marcuse, a contemporary critic who employs systems theory. Marcuse is just as certain as Easton that public affairs can best be analyzed by using units other than the concrete human being. In discussing his method of analysis, Marcuse relates: ". . . I do not refer to individually experienced social needs and consciously inaugurated policies: they may be thus experienced and inaugurated or they may not. I rather speak of *tendencies,* forces which can be identified by an analysis of the existing society and which assert themselves even if the policy makers are not aware of them. They express the requirements of the established apparatus of production, distribution, and consumption. . . ." These "requirements of the established apparatus," which include economic, technical, political, and mental requisites, must be met if this apparatus upon which the population depends for its very life is to continue functioning. Marcuse concludes that the most general requirement of contemporary industrial societies is to suppress the imaginative uses that people would make of the present and developing technologies. He believes that unless the imagination is suppressed and freedom to envision new alternatives is limited, both capitalist and communist societies as presently organized would disintegrate. In this view, these societies demand unreasonable sacrifices of human desires in the light of the potentialities of advanced technologies. Both of these societies use force and fraud to ensure that these sacrifices continue to be made. Marcuse, of course, believes that significant private problems are essentially public problems. It is the way the "apparatus" is organized that causes people to experience many of their frustrations. If the principle of social organization could be changed, there might be fewer situations which would cause frustration and more of a chance for people to exercise their freedom in creating desired objects and relationships. Marcuse thinks that such a change, which would have to be brought about by revolutionary activity, will be quite difficult to make. Contemporary technological societies have invented means of implanting wasteful and destructive needs in human beings which these human beings sacrifice themselves to satisfy. Advertising and propaganda are the modern means of exploitation.

Systems theory, when elaborated by either behavioralists or contemporary critics, tends to view private problems essentially as public problems. Moreover, systems theory does not normally make the concrete human being the primary unit of political analysis. On both of these counts, systems theory differs from psychological theory.

ROUSSEAU

Behavioralists and contemporary critics are not the only political theorists who have adopted a systems point of view for the analysis of public life. While the elaboration of the term "system" is a recent intellectual development, classical thinkers devised descriptions of politics in which they employed units of a scope beyond that of the concrete person. Of course, since classical theory is on the whole more eclectic than contemporary political thought, it is difficult to find any classical thinker who devised as pure and critically defined a systems theory as did Easton or Marcuse. We must remember that the classical theorists were frequently much less concerned with the logic of their task of inquiry than current political theorists tend to be. Just as the classicists often used many kinds of descriptive statements without distinguishing among them, they also employed a wide variety of units of analysis without caring which was the most important. Self-consciousness about approach, method, and theory is a mark of the present age rather than a characteristic of previous eras. Self-consciousness about the problems to be explored, however, has always been part of theorizing about public affairs. Therefore, when we say that Plato was a "psychological" theorist, Rousseau was a "systems" theorist, and Hobbes was a "conflict" theorist, we are identifying tendencies and trends in their work from our vantage point, rather than describing what they actually thought about their investigations.

Jean Jacques Rousseau, who was born in 1712 and grew up in Geneva, Switzerland, is the political theorist most responsible for advocating the romantic ideal which we find so important a source of contemporary problems of identity. In his *Confessions,* Rousseau attempted to give an account of his entire emotional and moral life, while in his treatise on education, *Emile,* he advanced the position that children should be educated in conformance to their "natures" rather than trained to act in accordance with repressive social roles. In both of these works, Rousseau emerges as a romantic individualist who discovers identity in the dynamic spontaneity of human beings. However, even in *Emile,* Rousseau shows a tendency to favor systems theory as the best description of civilized societies. "Civilized man is but a fractional unit that is dependent on its denominator, and whose value consists in its relation to the whole, which is the social organization. Good social institutions are those which are the best able to make man unnatural, and to take from him his absolute existence in order to give him one which is relative, and to transport the *me* into the common unity, in such a way that each individual no longer feels himself one, but part of the unit, and is no longer susceptible of feeling save when forming a part of the whole." In his *Social Contract*, Rousseau works this idea out by identifying two possible principles of social organization. First, he says, societies may be organized to serve the interests of particular groups or classes in the community at the expense of other groups or classes. Second, societies may be organized to serve the general interest of the community or to express the "general will." Rousseau was never completely clear about what the "general will" expressed. However, we can be certain that it did not express interests of any particular person or group that could only be satisfied at the expense of other individuals and groups. Full expression of the general will excluded the exercise of coercion by one private person over another. We may say that Rousseau's works contain two ideals, each of which has had a profound impact on both modern political thought and modern social movements. At times, Rousseau idealized spontaneity and the natural and free communion of human beings on an emotional level. He praised personal autonomy and advised people to follow their choices to completion with absolute sincerity. At other times, he said that the natural life could not be actualized in an era of civilization. Instead, he recommended a regime in which moral obligations would replace impulsive freedom and dispassionate justice would take the place of emotional communion. The ideal of spontaneity has been taken up by such varied groups as the hippies, the advocates of sensitivity training, and segments of the New Left. The ideal of dispassionate judgment has become embodied in many of our contemporary bureaucracies and complex organizations. Many of the current problems involved with identity, power, and change can be better understood once they are recognized as the result of a struggle to reconcile Rousseau's two ideals.

Identity*

Infancy—General Principles

Everything is good as it comes from the hands of the Author of Nature; but everything degenerates in the hands of man.[†]   He forces one country

---

*Pages 97-102 from *Emile* by J. J. Rousseau. Pages 102-114 from *Social Contract: Essays by Locke, Hume, and Rousseau,* trans. Gerard Hopkins with an introduction by Sir Ernest Barker; published by the Oxford University Press, New York, 1962.

[†]This is the keynote to Rousseau's theory of education, and is the central thought of all the writers of the Spencerian school, whose definition of education might be formulated as follows: *Education is adaptation to environment by environment.* By Nature, these writers seem to mean the world of matter and of physical forces, personified as an intelligent and infallible guide; and from environment they carefully exclude all the modifications of matter and force which have been made by human art.

Rousseau, who was ever inclined to adopt extreme views, and who was incapable of stating a case with judicial fairness, sought to divest the current education of its artificial and absurd forms by a return toward *primitive simplicity*; and so he sequesters Emile, his trial pupil from the abnormal society of the day, somewhat as a naturalist might remove a plant from an abnormal habitat in order to discover its real character and to restore it to proper conditions of growth. Rousseau believed that French society had become so bad, or so *unnatural*, that a child could not be trained into a real man while surrounded by so many to nourish the productions of another; one tree to bear the fruits of another. He mingles and confounds the climates, the elements, the seasons; he mutilates his dog, his horse, and his slave; he overturns everything, disfigures everything; he loves deformity, monsters; he will have nothing as Nature made it, not even man; like a saddle-horse, man must be trained for man's service—he must be made over according to his fancy, like a tree in his garden.

Plants are formed by cultivation and men by education. Had man been born tall and strong, his stature and strength would have been useless to him until he had been taught to use them; they would have been injurious to him by preventing others from thinking of assisting him; and, left to himself, he would have died of want before he had known his needs. People pity the lot of the child; they do now see that the human race would have perished if man had not begun by being a child.

We are born weak; we have need of strength; we are born destitute of everything; we have need of assistance; we are born stupid; we have need of judgment. All that we have not at our birth, but which we need when we are grown, is given us by education.

We derive this education from nature, from men, or from things. The internal development of our faculties and organs is the education of nature; the use which we learn to make of this development is the education of men; while the acquisition of personal experience from the objects that affect us is the education of things.*

Each one of us is thus formed by three kinds of teachers. The pupil in whom their different lessons are at variance is badly educated, and will never be in harmony with himself; while he in whom they all agree, in whom they all tend to the same end—he alone moves toward his destiny and consistently lives; he alone is well educated.†

Now, of these three different educations, that of nature is entirely independent of ourselves, while that of things depends on ourselves only in certain respects. The education we receive of men is the only one of which we are truly the masters; but even this is true only in theory, for who can hope to have the entire direction of the conversation and acts of those who surround a child?

As soon, then, as education becomes an art, it is well-nigh impossible for it to succeed, for no one has in his control all the conditions necessary for its success. All that can be done by dint of effort is to approach the

---

perverting and disturbing influences; but after he has received his training he is restored to society, protected against its allurements, and capable of working for its regeneration. Possibly his scheme of education may have been borrowed from Plato's Allegory of the Cavern.—(P.)

*This is a very crude statement. "The internal development of our faculties and organs" is not education in any intelligible and helpful sense; "the use which we learn to make of this development" is only a part of education, while "the acquisition of personal experience from the objects that affect us" is more properly the education of nature.—(P.)

†See Plutarch's Morals: Of the Education of Children.

final purpose as nearly as possible; but to attain it we must be guided by fortune.

What is this purpose? It is the very one proposed by nature, as has just been shown. Since the cooperation of the three educations is necessary for their perfection, it is to the one over which we have no control that we must direct the other two. But perhaps this word nature has too vague a meaning; we must here make an attempt to determine it.

Nature, we are told, is but habit.† What does this mean? Are there not habits that we contract only through compulsion, and that never stifle nature? Such, for example, is the habit of plants whose vertical direction is impeded. The plant, set at liberty, preserves the inclination it was forced to take; but the sap has not on this account changed its primitive direction, and if the plant continues to grow, its prolongation again becomes vertical. The same is true of the inclinations of men. So long as we remain in the same condition we can preserve those which result from habit and which are the least natural to us; but the moment the situation changes, habit ceases and the natural is restored. Education is certainly nothing but a habit. Now, there are people who forget and lose their education, and others who hold to it. Whence comes this difference? If we were to limit the term nature to habits that are in conformity with Nature, we might spare ourselves this nonsense.

We are born sensible, and from our birth we are affected in different ways by the objects which surround us. As soon as we have the consciousness, so to speak, of our sensations, we are disposed to seek or to shun the objects which produce them: first, according as they are agreeable or disagreeable to us; then, according to the congruity or the incongruity which we find between ourselves and these objects; and, finally, according to the judgments which we derive from them relative to the idea of happiness or perfection which is given us by the reason. These dispositions are extended and strengthened in proportion as we become more susceptible and enlightened; but, constrained by our habits, they change more or less with our opinions. Before this alteration, these dispositions are what I call our nature.

It is, then, to these primitive dispositions that everything should be referred; and this might be done if our three educations were merely different: but what are we to do when they are opposed to one another; when, instead of educating a man for himself, we wish to educate him for others? Then agreement is impossible. Compelled to oppose nature or our

---

†M. Formey assures us that this is not exactly what has been said; but yet it seems to me the very thing that is said in the following line to which I proposed to respond:

La nature, crois-moi, n'est rien que l'habitude.

M. Formey, who does not wish to make his fellow creatures proud, modestly gives us the measure of his own brain for that of the human understanding. This M. Formey was the author of an Anti-Emile, and edited an expurgated edition of the Emile, under the title of the Emile Chretien.—(P.)

social institutions, we must choose between making a man and a citizen, for we can not make both at once.*

The natural man is complete in himself; he is the numerical unit, the absolute whole, who is related only to himself or to his fellow man. Civilized man is but a fractional unit that is dependent on its denominator, and whose value consists in its relation to the whole, which is the social organization. Good social institutions are those which are the best able to make man unnatural, and to take from him his absolute existence in order to give him one which is relative, and to transport the *me* into the common unity, in such a way that each individual no longer feels himself one, but a part of the unit, and is no longer susceptible of feeling save when forming a part of the whole.

In order to be something, to be one's self and always one, we must act as we speak; we must always be decided on the course we ought to take, must take it boldly, and must follow it to the end. I am waiting to be shown this prodigy in order to know whether he is man or citizen, or how he manages to be both at the same time.

From these objects, necessarily opposed one to the other, there come two forms of institutions of contrary nature—the one public and common, the other private and domestic.

Would you form an idea of public education? Read the Republic of Plato. It is not a work on politics, as those think who judge of books by their titles, but it is the finest work on education ever written.†

When one would refer us to the land of chimeras, he names the educational system of Plato; though if Lycurgus had formed his only on paper, I should have thought it the more chimerical. Plato has done no more than purify the heart of man; but Lycurgus has made it unnatural.

A system of public instruction no longer exists and can no longer exist, because where there is no longer a country there can no longer be citizens. These two words, *country* and *citizen*, ought to be expunged from modern languages. I have a good reason for saying this, but I do not care to state it, as it has no bearing on my subject.

I do not regard as a system of public instruction these ridiculous estab-

---

*This is like the difficulty which Mr. Bain finds in "reconciling the whole man with himself" (Education as a Science, p. 2), and points to one of the most serious problems in education. There *is* some degree of incompatibility, as things go, between the artisan, or the citizen, and the *man*, and there is always occasion to readjust these relations on the basis of the higher claims of manhood. This is the explanation of "labor troubles," "civil-service reform," etc. Rousseau's doctrine is doubtless correct: education must have chief and direct reference to the future man, and only a subordinate and remote reference to the future artisan or citizen. In his famous "orders of activities" (Education, p. 32) Mr. Spencer would seem to reverse this order, placing the narrower aim first and the wider last.—(P.)

†Perhaps the reader need not be admonished that the Republic is a treatise on government, and that education is treated only as an incidental question; though the general doctrine of education as a function of the state is so profound, that this dialogue may justly be regarded as the first great educational classic in order of time.—(P.)

lishments called colleges.* Nor do I take into account the education of the world, because this education, tending toward two opposite ends, fails to reach either of them; it is fit only to make men double-faced, seeming always to attribute everything to others, but never attributing anything save to themselves. Now these pretenses, being common to everybody, deceive no one. They are so many misspent efforts.

Finally, there remains domestic education, or that of nature; but what would a man be worth for others who had been educated solely for himself? If perchance the double object proposed could be realized in a single individual by removing the contradictions in human life, we should remove a great obstacle to man's happiness. To form a conception of such a one, we should need to see him in his perfect state, to have observed his inclinations, to have seen his progress, and to have followed the course of his development. In a word, it would be necessary to know the natural man. I believe that my reader will have made some progress in these researches after having read this essay.

To form this rare creature, what have we to do? Much, doubtless, but chiefly to prevent anything from being done. When all we have to do is to sail before the wind, simple tacking suffices; but if the sea runs high and we wish to hold our place, we must cast anchor. Take care, young pilot, that your cable does not slip, that your anchor does not drag, and that your boat does not drift on shore before you are aware of it!

In the social sphere, where all have their destined places, each should be educated for his own. If an individual who has been trained for his place withdraws from it, he is no longer good for anything. Education is useful only so long as fortune accords with the vocation of parents. In every other case it is harmful to the pupil, were it only for the prejudices which it has given him. In Egypt, where the son was obliged to follow the vocation of his father, education at least had an assured object; but with us, where the classes alone are permanent, and where men are ever passing from one to another, no one knows whether, in educating his son for his own social order, he may not be working in opposition to the son's interest.

In the natural order of things, all men being equal, their common vocation is manhood, and whoever is well trained for that can not fulfill badly any vocation connected with it. Whether my pupil be destined for the army, the church, or the bar, concerns me but little. Regardless of the vocation of his parents, nature summons him to the duties of human life. .To live is the trade I wish to teach him.† On leaving my hands, he will

---

*In several schools, and particularly in the University of Paris, there are professors whom I love, whom I hold in high esteem, and whom I deem very capable of wisely instructing youth, if they were not compelled to follow the established usages. I have urged one of these to publish the plan of reform which he has thought out. Perhaps we may finally be tempted to cure the evil when we see that it is not without a remedy.

†*Qui se totam ad vitam instruxit, non desiderat particulatim admoneri, doctus in totum, non quomodo cum uxore aut cum filiis viveret, sed quomodo bene viveret.* —SENECA, Ep. 94.

not, I grant, be a magistrate, a soldier, or a priest. First of all he will be a man; and all that a man ought to be, he can be when the occasion requires it, just as well as any one else can; and fortune will make him change his place in vain, for he will always be in his own.*

Our real study is that of human destiny. He who knows how best to support the good and the evil of this life, is, in my opinion, the best educated; whence it follows that the real education consists less in precepts than in practice. Our instruction begins when we begin to live; our education begins with our birth; and our first teacher is our nurse.

We must, then, generalize our views, and consider in our pupil man in general—man exposed to all the accidents of human life. If men were born attached to their native soil, if the same weather lasted the whole year, if the fortune of each were so fixed that it could never change, the current practice would be good in certain respects; the child educated for his special vocation, and never withdrawing from it, would not be exposed to the inconveniences of another. But, considering the mutability of human affairs, and the restless, revolutionary spirit of this century, which overthrows the whole existing order of things once in each generation, can we conceive a more senseless method than that of educating a child as though he were never to leave his chamber, and were always to be surrounded by his attendants? If the unfortunate creature take a single step on the ground, or attempts to descend the stairs, he is lost. This is not teaching him to endure suffering, but is training him to feel it. . . .

Power

. . . Man is born free, and everywhere he is in chains. Many a man believes himself to be the master of others who is, no less than they, a slave. How did this change take place? I do not know. What can make it legitimate? To this question I hope to be able to furnish an answer.

Were I considering only force and the effects of force, I should say: "So long as a People is constrained to obey, and does, in fact, obey, it does well. So soon as it can shake off its yoke, and succeeds in doing so, it does better. The fact that it has recovered its liberty by virtue of that same right by which it was stolen, means either that it is entitled to resume it, or that its theft by others was, in the first place, without justification." But the social order is a sacred right which serves as a foundation for all other rights. This right, however, since it comes not by nature, must have been built upon conventions. To discover what these convictions are is the matter of our inquiry. . . .

. . . There will always be a vast difference between subduing a mob and

---

*Occupavi te, fortuna, atque cepi; omnesque aditus tuos interclusi, ut ad me aspirare non posses.—CICERO, Tuscul. v, cap. ix.

governing a social group. No matter how many isolated individuals may submit to the enforced control of a single conqueror, the resulting relationship will ever be that of Master and Slave, never of People and Ruler. The body of men so controlled may be an agglomeration; it is not an association. It implies neither public welfare nor a body politic. An individual may conquer half the world, but he is still only an individual. His interests, wholly different from those of his subjects, are private to himself. When he dies his empire is left scattered and disintegrated. He is like an oak which crumbles and collapses in ashes so soon as the fire consumes it.

"A people," says Grotius, "may give themselves to a king." His argument implies that the said people were already a people before this act of surrender. The very act of gift was that of a political group and presupposed public deliberation. Before, therefore, we consider the act by which a people chooses their king, it were well if we considered the act by which a people is constituted as such. For it necessarily precedes the other, and is the true foundation on which all Societies rest.

Had there been no original compact, why, unless the choice were unanimous, should the minority ever have agreed to accept the decision of the majority? What right have the hundred who desire a master to vote for the ten who do not? The institution of the franchise is, in itself, a form of compact, and assumes that, at least once in its operation, complete unanimity existed.

Of the Social Pact

I assume, for the sake of argument, that a point was reached in the history of mankind when the obstacles to continuing in a state of Nature were stronger than the forces which each individual could employ to the end of continuing in it. The original state of Nature, therefore, could no longer endure, and the human race would have perished had it not changed its manner of existence.

Now, since men can by no means engender new powers, but can only unite and control those of which they are already possessed, there is no way in which they can maintain themselves save by coming together and pooling their strength in a way that will enable them to withstand any resistance exerted upon them from without. They must develop some sort of central direction and learn to act in concert.

Such a concentration of powers can be brought about only as the consequence of an agreement reached between individuals. But the self-preservation of each single man derives primarily from his own strength and from his own freedom. How, then, can he limit these without, at the same time, doing himself an injury and neglecting that care which it is his duty to devote to his own concerns? This difficulty, in so far as it is relevant to my subject, can be expressed as follows: "Some form of association must be found as a result of which the whole strength of the community will be enlisted for the protection of the person and property of each constituent member, in such a way that each, when united to his fellows, renders obedience to his own will, and remains as free as he was before." That is the basic problem of which the Social Contract provides the solution.

The clauses of this Contract are determined by the Act of Association in such a way that the least modification must render them null and void. Even though they may never have been formally enunciated, they must be everywhere the same, and everywhere tacitly admitted and recognized. So completely must this be the case that, should the social compact be violated, each associated individual would at once resume all the rights which once were his, and regain his natural liberty, by the mere fact of losing the agreed liberty for which he renounced it.

It must be clearly understood that the clauses in question can be reduced, in the last analysis, to one only, to wit, the complete alienation by each associate member to the community of *all his rights*. For, in the first place, since each has made surrender of himself without reservation, the resultant conditions are the same for all: and, because they are the same for all, it is in the interest of none to make them onerous to his fellows.

Furthermore, this alienation having been made unreservedly, the union of individuals is as perfect as it well can be, none of the associated members having any claim against the community. For should there be any rights left to individuals, and no common authority be empowered to pronounce as between them and the public, then each, being in some things his own judge, would soon claim to be so in all. Were that so, a state of Nature would still remain in being, the conditions of association becoming either despotic or ineffective.

In short, whoso gives himself to all gives himself to none. And, since there is no member of the social group over whom we do not acquire precisely the same rights as those over ourselves which we have surrendered to him, it follows that we gain the exact equivalent of what we lose, as well as an added power to conserve what we already have.

If, then, we take from the social pact everything which is not essential to it, we shall find it to be reduced to the following terms: "each of us contributes to the group his person and the powers which he wields as a person, and we receive into the body politic each individual as forming an indivisible part of the whole."

As soon as the act of association becomes a reality, it substitutes for the person of each of the contracting parties a moral and collective body made up of as many members as the constituting assembly has votes, which body receives from this very act of constitution its unity, its dispersed *self*, and its will. The public person thus formed by the union of individuals was known in the old days as a *City*, but now as the *Republic* or *Body Politic*.[1] This, when it fulfils a passive role, is known by its members as *The State*, when an active one, as *The Sovereign People*, and, in contrast to other similar bodies, as a *Power*. In respect of the constituent associates, it enjoys the collective name of *The People*, the individuals who compose it being known as *Citizens* in so far as they share in the sovereign authority, as *Subjects* in so far as they owe obedience to the laws of the State. But these different terms frequently overlap, and are used indiscriminately one for the other. It is enough that we should realize the difference between them when they are employed in a precise sense. . . .

Each individual, indeed, may, as a man, exercise a will at variance with, or different from, that general will to which, as citizen, he contributes. His personal interest may dictate a line of action quite other than that demanded by the interest of all. The fact that his own existence as an individual has an absolute value, and that he is, by nature, an independent being, may lead him to conclude that what he owes to the common cause is something that he renders of his own free will; and he may decide that by leaving the debt unpaid he does less harm to his fellows than he would to himself should he make the necessary surrender. Regarding the moral entity constituting the State as a rational abstraction because it is not a man, he might enjoy his rights as a citizen without, at the same time, fulfilling his duties as a subject, and the resultant injustice might grow until it brought ruin upon the whole body politic.

In order, then, that the social compact may not be but a vain formula, it must contain, though unexpressed, the single undertaking which can alone give force to the whole, namely, that whoever shall refuse to obey the general will must be constrained by the whole body of his fellow citizens to do so: which is no more than to say that it may be necessary to compel a man to be free—freedom being that condition which, by giving each citizen to his country, guarantees him from all personal dependence and is the foundation upon which the whole political machine rests, and supplies the power which works it. Only the recognition by the individual

---

[1] The true meaning of the word "City" has been almost entirely lost by the moderns, most of whom think that a Town and a City are identical, and that to be a Burgess is the same thing as to be a Citizen. They do not know that houses may make a town, but that only citizens can make a City. This same error once cost the people of Carthage dear in the past. I have never anywhere read that the title *"cives"* could be conferred on the subject of a Prince, not even upon the Macedonians of ancient times, nor upon the English in our own day, though the latter are more nearly in the enjoyment of freedom than any other people. Only the French use *citizens* as a familiar word, the reason for this being that they have no true apprehension of its meaning, as may be seen by anyone who consults a French dictionary. Were it otherwise, they would fall, by adopting it, into the crime of *lèse-majesté*. In their mouths it is held to express not so much legal standing as quality. When Bodin speaks of "our citizens and burgesses" he commits a grave blunder in giving the same meaning to the two words. Not so deceived is M. d'Alembert, who, in his article on Geneva, properly distinguishes between the four Orders (five, if foreigners be counted) which go to make up our city, of which two only constitute the Republic. No French author known to me understands the meaning of the word "Citizen."

of the rights of the community can give legal force to undertakings entered into between citizens, which, otherwise, would become absurd, tyrannical, and exposed to vast abuses. . . .

Let us reduce all this to terms which can be easily comprehended. What a man loses as a result of the Social Contract is his natural liberty and his unqualified right to lay hands on all that tempts him, provided only that he can compass its possession. What he gains is civil liberty and the ownership of what belongs to him. That we may labor under no illusion concerning these compensations, it is well that we distinguish between natural liberty which the individual enjoys so long as he is strong enough to maintain it, and civil liberty which is curtailed by the general will. Between possessions which derive from physical strength and the right of the first-comer, and ownership which can be based only on a positive title.

To the benefits conferred by the status of citizenship might be added that of Moral Freedom, which alone makes a man his own master. For to be subject to appetite is to be a slave, while to obey the laws laid down by society is to be free. But I have already said enough on this point, and am not concerned here with the philosophical meaning of the word *liberty*. . . .

Whether the General Will Can Err

It follows from what has been said above that the general will is always right and ever tends to the public advantage. But it does not follow that the deliberations of the People are always equally beyond question. It is ever the way of men to wish their own good, but they do not at all times see where that good lies. The People are never corrupted though often deceived, and it is only when they are deceived that they appear to will what is evil.

There is often considerable difference between the will of all and the general will. The latter is concerned only with the common interest, the former with interests that are partial, being itself but the sum of individual wills. But take from the expression of these separate wills the pluses and minuses—which cancel out, the sum of the differences is left, and that is the general will.[2]

If the People, engaged in deliberation, were adequately informed, and if

---

[2] "Every Interest," says the Marquis d'Argenson, "has different principles. An identity of interests between any two given persons is established by reason of their opposition to the interests of a third." He might have added that the identity of the interests of all is established by reason of their opposition to the interests of each. Did individual interests not exist, the idea of a common interest could scarcely be entertained, for there would be nothing to oppose it. Society would become automatic, and politics would cease to be an art.

no means existed by which the citizens could communicate one with another, from the great number of small differences the general will would result, and the decisions reached would always be good. But when intriguing groups and partial associations are formed to the disadvantage of the whole, then the will of each of such groups is general only in respect of its own members, but partial in respect of the State. When such a situation arises it may be said that there are no longer as many votes as men, but only as many votes as there are groups. Differences of interest are fewer in number, and the result is less general. Finally, when one of these groups becomes so large as to swamp all the others, the result is not the sum of small differences, but one single difference. The general will does not then come into play at all, and the prevailing opinion has no more validity than that of an individual man.

If, then, the general will is to be truly expressed, it is essential that there be no subsidiary groups within the State, and that each citizen voice his own opinion and nothing but his own opinion.[3] It was the magnificent achievement of Lycurgus to have established the only State of this kind ever seen. But where subsidiary groups do exist their numbers should be made as large as possible, and none should be more powerful than its fellows. This precaution was taken by Solon, Numa, and Servius. Only if it is present will it be possible to ascertain the general will, and to make sure that the People are not led into error. . . .

That the General Will Is Indestructible

So long as a number of men assembled together regard themselves as forming a single body, they have but one will, which is concerned with their common preservation and with the well-being of all. When this is so, the springs of the State are vigorous and simple, its principles plain and clear-cut. It is not encumbered with confused or conflicting interests. The common good is everywhere plainly in evidence and needs only good sense to be perceived. Peace, unity, and equality are the foes of political subtlety. Upright and simple men are hard to deceive by the very reason of their simplicity. Lures and plausible sophistries have no effect upon them, nor are they even sufficiently subtle to become dupes. When one sees, in the happiest country in all the world, groups of peasants deciding the affairs of State beneath an oak tree, and behaving with a constancy of wisdom, can one help but despise the refinements of other nations which,

---

[3] "Vera cosa," says Machiavelli, "che alcuni divisioni nuocono alle republiche e alcune giovano: quelle nuocono che sono dalle sette e da partigiani accompagnate: quelle giovano che senza sette, senza partigiani si mantengono. Non potendo adunque provedere un fondatore d'una repubblica che non siano nimizichie in quella, ha da proveder almeno che non vi siano sette." (History of Florence, Book VII.)

at so great an expense of skill and mystification, make themselves at once illustrious and wretched?

A State thus governed has need of very few laws, and when it *is* found necessary to promulgate new ones, the necessity will be obvious to all. He who actually voices the proposal does but put into words what all have felt, and neither intrigue nor eloquence are needed to ensure the passing into law of what each has already determined to do so soon as he can be assured that his fellows will follow suit.

What sets theorists on the wrong tack is that, seeing only those States which have been badly constituted from the beginning, they are struck by the impossibility of applying such a system to *them*. The thought of all the follies which a clever knave with an insinuating tongue could persuade the people of Paris or of London to commit, makes them laugh. What they do not know is that Cromwell would have been put in irons by the people of Berne, and the Duc de Beaufort sent to hard labor by the Genevese.

But when the social bond begins to grow slack, and the State to become weaker; when the interests of individuals begin to make themselves felt, and lesser groups within the State to influence the State as a whole, then the common interest suffers a change for the worse and breeds opposition. No longer do men speak with a single voice, no longer is the general will the will of all. Contradictions appear, discussions arise, and even the best advice is not allowed to pass unchallenged.

Last stage of all, when the State, now near its ruin, lives on only in a vain and deceptive form, when the bond of society is broken in all men's hearts, when the vilest self-interest bears insolently the sacred name of Commonweal, then does the general will fall dumb. All, moved by motives unavowed, express their views as though such a thing as the State had never existed, and they were not citizens at all. In such circumstances, unjust decrees, aiming only at the satisfaction of private interests, can be passed under the guise of laws.

Does it follow from this that the general will is destroyed or corrupted? No; it remains constant, unalterable and pure, but it becomes subordinated to other wills which encroach upon it. Each, separating his interest from the interest of all, sees that such separation cannot be complete, yet the part he plays in the general damage seems to him as nothing compared with the exclusive good which he seeks to appropriate. With the single exception of the particular private benefit at which he aims, he still desires the public good, realizing that it is likely to benefit him every whit as much as his neighbors. Even when he sells his vote for money, he does not extinguish the general will in himself, but merely eludes it. The fault that he commits is to change the form of the question, and to answer something which he was not asked. Thus, instead of saying, through the medium of his vote, "This is of advantage to the State," he says, "It is to the advantage of this or that individual that such and such a proposition become law." And so the law of public order in assemblies is not so much the maintenance of the general will, as the guarantee that it shall always be asked to express itself and shall always respond. . . .

As particular wills act constantly in opposition to the general will, so does the Government make an incessant effort against Sovereignty. As this strife becomes more marked, the constitution changes for the worse. And since there is here no corporate will which, by resisting the will of the Prince, can achieve equilibrium, it must happen that, sooner or later, the Prince will oppress the Sovereign and break the social treaty. This is the inherent and inevitable vice of the body politic which, from the moment of its birth, tends consistently to its destruction, just as old age and death ultimately destroy the human body. . . .

Change

Of Divers Systems of Legislation

Should we inquire in what consist the greatest of good of all, the ideal at which every system of legislation ought to aim, we shall find that it can be reduced to two main heads: *liberty* and *equality*: liberty, because when a subject is in a condition of dependence, by so much is the State cheated of part of his strength: equality, because without it there can be no liberty.

I have already described the nature of civil liberty: I turn now to equality. Let it be clearly understood that, in using the word, I do not mean that power and wealth be absolutely the same for all, but only that power should need no sanction of violence but be exercised solely by virtue of rank and legality, while wealth should never be so great that a man can buy his neighbor, nor so lacking that a man is compelled to sell himself.[4] The great should be moderately endowed with goods and credit, the humble should be free of avarice and cupidity.

But such equality, it will be said, is but an airy daydream, and cannot exist in practice. Does it, then, follow that because abuses will come, they should not at least be regulated? It is just because the pressure of events tends always to the destruction of equality that the force of legislation should always be directed to maintaining it.

But these general truths of all good statecraft have to be modified in each country to suit local conditions and the character of the people. A system must be found which is suited to these differences. It may not be

---

[4] If you would have a solid and enduring State, you must see that it contains no extremes of wealth. It must have neither millionaires nor beggars. These are inseparable from one another, and both are fatal to the common good. One produces the makers of tyrants, the other, tyrants themselves. Where they exist public liberty becomes a commodity of barter. The rich buy it, the poor sell it.

the best in any absolute sense, but it will be the best that can be found for the country destined to make use of it. . . .

The structure of the State is truly solid and durable only when, as the result of careful adaptation, natural conditions and man-made laws are ever in agreement, so that the latter do but ratify, so to speak, accompany, and adjust the former. But should the legislator who is uncertain of his object flout the nature of the material in which he has to work, attempting to impose liberty in conditions which make for slavery, to favor the amassing of wealth where he should be giving his attention to problems of population, to plan conquest where a policy of peace is indicated— the authority of the laws will insensibly diminish, the structure of the community will change for the worse, and unrest will grow to a point at which the State will have to choose between death or change, and nature, which can never be defeated, will reassert her empire. . . .

Of the Legislator

In order to discover what social regulations are best suited to nations, there is needed a superior intelligence which can survey all the passions of mankind, though itself exposed to none: an intelligence having no contact with our nature, yet knowing it to the full: an intelligence, the well-being of which is independent of our own, yet willing to be concerned with it: which, finally, viewing the long perspectives of time, and preparing for itself a day of glory as yet far distant, will labor in one century to reap its reward in another.[5] In short, only Gods can give laws to men.

The same argument which Caligula applied in practice Plato used in theory when, in his dialogue of *The Statesman*, he sought to define the nature of the Civil or "Royal" man.[6] But if it be true that a great prince occurs but rarely, what shall be said of a great Lawgiver? The first has but to follow the rules laid down by the latter. The Lawgiver invents the machine, the prince merely operates it. "When societies first come to birth," says Montesquieu, "it is the leaders who produce the institutions of the Republic. Later, it is the institutions which produce the leaders."

Whoso would undertake to give institutions to a People must work with full consciousness that he has set himself to change, as it were, the very stuff of human nature; to transform each individual who, in isolation, is a complete but solitary whole, into a part of something greater than himself,

---

[5] A nation becomes famous only when its legislation begins to decline. We know not for how many centuries the institutions of Lycurgus gave prosperity to Sparta before she became involved in the general destinies of Greece.

[6] See Plato's dialogue which, in its Latin version, is called *Politicus* or *The Citizen*. It is occasionally entitled *The Statesman*.

from which, in a sense, he derives his life and his being; to substitute a communal and moral existence for the purely physical and independent life with which we are all of us endowed by nature. His task, in short, to take from a man his own proper powers, and to give him in exchange powers foreign to him as a person, which we can use only if he is helped by the rest of the community. The more complete the death and destruction of his natural powers, the greater and more durable will those be which he acquires, and the more solid and perfect will that community be of which he forms a part. So true is this that the citizen by himself is nothing, and can do nothing, save with the cooperation of his neighbors, and the power acquired by the whole is equal or superior to the sum of the powers possessed by its citizens regarded as natural men. When that result has been achieved, and only then, can we say that the art of legislation has reached the highest stage of perfection of which it is capable.

The Legislator must, in every way, be an extraordinary figure in the State. He is so by reason of his genius, and no less so by that of his office. He is neither magistrate nor sovereign. His function is to constitute the State, yet in its Constitution it has no part to play. It exists in isolation, and is superior to other functions, having nothing to do with the governance of men. For if it be true that he who commands men should not ordain laws, so, too, he who ordains laws should be no longer in a position to command men. Were it otherwise, the laws, mere ministers to his passions, would often do no more than perpetuate his acts of injustice, nor could he ever avoid the danger that his views as a man might detract from the sanctity of his work.

When Lycurgus gave laws to his country, he began by abdicating his royal powers. It was a custom obtaining in most of the Greek city-states, that the framing of their constitutions should be entrusted to foreigners. This practice has not seldom been copied in modern times by the republics of Italy, and was adopted by the State of Geneva, where it worked well.[7] Rome, in her greatest age, saw all the crimes of tyranny revive within her frontiers, and was near to perishing, simply because she had united in the same hands legislative authority and sovereign power.

For all that, the Decemvirs never arrogated to themselves the power to establish any law on their own authority. "Nothing of what we propose," they said to the People, "can become law without your consent. Romans, be yourselves the authors of those laws which are to ensure your happiness."

Whoso codifies the laws of a community, therefore, has not, or should not have, any legislative right, a right that is incommunicable, and one of

---

[7] Those who think of Calvin only as a theologian know very little of the full extent of his genius. Our wise edicts, in the framing of which he played a large part, do him no less honour than his *Institutes.* Whatever changes time may bring to our religious observances, so long as the love of country and of liberty is a living reality with us, the memory of that great man will be held in veneration.

which the People, even should they wish to do so, cannot divest themselves. For, by reason of the social compact, the general will alone can constrain the individual 'citizen: nor is there any other way of making sure that the will of the individual is in conformity with the general will, save by submitting it to the free votes of the People. This I have said once already; but it is well that it should be repeated.

Two things, therefore, seemingly incompatible, are to be found within the operation of lawmaking—it is a task beyond the capabilities of mere humans to perform: for its execution we are offered an authority which is a thing of naught.

There is another difficulty, too, that demands attention. Those wise men who, in speaking to the vulgar herd, would use not its language but their own, will never be understood. Many thousands of ideas there are which cannot be translated into popular phraseology. Excessive generalizations and long-range views are equally beyond the comprehension of the average man, who, as a rule, approves only such schemes, in matters of government, as will redound to his personal advantage. He finds it difficult to see what benefit he is likely to derive from the ceaseless privations which good laws will impose upon him. For a young people to understand fully the pondered maxims of the statesman and to follow the rules of conduct which are essential to healthy community life, would be for the effect to precede the cause. For such a thing to happen, the social spirit which can be the product only of a country's institutions would have, in fact, to be present at their birth, and, even before the laws are operative, the citizen would have to be such as those same laws would make him. Since, then, the legislator can use neither force nor argument, he must, of necessity, have recourse to authority of a different kind which can lead without violence and persuade without convincing.

That is why, in all periods, the fathers of their country have been driven to seek the intervention of Heaven, attributing to the Gods a Wisdom that was really their own, in order that the People, subjected to the laws of the State no less than to those of nature, and recognizing in the creation of the City the same Power at work as in that of its inhabitants, might freely obey and might bear with docility the yoke of public happiness. The legislator, by putting into the mouths of the immortals that sublime reasoning which is far beyond the reach of poor mankind, will, under the banner of divine authority, lead those to whom mere mortal prudence would ever be a stumbling block.[8] But it is not within the competence of every man to make the Gods speak, nor to get himself believed when he claims to be their interpreter. The real miracle, and the one sufficient proof of the

---

[8] "E veramente," said Machiavelli, "mai non fù alcuno ordinatore di leggi straordinarie in un popolo, che non ricorresse a Dio, perche altrimenti non sarebbero accettate; perchè sono molti beni conosciuti da uno prudente, i quali non hanno in se ragioni evidenti da potergli persuadere ad altrui . . ." (Discourses on Titus Livius, Book I, ch. xi).

Legislator's mission, is his own greatness of soul. Anyone can incise words on stone, bribe an oracle, claim some secret understanding with a high divinity, train a bird to whisper in his ear, or invent other ways, no less crude, for imposing on the People. He whose powers go no farther than that, may, if he be fortunate, hold the attention of a superstitious mob: but he will never found an empire, and his extravagant production will, in no long time, perish with him. Authority which has no true basis forms but a fragile bond. Only in wisdom can it find hope of permanence. The Jewish Law still lives, and the Law of the child of Ishmael which, for ten centuries, has regulated the conduct of half the world. They bear witness, even today, to the great men who gave them form. To the eyes of pride bred of philosophy or the blind spirit of Party, they may seem no more than fortunate impostors, but true political wisdom will ever admire in their institutions the great and powerful genius which watches over the birth of civilizations destined to endure.

We should not, from all this, conclude, with Warburton, that politics and religion have, in the modern world, the self-same aim, but rather that, in the forming of nations, the one serves as the other's instrument. . . .

But there is a purely civil profession of faith, the articles of which it behoves the Sovereign to fix, not with the precision of religious dogmas, but treating them as a body of social *sentiments* without which no man can be either a good citizen or a faithful subject.[9] Though it has no power to compel anyone to believe them, it can banish from the State all who fail to do so, not on grounds of impiety, but as lacking in social sense, and being incapable of sincerely loving the laws and justice, or of sacrificing, should the need arise, their lives to their duty. Any man who, after acknowledging these articles of faith, proceeds to act as though he did not believe them, is deserving of the death penalty. For he has committed the greatest of all crimes, that of lying before the law.

The dogmas of this civil religion should be few, clear and enunciated precisely, without either explanation or comment. The positive clauses are: —the existence of a powerful, intelligent, beneficent, and bountiful God: the reality of the life to come: the reward of the just, and the punishment of evildoers: the sanctity of the Social Contract and of the Laws. The negative element I would confine to one single article—intolerance, for that belongs to the creeds which I have excluded.

Those who draw a distinction between civil and theological intolerance are, in my opinion, guilty of error. The two things are inseparable. It is impossible to live in peace with those whom we believed to be damned.

---

[9] Caesar, when speaking in defence of Catiline, tried to establish the dogma that the soul is mortal. Cato and Cicero, in rebuttal, did not involve themselves in the pleasing complexities of philosophical disputation, but confined their efforts to proving that Caesar had pleaded as a bad citizen, having advanced a doctrine pernicious to the State. That, indeed, was what the Roman Senate was called upon to decide, not a point of theological theory.

To love them would be to hate God who punishes them. It is essential that they be either converted or punished. Wherever theological intolerance enters it cannot but have an effect on civil life,[10] and when that happens the Sovereign is no longer sovereign, even in temporal affairs. From then on, the priests are the real masters, the kings no more than their officers.

Now that there are, and can be, no longer any exclusive national religions, we should tolerate all creeds which show tolerance to others, so long as their dogmas contain nothing at variance with the duties of the citizen. But anyone who dares to say "Outside the Church there can be no salvation," should be banished from the State, unless the State be the Church and the Prince the Pontiff. Such a dogma is good only where the government is theocratic. In any other it is pernicious. The reason for which, according to the popular story, Henry IV embraced the religion of Rome would make any honest man leave it: and especially any Prince who was capable of using his brain. . . .[11]

DAVID EASTON

Until recently, systems theory in American political science has been considered synonymous with the works of David Easton. In fact, Easton, who is currently at the height of his career, introduced the term "political system" into the discourse of political theory. Of course, there were systems theories of public life devised in America before Easton's efforts were published. However, they went relatively ignored for reasons deeply embedded in the

---

[10] Marriage, for instance, being a civil contract, has civil consequences; and without them it is impossible for society even to subsist. If we assume that the clergy succeed in arrogating to themselves the sole right to perform the act of marriage, a right which, of necessity, they will usurp whenever they serve an intolerant religion, is it not obvious that, by establishing the authority of the Church in this matter, they will render that of the Prince null, and create a situation in which the Prince will have as subjects only such as the clergy shall see fit to give him? Being in a position to permit or to refuse marriage, according as whether those concerned do, or do not, hold certain doctrines whether they admit or denounce the validity of this or that formula, whether they be more or less devout, the Church, surely, if only it use a little tact and refuses to yield ground, will be the sole controller of inheritances, offices, citizens, and the State itself, which could not continue were it composed only of bastards. But, I shall be told, men will appeal against abuses, will adjourn decisions, will issue decrees and lay hold on the temporal power. How sad! The clergy, no matter how little they may have of, I do not say courage, but good sense, will stand aside from all such agitations and will quietly go their own way. They will blandly acquiesce in claims and adjournments, in decrees and seizures—and will still be masters in the end. It is not, I think, any great sacrifice to surrender a part when one is sure of getting possession of the whole.

[11] We are told by an historian that the king, having ordered a conference to be held in his presence between the doctors of the two Churches, and hearing a Protestant pastor admit that a man might be saved even though he were a Catholic, interrupted the debate with these words: "What, do you then agree that a man may be saved even if he holds to the religion of these gentlemen opposite?" The pastor replied that there was no doubt he could, provided he lived a good life. The King then continued as follows: "In that case, if I listen to the voice of prudence, I shall profess their religion and not yours, thereby making certain that I shall be saved in the eyes of both of you. For were I to become a Protestant, I might be saved in your view, but not in theirs, and prudence ordains that I take the safest road."

American political culture. This culture has been characterized by a suspicion of government and politics and an emphasis on individualism. Thus, American political theories have tended to stress the psychological and conflict points of view. This tendency is still present in contemporary political thought, and it partially accounts for the wide impact of behavioral approaches, which concentrate on the analysis of individual activities. However, since the Depression and the New Deal, many political theorists in the United States have felt impelled to employ units of analysis that go beyond the activities of concrete individuals. In a society characterized by large concentrations of organized power, it becomes difficult to account for all of public activity in terms of collections of human beings. Easton, thus, can be considered a leader of the countertrend against the individualistic and antipolitical assumptions which were once widely accepted in American society.

Like Rousseau, Easton stresses the themes of socialization (education) and social organization in his work. As a political theorist his major question has been: Why do political systems hold together and persist? Why do political systems not collapse more often into chaos? Attempting to answer the latter question by investigating the ways in which children learn to perform public roles, he has found that in America "by the time children have reached second grade (age 7) most of them have become firmly attached to their political community." He has also found that children in America idealize political authority quite early in their lives. When he was in his romantic phase, Rousseau, who reached similar conclusions about socialization in a civilized country, thought that such efficient inculcation of loyalty was the greatest barrier to spontaneity. Easton is inclined to think of socialization as one of the most important forces in securing democracy.

Identity*

The Formative Years in Politics

The following analysis is based on extensive pretesting data collected over the last five years and most recently in connection with a national study of over twelve thousand elementary school children in selected areas of political socialization. The results of the pretesting reported here involve certain limitations. For example, they do not take into account important variations due to ethnicity, religion, region, educational systems, family political background, and the like, characteristics that will receive considerable attention in our final study. But our preliminary data do yield some important

*Pages 115-125 reprinted from *Midwest Journal of Political Science* 6 (August 1962): 3. Written by David Easton and Robert D. Hess and reprinted by permission of the Wayne State University Press and the authors. A final analysis of the research referred to in this article appears in D. Easton and J. Dennis, *Children in the Political System: Origins of Political Legitimacy* (New York: McGraw-Hill Book Company, 1969). Pages 125-132 from *The Political System*, by David Easton. Copyright © 1953 by Alfred A. Knopf, Inc. Reprinted by permission of the publisher. Pages 132-142 from David Easton, *A Framework for Political Analysis* (Englewood Cliffs, N.J.: Prentice-Hall, Inc., 1965). Reprinted by permission.

impressions worth opening up for discussion at this early stage in our research, especially with regard to trends and possible relationships among significant variables.

Existing research on young people has put its main emphasis on the adolescent during his high school years (age 14—17), perhaps on the assumptions that it is only the older child who displays the first glimmerings of an interest in politics and that this is where political development is likely to occur. Our preliminary investigations bear out neither of these premises. Every piece of evidence indicates that the child's political world begins to take shape well before he even enters elementary school and that it undergoes the most rapid change during these years.

A little-recognized fact is that political learning gets a good start in the family during the preschool period. When the child first asks his parents a question typical in our society: "Daddy, who pays the policeman?" or "Why can't you park your car there?" and when the father replies: "The city or mayor pays him," or "It is against the law to park there," the child has here received from a trusted source an early and important introduction to politics broadly conceived. In effect he is being gently exposed to the notions that in the given regime there is a difference between public and private sectors of life, that there is a need to obey rules and regulations regardless of individual whim or desire, and that there exists some higher authority outside the family to which even all-powerful parents are subject. Through indirect and casual ways like these, the child at a tender age begins to build up his conception of political life. This is so even though, according to our preliminary data, the words *politics* and *politician* usually do not become part of his vocabulary until he is 11 or 12 years old and even though politics has a relatively low salience compared to school, sports, and other play activities and interests.

Our pretesting also suggests that by the time the child has completed elementary school, many basic political attitudes and values have become firmly established. What is even more important, and dramatically contary to expectations and implications of existing literature, it appears that by the time the child enters high school at the age of 14, his basic political orientations to regime and community have become quite firmly entrenched so that at least during the four years of high school little substantive change is visible. In that period his own interest in politics may be stimulated—although our data indicate that the high-point in reported political interest may occur in 7th and 8th grades—and, as we would expect, he learns much more about the structure and practices of government and politics. Formal education bolstered by the mass media is likely to be the source of such knowledge. But for most young people, there is little evidence that fundamental attitudes and values with respect to the regime and political community are any different when they leave high school than they were upon entrance.

The truly formative years of the maturing member of a political system would seem to be the years between the ages of three and thirteen. It is this period when rapid growth and development in political orientations take place, as in many areas of nonpolitical socialization.

Attachment to the Political Community

By the time children have reached second grade (age 7) most of them have become firmly attached to their political community. Imperceptibly they have learned that they are Americans and that, in a way they find difficult to define and articulate, they are different from members of other systems. As we find in most other aspects of the child's political world, and as we would expect, the responses are highly colored with emotion and occur long before rational understanding or even the capacity to rationalize political orientations are evident.

Thus the sentiments of most children with respect to their political community are uniformly warm and positive throughout all grades, with scarcely a hint of criticism or note of dissatisfaction. When interviewed about where they would like to live for one week, a year, or the rest of their lives, some children favor travel for a shorter or longer time. But in most cases it is beyond their capacity to imagine themselves living anywhere other than the United States for the rest of their lives. And a high proportion would not even like to take permanent leave of the immediate places where they happen to live.

One of the processes contributing to this outcome we could easily have anticipated. The feelings initially aroused by immediate but diffuse social objects are extended to include specifically political ones. It would appear that national sentiment, loyalty, patriotism, or love of country—all ingredients of attachment to political community—may rest on such unpretentious foundations as these.

In the development of this attachment, the child early learns to admire and cherish those things and persons that are local and close, that form part of his personal experience and are therefore meaningful to him, and that in most cases represent undifferentiated social objects. Thus when the political context of the question is not concealed from the child, and he is asked to list the three best things about America, children in the lower grades (ages 7–9) consistently speak about such general social objects as their schools, the beauty of their country, its animals and flowers, and the goodness and cleanliness of its people. Very few politically differentiated items appear. Those that do, convey pride in the President, the policeman, the flag, and freedom.[1] The President and the policeman

---

[1] Even though children in grade 2 are already able to associate themselves with the label Republican or Democrat, this touches on the regime rather than the community level and will be discussed later.

are two authority figures with which the child is quite familiar and, at the early grades, just about the only two for most children. Only one impersonal abstract symbol, that of freedom, regularly appears at this age level. The meaning attributed to it is quite nonpolitical and diffuse, however. A person is conceived to be free when he can do whatever he wishes, an appealing thought to the adult dominated child.

Only as the child grows older do the warm feelings already generated with respect to these things of personal significance spread to impersonal political symbols, to differentiated political objects, and to the broader and more inclusive aspects of the political community. Thus although in the higher grades (ages 12–13) children continue to mention schools, the moral worth of people in the United States, and the like, by that time reference to items such as these declines sharply. The majority of responses to the same question now include such specifically political items of an abstract or impersonal character as democracy, government, voting, and elaborations of freedom to mean freedom of speech, press, religion, and choice of occupation. The same pride and positive feelings that were displayed more diffusely at an earlier age are now also invested in a distinctively political direction. The feelings stimulated by the concrete, personally experienced part of the child's immediate world seem to be transferred, as the child grows older, to abstract political symbols. "America" itself as a symbol of the political community now becomes laden with specifically political content, and an early nonpolitical attachment to general social aspects of the community is transformed into a highly political one.

A second process joining forces with fondness for the immediate concrete environment quite unexpectedly proved to be religious in nature. In a secular society that adults have frequently described as essentially materialistic and where adults have sought to maintain a clear separation between church and state, there was little reason for suspecting that in the early grades religious sentiments would be instrumental in generating support for the political community. As it turns out, however, not only do many children associate the sanctity and awe of religion with the political community, but to ages 9 or 10 they sometimes have considerable difficulty in disentangling God and country.

In many schools it is customary to pledge allegiance to the flag each morning as classes begin or at other regular intervals.[2] The pledge is brief but it is said in a formal, solemn atmosphere. Levity brings down sanctions from the school authorities and sincerity is approved. The exact procedures associated with the pledge may vary. In some cases the flag is saluted; in others, the right hand is held over the heart. But the repetition of the pledge assumes the character of a ritual.

---

[2] "I pledge allegiance to the flag of the United States of America and to the Republic for which it stands, one nation under God, indivisible, with liberty and justice for all."

When the children in grades two and three were interviewed around the question, "To whom do take the pledge of allegiance?" the answers were distributed among flag, country, and for the single largest minority, God. Not only do we find the explicit statement that God is the object of the pledge, but when probed with regard to its functions, many children interpreted the pledge as a prayer. They saw it as a request either to God or to some unidentified but infinite power for aid and protection. At times it is even understood as an expression of gratitude, again to some unspecified being, for the benefits already received. Only when we reach the fourth or fifth grade in our pretest interviews, and more rapidly thereafter, do we find a tendency for children to stress the pledge as an assertion of the need to perform one's duties as a citizen. The religious theme does not disappear entirely, but over the sample it becomes subordinate to the political.

Although our limited data do not permit full interpretation of the processes at work here in linking the child to the political community and its symbols such as the flag, in all likelihood there is an association in the child's mind of the form and feeling tone of religious ritual with the political ceremony of pledging allegiance. Specific invocation of God in the pledge itself would clinch the point for the child.

Religious affect, it appears, is being displaced upon political object, less by design than by the natural assimilation of political with religious piety and ritual. We might infer that the depth and peculiar strength of religious sentiments, if only because of their early introduction to the child and numerous social sanctions enlisted in their aid, become subtly transferred to the bond with the political community. The fact that as the child grows older he may be able to sort out the religious from the political setting much more clearly and restrict the pledge to a political meaning, need not thereby weaken this bond. The initial and early intermingling of potent religious sentiment with political community has by that time probably created a tie difficult to dissolve.[3]

Attachment to the Structure and Norms of the Regime

As we have seen, when we refer to the maintenance or change of a political system, it is imperative to specify the level with respect to which we are speaking. Adequate provision may be made for the persistence of the political community, but it is not at all clear that attachment at this

---

[3] For such political systems as we find in the USSR where religious sentiment is discouraged or in many African societies where religion is not so clearly associated with newly developing political systems, it would be interesting to search for substitute mechanisms that come into play in the early years of the child to mold his sentiments with respect to the political community.

level must necessarily include positive affect towards other levels such as the regime. As a case in point, the French metropolitan political community has remained relatively intact for an historically lengthy period even though it has witnessed the rise and fall of numerous regimes.

Undoubtedly the degree and extent of support directed to the community or to the regime will each affect the other in important ways. But if we are to understand the early sources of support for either level, it is necessary to begin by viewing them separately and independently. We therefore turn now to an examination of some of the concrete ways in which members of a political system form attachments to the structure and norms of the regime in the United States.

Our pretesting suggests that, as with regard to the political community, in a relatively stable system such as the United States firm bonds are welded to the structure of the regime quite early in childhood. By the time children reach the 7th and 8th grades, most of them have developed highly favorable opinions about such aspects of the political structure as the Presidency, Congress, or "our government" in general. The Constitution has become something of the order of a taboo that ought not be tampered with in its basic prescriptions. Yet children know very little about the formal aspects of the regime and much less, if anything, about its informal components. How then do they acquire and develop ties to the structure of a regime about which they have negligible and blurred information and equally little understanding?

Our data indicate several things. First, what is most apparent to most children in the realm of politics is the existence of an authority outside the family and school. Second, initially and continuously through the elementary school years, this external authority is specifically represented in the Presidency and the policeman, a local appointed official. Although as the child grows older he becomes increasingly aware of other institutions of authority, such as the courts, Congress, and local elected officials, the President and the policeman remain extremely visible. And third, emotional rather than rational processes are at work on these cognitions. They enable children to develop favorable feelings for the presidential form of authority in the United States long before they know very much of a concrete nature about it.

Interviews and questionnaires reveal that the first point of contact children are likely to have with the overall structure of authority is through their awareness of the President.[4] When children at a young age are asked in separate items about who makes the laws, runs the country, helps the country most, best represents the government, or, in a political context, who helps you most, the responses consistently favor the President.

---

[4] For similar findings in an important contribution to research on political socialization see F. I. Greenstein, "The Benevolent Leader: Children's Images of Political Authority," *American Political Science Review*, 54 (December, 1960), 934-43.

Authority figures at the lower reaches of the regime, such as the policeman or mayor, will be very familiar to most younger children. On occasion the Senate, Congress, or the courts will cross their cognitive horizon. But in general, between the polar extremes of the policeman and the President, it is the rare child in the early grades who sees anything but a truly blooming, buzzing political confusion. For most children at this stage the President *is* the political structure. Even where the child knows about the Vice-President, he is frequently seen as an aid to the President; and the Senate and House of Representatives as well are considered to be subordinate and subject to the orders of the President.

In the acquisition of attachments to the regime as a whole, it turns out to be critical that there is this well-defined point in the political structure that is highly visible and important for the children, whether young or old. Without it or some comparable institution we might have difficulty in understanding how the child would be able to formulate some introductory, if curde conception of political authority and some early feelings with regard to its worth. It provides the child with a means for "seeing" the structure in a clear and simple way and possibly identifying with it. Although in the United States the Presidency may be the vehicle for these purposes, in other systems of course we might suspect it to be a king, a chief, or a great leader.

In an earlier paper [5] we have shown that it is likely that the child's attachment to the structure of the regime is mediated through the attitudes he acquires towards this focal point, the Presidency. From grade 2, the earliest grade it was feasible to test, most children in a group of approximately 350 reported highly positive feelings about the President. When children through grade 8 were asked to compare the President to most men with regard to such personal and moral characteristics as honesty, friendliness, overall goodness, and liking for others, and such performance qualities as his knowledge and application to work, the vast preponderance see him as measuring up to most men or surpassing them. And even when father was compared to the President with regard to these characteristics, few rate father higher, and in some role performance qualities they rank him even lower. In subsequent tests of other children, they uniformly see the President possessed of all the virtues: benign, wise, helpful, concerned for the welfare of others, protective, powerful, good, and honest.

It is not surprising to find that a high percentage of children hold as strongly positive feelings about their father as they do about the President. What is unexpected is that even though the President is subject to intense partisan dispute, children should have at least as high an opinion of the President, and an even higher one with regard to some qualities. As we

---

[5] R. D. Hess and D. Easton, "The Child's Changing Image of the President," *Public Opinion Quarterly*, 24 (Winter, 1960), 632-44.

have shown,[6] part of this can be explained by the increasing capacity of the child, as he grows older, to differentiate the role of President from that of father. But part is probably a function of other socializing processes at work.

These varied processes concern what we have found to be typical ways in which children may respond to all figures of authority. In the first place, children display a strong tendency to generalize attitudes developed in connection with authority in their immediate experience to perceived authority beyond their knowledge and direct contact. The authority figures with which they have earliest and most intimate contact are of course their parents, and it is this image of authority that they subsequently seem to transfer to political figures that cross their vision. The child not only learns to respect and admire political authorities, but with regard to many characteristics sees them as parents writ large.

But more than that is involved. As noted already, maturing children develop the capacity to discriminate between qualities that are appropriate to the role of the President, and they see the latter as quite different from father in these respects. But with regard to those qualities of moral and personal worth already mentioned, even though there is a linear decline for children in successively higher grades, the absolute level of response remains quite high—at or above 50 percent.

These data suggest that in attributing so much personal and moral worth to both parental and political authority the child is responding not to what the authority figures are, but in terms of what he would expect them to be. Parents and President together are reported less in the image of any real parent than of one strongly reflecting the ideal expectations of our culture. Indeed additional testing that had the child compare teacher, father, President, and policeman bears out the broader hypothesis that children tend to view all significant and approved authority, political or otherwise, as similar to an ideal parental model.

The probable consequences of this idealization are apparent. In the first place, it should contribute to the ease with which maturing members of the American political system develop a strong attachment to the structure of the regime. The part that is initially visible and salient for the child represents everything that is good, beneficial, and worth cherishing. In the second place, in so far as feelings generated with respect to the Presidency as a focal point are subsequently extended to include other parts of the political structure—an area that still needs to be investigated—this may well be the path through which members of the system come to value the whole structure. If so, it would be a vital determinant contributing to the stability of the regime.

What still needs to be explained, however, is the origin of this impetus towards idealization. Here our preliminary data permit us to speculate

---

[6] Ibid.

broadly about the nature of the socializing processes.

In part, the high idealization of approved authority may reflect important psychological needs of the child. Confronted with the pervasive and inescapable authority of adults, and realistically aware of his own helplessness and vulnerability, the child must seek some congenial form of accommodation. For a small minority, rebellion, aggression, and mistrust may be the chosen avenue. But for most, adaptation is more likely to take the form of imputing to authority qualities that would permit the child to construe the authority in a most favorable light. By idealizing authority and by actually seeing it as benign, solicitous, and wise, the child is able to allay the fears and anxieties awakened by his own dependent state. A potentially threatening figure is conveniently transformed into a protector. Hence in spite of what he may learn about authority figures, about their foibles and shortcomings, he has a strong incentive to continue to idealize. As our data show, even though as they grow older fewer children hold the same high opinion of the President, the absolute level remains high. The security needs of the child in this way become an important ingredient in the socializing process.

In addition, however, the impetus to idealize authority also has its origin in the learning process itself, that is, in the attitudes children learn from adults. However little it may have been recognized, adults in the United States show a strong tendency to shelter young children from the realities of political life. In many ways it is comparable perhaps to the prudery of a Victorian era that sought to protect the child from what were thought to be the sordid facts of sex and parental conflict. In our society politics remains at the Victorian stage as far as children are concerned. Some adults—and there is reason to believe they are numerous—feel it is inappropriate to let the child know about what is often felt to be the seamy and contentious side of politcs. He is too young, he will not understand, it will disillusion him too soon, awareness of conflict among adults will be disturbing, are some of the arguments raised against telling the whole truth. The child has to learn as best he can that in politics the stakes are high, passions are strong, motivations may be less than pure and altruistic, conflict is endemic, and men have the capacity to place self, party, or occupation above country. Adults tend to paint politics for the child in rosier hues. And the younger the child the more pronounced is this protective tendency.

What this means is that in addition to learning political ideals from adults the child may also learn to idealize or romanticize politics. For example, some testing at the high school level (ages 14—17) indicates that romantic notions about politics are not fully or largely dissipated even by that stage. The child's inner need to create a benevolent image of authority coincides with and is thereby strongly reinforced by the partial, idealized, and idealizing view of political life communicated to him by protective adults.

But in spite of these forces working in the direction of idealization, our data do suggest that, contradictory as it may seem, at least in some areas the child is quite capable of facing up to the passions and conflict in political life and that he is equally capable of tolerating such stress without succumbing either to cynicism or to disenchantment with political authority. The area of conflict to which the child is particularly exposed at the youngest age is the presidential electoral campaign. In an age of television, it is an area which cannot be concealed from him. He is aware of the acrimony of debate over the merits of alternative candidates, and more important, he easily learns that people align themselves on different sides and that it is proper for people so to commit themselves. The child even goes further. Simultaneous with the emergence of high positive affect with regard to the President, it is quite revealing to discover that young as they are, children in the early grades learn to tolerate partisan commitment on their own part and to accept alternative partisanship on the part of others as one of the rules of the game. Partisan differences—and at times even conflict—so generated are not interpreted as hampering the acceptance of the outcome of electoral campaigns, esteem for the victor, or the legitimacy of the authority so established. This constitutes the beginning of what later in life becomes a rather complex set of attitudes and represents an introduction to a major norm of democratic society.

Most children do not become familiar with the term political party until the fourth and fifth grade at the earliest. But before this, as early as the second grade, large numbers are nevertheless able to assert a party identification. In a pretest sample of about 700 children, a strong majority in each grade from two through eight state that if they could vote they would align themselves with either of the two major parties in the United States. Interviews around responses such as these indicate that in the early grades—the point at which party preference becomes well established—the children may be adopting party identification in much the same way that they appropriate the family's religious beliefs, family name, neighborhood location, or other basic characteristics of life.

Nor do most children display partisan feelings in a purely formal way. They seem to be aware of the implications of party preferences as an expression of explicit commitment to a point of view, however superficial their understanding of this point of view may be. Thus of a pretest sample of over 300 children, a large majority reported that they participated in a partisan spirit in the last presidential campaign by wearing candidate buttons. Most of these children who were in grades 4 through 8 responded that they did so as a way of taking sides or for purposes of helping their candidate win. A minority were less sensitive to the expression of partisan commitment involved, but said they took sides because they thought it was fun to do so, or because they were simply imitating their friends or parents. But they did feel the pressure to adopt a partisan posture, however apolitical its meaning was for them.

But partisanship does not seem to interfere with what we may interpret as the early origins of a belief in the legitimacy of political authority. When some 200 pretest children were asked whether the candidate who loses an election should ask his followers to help the winner, an overwhelming majority beginning in the early grades and increasing with age responded in the affirmative. The dissenting minority here is of course interesting and needs to be explored.

Thus even though the child idealizes political authority as the result of the socializing processes to which he is exposed, at the same time he acquires regime norms that make it possible for him to tolerate comfortably the campaign conflict surrounding the choice of these authorities. As a result, the attachment to authority achieved through the mechanism of idealization is not disturbed or displaced by electoral passions and cleavage. The importance of this type of socialization for the stability of a democratic regime needs no elaboration.

Conclusion

We have touched on only a few selected topics of socialization of knowledge and attitudes with respect to two major objects, the political community and the regime. We have reported only from tentative and limited preliminary data. But what this theoretically determined approach does reveal is that processes of attachment to the political community and the regime begin at a considerably earlier age than one would expect. The political content that is socialized shows signs of being buttressed by powerful sentiments linked to religion, family, and internal needs of the dependent child. If what is learned early in life is hard to displace in later years, we have here an important increment to our understanding of the sources of stability in the American political system. Comparative research in systems experiencing considerable change and in those developing nations moving toward a unified entity for the first time should help us in better understanding the contribution of socialization to political instability and change. . . .

Power

If political science sought to explore the total value pattern of society it would have to embrace all social science. The reason for this is that all social mechanisms are means for allocating values. The structure and processes of society determine the social statuses that we have and the roles that we perform; these in turn enable us to acquire certain benefits or rewards not available to others. Our economic statuses and roles, for example, help to determine the economic benefits that we get in the processes of production and exchange. Similarly our class, educational, religious, and other institutions help to distribute unequally other advantages available in a society.[7] Every other set of institutions helps in one way or another to distribute the values in a society.

But none of these modes for allocating desirable or undesirable things need be authoritative. Political science can learn much from the other social sciences because they are all interested to some degree in how institutions distribute what we consider to be advantages or disadvantages. I am suggesting, however, that political research is distinctive because it has been trying to reveal the way in which values are affected by authoritative allocation. We must inquire, therefore, into the characteristics that lend the color of authority to policies. This brings us to the second of the three concepts just mentioned.

Although the literature is replete with discussions about the nature of authority,[8] the meaning of this term can be resolved quickly for our purposes. A policy is authoritative when the people to whom it is intended to apply or who are affected by it consider that they must or ought to obey it. It is obvious that this is a psychological rather than a moral explanation of the term. We can justify its use in this way because it gives to the term a meaning that enables us to determine factually whether a group of people do in practice consider a policy to be authoritative. . . .

As we shall shortly see, it is a necessary condition for the existence of a viable society that some policies appearing in a society be considered authoritative. But a moment's reflection will reveal that political science is not initially and centrally interested in all authoritative policies found in a society. For example, the members of any association, such as a trade union or a church, obviously consider the policies adopted by their organization authoritative for themselves. The constitution and by-laws of an association constitute the broad formal policy within the context of which members of the organization will accept lesser policies as authoritative. Minorities within the group, while they remain as members, will accept the decisions and practices of the group as binding, or authoritative, for the whole membership.

In organizations that are less than society-wide we have, therefore, the existence of a variety of authoritative policies. And yet, in spite of the fact that for the members of the organization these policies carry the weight of authority, it is at once apparent that political science does not undertake to study these policies for their own sake. Political science is concerned rather with the relation of the authoritative policies, made in such groups

---

[7] P. Sorokin, *Social Mobility* (New York: Harper, 1927).

[8] For a discriminating bibliography see H. Simon, D. Smithburg, V. Thompson, op. cit., pp. 571-572.

as associations, to other kinds of policies, those that are considered authoritative for the whole society. In other words, political research seeks first and foremost to understand the way in which values are authoritatively allocated, not for a group within society, but for the whole society. . . .

The Need for Authoritative Allocations in Society

If it is true, as I have maintained, that from time immemorial men have been asking questions that lead them to seek an understanding of the way values are authoritatively allocated, this has not been just a matter of accident. A minimum condition for the existence of any society is the establishment of some mechanisms, however crude of inchoate, for arriving at authoritative social decisions about how goods, both spiritual and material, are to be distributed, where custom fails to create other patterns. Because every society must fulfill this task there has recurred in every literate society the kind of question political scientists ask today. Let us examine for a moment why this need arises; we will then be in a position to probe more fully into just what is meant by the phrase authoritative allocation of values for a society, and therefore into what gives coherence to political research.

The need for social policy stems from the very character of a society.[9] As a social system, a society is a special kind of human grouping the members of which continually interact with one another and in the process develop a sense of belonging together. This common consciousness, as it is often called, reflects the fact that the members of the social system have a basic similarity in their culture and social structure. But a society consists of more than these characteristics. Dependent nationality groups, for example, experience this feeling of togetherness induced by a common culture and social structure. The societal group, however, is further distinguished by the fact that it seeks to solve all the problems usually associated with the survival and perpetuation of a group of people. The activities of a society, in other words, are broader than those of any of its component groups. Briefly, the broadest grouping of human beings who live together and collectively undertake to satisfy all the minimum prerequisites of group life is what we refer to when we speak of a society.

Various groups may be devoted to special tasks important for the continuity of any society. Groups may devote themselves to tasks such as those of production and exchange for purposes of physical sustenance, the dissemination and communication of knowledge, the maintenance of

---

[9] See a suggestive analysis of the characteristics of a society in J. W. Bennett and M. M. Tumin, *Social Life* (New York: Knopf, 1949).

order, the inculcation of a sense of common purpose and destiny, or provision for the common defense. It is however the peculiar task of no one group within a society to undertake to fulfill all these conditions for existence. Any one group may help to meet some of the conditions; no group aside from society meets them all. The religious and philosophical institutions, for instance, help to instill purpose; the army and foreign policy associations devote themselves to defense; trade unions, business, and consumers' organizations are involved with problems of exchange and distribution of wealth. Each group has sets of tasks, the scope of which embraces something less than all those conditions demanded for the survival of society as a whole. Only a society casts its net over all these tasks.

As I have suggested, wherever we have such a grouping of people who seek to satisfy all these conditions for collective existence, there we find that one of these conditions calls for authoritative allocation of values. The reason for this is elementary. In spite of the glowing early liberal picture of a future when all social relations would be automatically adjusted without intervention in the name of the collectivity, in no society that has yet existed has this occurred. The grain of truth in the late eighteenth-century liberal view lies in the fact that in every society custom does provide for the private solution of a vast variety of differences and conflicts among individuals with regard to their share of the values. But the greater the size and complexity of a society, the narrower does the scope of private negotiation become, and conversely, even in the smallest and simplest society someone must intervene in the name of society, with its authority behind him, to decide how differences over valued things are to be resolved.

This authoritative allocation of values is a minimum prerequisite of any society, even though it is not the only prerequisite. When individuals or groups dispute about the distribution of things considered valuable, whether they be spiritual or material, and when these disputes are not resolved to the satisfaction of the parties through some customary process of private negotiation, then a policy is enunciated with the authority of society behind it and with its acceptance by society as authoritative. It is patent that without the provision for some means of deciding among competing claims to limited values, society would be rent by constant strife; the regularized interaction which distinguishes a society from a random mob of individuals could not exist. Every society provides some mechanisms, however rudimentary they may be, for authoritatively resolving differences about the ends that are to be pursued, that is, for deciding who is to get what there is of the desirable things. An authoritative allocation of some values is unavoidable.

This conclusion may appear to be at odds with the undeniable facts about our international society today or about nonliterate societies where there are no central organs, the policies of which are recognized as authoritative for the whole group. This does appear to raise a difficulty. The trouble flows, however, from an assumption that I have not intended, namely, that authoritative allocations require the existence of a well-defined organization called government.

The question we must ask is this: To what extent does government as we know it today in any unified nation need to exist in order to be able to say that social life has a political aspect? To this point I have said little about the kind of institutional mechanisms necessary for the translation of social power into social policy. The fact that policies recognized as authoritative for the whole society must exist does not imply or assume that a central governmental organization is required in order to make decisions and effectuate them. Institutional devices for making and executing policy may take an infinite variety of forms. The clarity and precision with which the statuses and roles of legislators and administrators are defined will depend upon the level of development of a particular society. Societies could be placed on a continuum with regard to the degree of definition of such roles. Well-defined organizations, which we call government, exist in the national societies of western Europe; scarcely discernible statuses and roles of which a governmental organization is constituted exist in international society and in nonliterate societies.

In the interaction among nations today, for example, when they are viewed as units, we have a genuine society even though it is at a less integrated and less rationalized stage of development than in national societies. Nevertheless, it is a separate society. The fact of the continuing contact that we associate with a society, a minimum feeling of similarity which has been growing with the increase in the material and cultural exchanges of a shrinking world, and the obvious need to solve the basic conditions of social coexistence among national units all require that some mechanisms be established for the solution of differences. This is demanded by virtue of the fact that not all disputes are automatically settled through the efforts of individual nations along customary lines. As in the domestic sphere, the solution of differences is in large measure left to the individual national units through bilateral or wider negotiations. Private negotiation is a major mechanism, just as within any national unit there are far more differences over the distribution of values solved by the interacting parties alone than by any authoritative agency acting in the name of society.

But without an explicit statement to the effect, it is patent that the general atmosphere or set of relations within which the individual national units are able to conduct their private negotiations about the distribution of values is dominated and supervised by the great powers. In the last resort, if any specific pattern of distribution of values, or if the general pattern emerging from individual private negotiations over time, does not accord with their conception of a desirable disposition of resources internationally, it has been normal for the great powers to step in to speak with the voice of the international society. We generally associate the collective action of the great powers with crisis situations such as the historic conferences at Westphalia, Vienna, The Hague, Versailles, Teheran, or Potsdam. But between crises it is obvious that the international allocation of values is closely scrutinized by the great powers; therefore, the political matrix within which international activity takes place reflects their outlook.

Within the last fifty years periodic attempts have been made, especially through the structures of the League of Nations and the United Nations, to broaden the base of the organs responsible for speaking with the authoritative voice of the international society. To this extent we have been seeking to rationalize or define more clearly the institutional mechanism for making authoritative allocations of values. These new organizations do not introduce for the first time the idea of providing a formal policy-making and policy-executing mechanism for the international society. The great powers, with lesser powers at the fringe, have always themselves assumed the obligation of fulfilling an obvious condition for the existence of any international contact. The new organizations were designed only to take the place of the earlier device of periodic meetings among the great powers. No less than within national units themselves, the fact of persisting international contact lays down as one of the conditions for its continuation the creation of means for the authoritative settling of differences. For this reason the study of international politics is integral with the study of politics in general; it concerns the same genus of subject matter. It deals with the functioning and determinants of those policies, both formal, legal decisions as well as practices, which have most influenced the allocation of social goods—or we might say analogically, with the functioning and the determinants of authoritative policy in the international society. It differs from political research in domestic matters only with regard to the society to which it refers.

A glance at nonliterate societies indicates even more clearly that the kind of institutional mechanisms for making authoritative policies or the clarity with which the roles of policy makers are defined is irrelevant to the fact of the existence of such policies. Consider the case of two Bantu tribes living in western Kenya, the Logoli and the Vugusu[10] of approximately 45,000 inhabitants each, as they functioned before the intrusion of Western civilization. Each tribe is divided into clans, subclans, and lineages. Neither of these tribes has a formal political organization, either for the resolution of disputes among the members of the tribe or between the tribe and some outsider. To the casual observer it might appear that

---

[10] See the account of the political organization of these tribes in M. Fortes and E. E. Evans-Pritchard (eds.) *African Political Systems,* pp. 197-238; K. Davis, *Human Society* (New York: Macmillan, 1950), pp. 481 ff., draws on this material in his discussion of political institutions. The whole of *African Political Systems* is of exceptional value to political scientists because of the theoretical problems it raises in an empirical context.

no political activity goes on here at all since there is clearly no central body to make authoritative policy. Political statuses and roles are hardly distinguishable; there is no institution that at first glance seems to undertake the tasks of government as we know it. Interpersonal private negotiation, dominated by custom, regulates the largest part of the life of the tribes, so that where differences arise they are automatically resolved without recourse to the kind of special deliberation we associate with government.

But as is usual in these circumstances, custom is never strong enough to bind all men equally; and, in addition, novel situations arise where the rule to be invoked is in doubt. The political function is here taken over by the elders of a subclan when the dispute is confined to members of the same subclan; and when it involves members of different subclans, by the elders of the clan as a whole. There is normally no formal meeting of the elders in the subclan, who can be found talking over local problems in the pasture every morning. Only when the elders of the entire clan are required, is a special meeting called. If these individuals agree on a policy, means are available through their prestige to enforce it; but if the elders are divided on the solution, then it is possible that the minority may secede from the clan and join another. In cases of inter-clan friction, it is the elders of the offender's clan who are expected to settle the policy; if they fail to produce a satisfactory solution then the clans may enter into violent conflict. This sets in motion attempts by the elders of neutral clans to arbitrate and seek a reconciliation.

It is clear that in all these procedures we have a mechanism, at times peaceful, at others violent, for arriving at authoritative policy, a condition for the continuation of the society. We are accustomed to associate the mechanisms for deciding political issues with peaceful, even perhaps rational, procedures; but there is no prior reason why this must be the case. As we know from our own strife, industrial, civil, and international, violence itself is a recognized, even though usually a deplored, procedure for arriving at authoritative policy. It is, however, as much a part of the political process as peaceful means; hence, it has become a significant part of political research. Among these Bantu tribes, as in contemporary international society, the decisions may not meet with the approval of all parties, but what is accepted is the fact that in the elders, as in the great powers, there is a group which normally undertakes the task of dealing authoritatively with policy when other means of solving differences over values fail.

It is clear, therefore, that even in societies peripheral to ours, a process that corresponds to what in our own society we call the making and execution of policy for society must take place, even though the devices may be less formal and even though there may be few, if any, legally recognized means for enforcing decisions. The form of the mechanism and the kind of sanctions are, however, matters for empirical investigation;

they do not invalidate the conclusion that there is discernible a process whereby values are authoritatively allocated for the whole society. . . .

Change

General Sources of Stress

The sources of stress need not always be quite so dramatic as wars, revolutions, or other social traumas. Indeed, normally they are much more prosaic. They are just as likely to stem from the constant, daily pressures of political life. Without any aid from special crises, they seem capable of imposing serious strains on the ability of any political system to survive or on the ability of the members of a society to assure any arrangement for making and implementing authoritative decisions. On the face of it, it is little short of miraculous that the basic political functions are met in some way, so great are the internal strains to which any system is typically and normally subjected and so overpowering the external changes that they frequently must be capable of absorbing. . . .

Stress on a System

We can further improve our grasp of the meaning of persistence and its implications for our mode of analysis if we consider what is involved in the idea of stress, those conditions that challenge the capacity of a system to persist. I have been suggesting that it is the results of the operation of stress and the inability of a system to cope with it that lead a system to collapse. A system will be able to persist if its members are able to undertake adequate action in the face of stress. By understanding the general conditions that are created when stress occurs or that we may identify as stressful, we shall be able to reveal the full implications of persistence as a central concept in systems analysis.[11]

Disturbance as the Cause of Stress

How do we know when a system is operating under stress? To be able to answer this question, two preliminary remarks are necessary. In the first place, stress may have occurred, in which case it would not be difficult to document. But the kind of stressful condition that will be of primary interest for us is that which is potential. It represents a threat to a system, endangering its capacity to survive but not necessarily destroying the

---

[11] In this volume the discussion on stress will be confined to those conditions that define stress. The specific circumstances that promote stress will not be investigated.

system. It offers the members of a system a chance to regulate or eliminate the stressing conditions or to shield the system from them. Whether or not the potential is actualized to the detriment of the system will depend upon the ability of the members of the system to deal with the conditions creating the stress.

In the second place, stress may imply a change from a prior condition of some sort that was hospitable to the persistence of a system. This is not to be understood, however, as suggesting that every internal or environmental change will necessarily be stressful. From the point of view of the survival probabilities of a system, changes will range from insignificant to those that are either highly beneficial or damaging.

In order to identify those events or occurrences within a system or its environment that in some way can be expected to bring about, or have brought about, a change in the way a system operates, we may reserve for them the concept *disturbance*. Disturbances will refer to all activities in the environment or within a system that can be expected to or do displace a system from its current pattern of operations, regardless of whether or not it is stressful for the system.

Disturbances will vary enormously both in numbers and variety. They will also vary with respect to their consequences; hence, they may be classified as neutral, benign, or stressful according to the degree to which they affect the chances for some or any kind of political system to persist. In some cases an activity may take place that simply makes no difference to the operations of a political system; or the effects are so slight as to be negligible. In other instances the distubrance may be of such a nature as to enhance the chances of the system for surviving as some kind of system. The discovery in the economic sector of society of new material resources or the invention of new technologies that markedly improve the general standard of living may so contribute to the satisfactions with the system as to reinforce existing support for it. The disturbances with which we shall be particularly preoccupied are those that threaten to prevent a system from functioning and that can, therefore, be designated as stressful.

Threaten or endanger are the key words. If allowed to run its course, a disturbance might lead to the complete destruction of the system and even prevent its continuity through resurrection in any other form. But if a system survives, *ipso facto* it must have been able to abort such a tendency. Then the disturbance presented a threat rather than an accomplished fact; it stressed the system without destroying it. Most of the kinds of stress we shall be analyzing are of this sort.

Stress as Variation from the Normal Range of Operation

At the outset it is necessary to recognize that the precise identification of a stressful condition in a system raises major problems, some of which are not amenable to solution, given the level of data and understanding we presently have about political life. Since the task of theory is to extend the frontiers of knowledge and not simply to codify what we already know, this handicap in itself need not deter us.

We can appreciate the plausibility of stress as a useful concept if we are willing to recognize that, as an idea, it at least makes intuitive good sense. This is a sufficient, if not always necessary, starting point in seeking to ascribe a more technical meaning to a term. In a loose but meaningful way, we are prone to talk of political systems undergoing stress. In doing so we generally have in mind conditions that may lead to the destruction and transformation of a system. Much has been written of democracy in crisis, the horse and buggy political structures in an age of streamlined jets, the inability of tribal political systems to withstand the impact of colonizing cultures, the dangers of democracy inherent in the cleavages associated with pluralistic societies, or the threats posed to authoritarian and totalitarian systems by fissures in their elites.

In characterizing systems in this way, whether or not we are conscious of it, we seem to be implying that for the specific types of system under consideration there is some *normal* pattern of operation which has been displaced. But if we were asked to spell out the normal level of operation that is thus being modified, we might have considerable difficulty in providing a measure that would be generally accepted. For example, what is the normal range of operation of a totalitarian system such as the Soviet Union? Would the entrenchment of an orderly and peaceful pattern of leadership succession stress the system enough so as to push it beyond its normal range with the result that it could no longer be considered totalitarian? Has the French democratic system disappeared under the stress of the Gaullist regime or does it continue to operate within what we would consider to be the normal range of democracy?

The idea of stress driving a system beyond some normal range of operation is at least applicable to given types of systems. It is certainly implicit in much of the analysis traditionally undertaken with respect to them. Theoretically, the identification of a point of stress is relatively simple for given types. Any time a disturbance leads to the change of the essential characteristics of a type of system—those that best define the characteristic way in which the system operates—we can say that the system has been put under stress and has succumbed to it. Empirically it might be somewhat more difficult to establish when this point has been reached. Even here the contrasts are clear; it is only the thresholds that would remain ambiguous. Certainly, if Spain were to introduce free popular elections and freedom of speech and association in the Western pattern or if the French regime were to restore the Presidency to a less dominant role and parties to a more prominent one, there would be little question that the systems fell within what would be explicitly considered the normal range of variation of a democratic system.

If, temporarily, we continue to use given types of systems as a point of departure, it is clear, that latent in our description of them as operating within a normal range, beyond which stress may push them, is the idea that there are certain *essential variables*[12] that are thus being displaced beyond their normal range. For democracies these might be conceived to be some vaguely defined degree of freedom of speech and association and popular participation in the political process. For a totalitarian system the essential variables might consist of some minimal degree of exclusion of popular participation, dominant power in the hands of a political elite, coercion of the individual, and controlled and highly restricted freedom of speech and association. But our criteria for classifying political systems are sufficiently imprecise to leave considerable room for dispute as to what the essential variables are that help to distinguish one type of system from another.

Regardless of the theoretical problems of classification encountered in any effort to single out the essential identifying variables of a particular type of system, we tend to operate on the assumption that it is possible to distinguish two different aspects of a system. The one identifies those features of a system that enable it to operate in a characteristic way and that thereby distinguish it fundamentally from other systems. By classifying systems as democratic, authoritarian, totalitarian, traditional, or modernizing, we are attributing to each type of system different characteristic modes of operation. Presumably, this difference can be specified through the kinds of relationships or patterns of interaction that we consider central properties of the system. We may call these differences, whatever their specific character may be, the essential variables.

In most types of systems the system will retain its characteristic properties, say, as a democracy or totalitarian system, as long as the essential variables remain within a given range, what I have called the normal range. Again, empirically it may be difficult to discern when the system is moving toward the critical point, one beyond which it becomes transformed into a different system. For some observers Gaullist France has moved beyond the critical limits of a democracy; but persons may differ at least empirically on this score. However, theoretically it is clear that the essential variables of a type of system need not just be present or absent. They will usually be of a type that can be present in greater or lesser degree. Only when they function within some normal or critical range can the system be described as conforming to the criteria of a given type. For example, if a system is to be labeled democratic, the presence in politics of freedom of speech or popular participation in a small measure

---

[12] This concept has been adapted from W. R. Ashby, *An Introduction to Cybernetics* (New York: John Wiley & Sons, Inc., 1956), p. 197.

may not be enough. The amount is critical. Few systems eliminate all freedom, and in modern mass societies, some forms of popular participation are almost mandatory.

The persistence of a given type of political system requires more than the presence of essential variables. They need to operate above a certain level. In other words, there is a critical range and if disturbances displace the system beyond it, the entire system will change its character.

By implication, there must be a second aspect to systems. This aspect may change without altering the characteristic mode of operation of the system. It will consist of the nonessential features of a system. For example, in light of the customary classification I am using, the United States would continue to function characteristically as a democracy regardless of the many changes in its political structure in the last fifty years. Many modifications in a type of political system are possible without leading to the transformation of the type.

Perhaps an illustration from biology will help to illuminate the difference between essential and nonessential variables. Let us turn to the human organism, if we may do so without being accused of thinking that a political system corresponds in most respects to this biological system. Changes in certain variables internal to the organic system may occur without destroying the normal mode of operation of the body as a whole. The loss of an eye, a limb, or other duplicated organs may reduce the flexibility with which the organism can cope with any succeeding disturbances, but it need not destroy the typical way in which the organism functions. We may describe this situation by saying that the essential variables of the organic system have remained within their normal range. If the blood pressure had been displaced beyond a certain level or the sugar content of the blood fell below a specified point, there would be more serious consequences. These constitute two essential variables of the organic system that must be kept within critical limits if the system as a whole is to persist.

Stress and the Critical Limits of the Essential Variables

Once we recognize that there is this difference between variables essential to the characteristic mode of operation of a system and those that are of secondary importance and that the former operate within normal ranges, we have a clue toward a useful way of describing stress on a system. It can now be said to be a condition that occurs when disturbances, internal or external in origin, threaten to displace the essential variables of a political system beyond their normal range and toward some critical limit. Thereby it prevents a political system from operating in its characteristic way.

Two things need to be said about this description of the stress potential of a disturbance. First, empirically we may not have adequate measures or indices of when a disturbance becomes stressful and threatens to destroy a system. But, as I have indicated, the task of theory is to point out what is necessary. As long as in principle it is possible to achieve, empirically, what is necessary, it becomes a separate although important matter to locate empirical indicators of theoretically important phenomena. No more than at many other points in our analysis need we be perturbed here by the current lack of such indicators.

Second, since stress is a potential in the form of a present danger or threat, we may need to assess a disturbance as stressful even though the essential variables do not pass beyond their critical limits. The fact that such a stressful disturbance did not push the essential variables this far would not necessarily be proof of an erroneous assessment. It could be an indication that at some point the members of a system were able to intervene constructively so as to prevent the disturbance from continuing to operate in a stressful manner, at least to the point of destroying the system. This is typically what happens when political systems do survive; every persisting system has homeostatic devices to help it cope with stress. But as long as a disturbance hinders rather than helps an essential variable, we may consider it to be stressful.

To reiterate, not every disturbance need result in stressing a system. Some may, in fact, reinforce the operation of its essential variables within the normal range and thereby help the system to continue functioning in its typical way. Let us return to democracy as a type of system for purposes of this illustration. If we accept the plausible hypothesis that the conditions for the functioning of democracy include a high level of literacy, acceptance of negotiation and compromise in the general culture, minimal levels of economic productivity, and the emergence of a strong middle class, changes among the parametric systems that encourage these conditions may well increase the probability that the essential variables of an existing democratic system will continue to operate within their normal range. By virtue of the same argument, any movement of these parameters in opposite directions will act as disturbances on a democratic system and will impose stressful consequences.

The Essential Variables of Political Systems as Such

Whatever the situation may be with regard to the ease of identifying stress in particular types of systems, it is now time to recall that our primary focus is not on the persistence of such types. Rather, it concerns any and all systems, regardless of type. How shall we establish when the capacity of a political system to continue as such a system is being put under stress, regardless of the capacity of the society to sustain any particular kind of political system? That is to say, if a political system under stress transforms itself from a democratic to a totalitarian one or from a weak to a strong presidential democratic system, the capacity of the society to sustain some kind of political system has not been impaired. However, if one after another kind of political system were tried and found wanting, it is conceivable that the members of the society might find themselves unable to support any political system, regardless of type. This would result in the destruction of all political life for that society and without doubt, the demise of the society as well. The very life processes of any political system in that society would be extinguished.

What, then, are the essential variables, not of a given type of system, but of any and all systems? When posed in this way, the question virtually answers itself. I have already identified a political system as those patterns of interaction through which values are allocated for a society and these allocations are accepted as authoritative by most persons in the society most of the time. It is through the presence of activities that fulfill these two basic functions that a society can commit the resources and energies of its members in the settlement of differences that cannot be autonomously resolved.

By definition, therefore, whatever type of system we may be considering, its characteristic mode of behaving as a political system, as contrasted, say, with an economic or religious system, will depend upon the capacity of the system to allocate values for the society and assure their acceptance. It is these two major variables or sets of variables—the behavior related to the capacity to make decisions for the society and the probability of their frequent acceptance by most members as authoritative—that are the essential variables and that therefore distinguish political systems from all other types of social systems. Once events occur leaving it impossible for members of a system to arrive at political decisions, or, if after they have been taken, they are regularly rejected by large segments of the membership, no political system (democratic, totalitarian, or authoritarian) can function. The system must either crumble into a variety of smaller units as seemed to be threatening in the Congo during the sixties, or it must be absorbed into another society subject to a different political system.

From this point of view all other variables may be considered nonessential or incidental. It must be emphasized that if we were directing our attention to an analysis of varying classes of systems, such as democracies, we would redefine the essential variables to include whatever characteristic patterns of political relationships we associated with this kind of system. But if we continue to take as our level of analysis the persistence of some kind of political system, regardless of the type involved—that is, the study of the underlying processes of all political life—the variables essential to the persistence of a specific type, such as democracy, become incidental with respect to all types of political systems considered as a species of social system. Thus, we establish the two essential variables for all and any kinds of political system as "the making and execution of decisions for a society" and "their relative frequency of acceptance as authoritative or binding by the bulk of society."

The operation of essential variables need not be an all or nothing matter. A system may be more or less able to make decisions, put them into effect, and get them accepted as binding. The behavior involved varies on a range of effectiveness, and within that normal range a system may be able to persist. Thus, the authorities are not always able to make decisions; varying degrees of paralysis may occur as the history of the Weimar Republic and of France during the Third and Fourth Republics so clearly indicates. It is always a question of whether the capacity to make decisions has dropped below some critical point. Such a condition would signalize the loss of power to make some presently indeterminable minimum of decisions for the given system. Beyond that point the system diasppears since it is no longer minimally effective in resolving differences among the members of a system. The critical point will vary with type of system and with time and place; in general, we would need to bear in mind that each system or type of system does have a critical point.

Similarly, even where the authorities are fully capable of making decisions and of seeking to implement them, compliance will vary on a continuum. The probability of the members accepting all decisions as binding is usually less than one, at least in any significant historical interval of time. Yet it must certainly be higher than .5. A system would be in a state of constant turmoil and confusion and might well be on the threshold of disappearance if there were just an equal probability that the decisions and associated actions of its authorities would be accepted or rejected. The ratio of rejection to acceptance must fall within a limited range well above that of chance. Below that level the system would collapse for want of sufficient authority being attached to its allocations.

Accordingly, as long as the disturbances operating on a system lead to changes in the system that do not affect its capacity to maintain these two essential variables within their indeterminate but, in principle, determinable normal range, they will not be considered stressful. They will, rather, just induce changes in the state of the system. The system may change, but not in any way that affects its characteristic mode of functioning as a political system. Where the disturbance can be interpreted as introducing changes in a system that are driving either of the essential variables beyond their critical range, we can designate them as stressful. If the disturbances can just be assessed as having the potential for doing so, that is, as representing a threat or pressure in that direction, they will also be noted as stressful.

It will be crucial to bear in mind the distinction I am attempting to make between the persistence of a type of system such as a democracy and any or all systems. It is easy to slip from the general to the type level, that is, from all and any systems to a special type such as democracy. Indeed, it is hard to resist the temptation to drop to a lower level of generality because, typically, in thinking about political life, political science has been concerned with the conditions for survival of democratic systems of varying subtypes and with the conditions for the elimination or self-destruction of dictatorial or nondemocratic systems of equally varying subtypes. From a policy-oriented point of view, and in the light of many alternative kinds of ethical considerations, this is as it should be. However, from the perspective of seeking to develop general theory, we are setting aside such ethically oriented questions. It should be evident that this is not because they are unimportant questions, but because in terms of the strategy of research the ethical and policy considerations will ultimately be better and more reliably answered if we have useful general theory as a point of departure.[13]

In any event, in view of my focus on general theory, it will be vital to bear in mind that what I designate as stressful for political systems as such will necessarily be equally so for any type. The converse, though, is not equally true. Disturbances stressful to a particular type of system need not be stressful to the essential variables of the political system as such. The destruction of the system type may well be one way of coping with stress so that at least *some* kind of system will endure. This need not mean that alternative methods for coping with the stressful disturbances are lacking. No one can say that the Nazi regime presented the only alternative to the Weimar Republic as a means of sustaining the essential variables of a German political system. There were probably many alternative ways of keeping the essential variables within their critical range. Even if there were not, the fact that systems analysis leads to a discussion of how systems typically seek to avoid stress is no indication that any outcome, even if it is the only one possible, is necessarily desirable according to my own value criteria. Both the ethical value of the transformations in a system and their impact on the probabilities of survival are vital considerations; at the same time they can be treated as quite different and separate matters.

The Regulation of Stress

Persistence in a stable or changing world will thus be found to be in part a function of the presence of stressful disturbances. We have seen that it is in the very nature of political life that these cannot be avoided. But the consequences of disturbances on the fortunes of the system itself—

---

[13] See my volume, *The Political System,* where this point is fully developed.

whether it survives and in what form—will depend upon the capacity and readiness of a system to cope with such stress.

It is a critical property of social systems, including political systems, that they are able to respond to the influences acting upon them. They can cope with such disturbances and seek to regulate them in some way. The members of a political system need not sit back, as it were, to accept stress supinely, through some mechanistically conceived way of adapting to changes taking place in the environment. This is what has long been unwittingly implied in equilibrium analysis as a theory of political life, a kind of conceptual posture that has been characteristic of much political research in the last half century.[14] The members of a system are able to react constructively in one or all of several directions so as to regulate the disturbances that have been thrust upon the system and, thereby, to seek to alleviate existing or potential stress.

Over time political systems in general, and each system in particular, have developed extensive repertoires of techniques for coping with possible stress. It is the fact that social systems have such repertoires at their disposal that dramatically distinguishes them from other kinds of systems. It builds a flexibility into them that not even the most complex biological systems, and therefore the most versatile of them, have ever possessed.

Although I shall reserve for a succeeding volume my discussion of the particular kinds of regulative responses that characterize all systems, here it will be useful to point to the general classes of responses that are to be found. Like human biological systems, political systems may be able to keep themselves intact, at least for brief periods, by insulating themselves from all change. Like human biological systems, political systems may even seek to control environmental and internal changes in such a way that they do not become stressful; or if they have already become so, so as to ward off the dangers already present.

What political systems as a type of social system possess uniquely, when compared to both biological and mechanical systems, is the capacity to transform themselves, their goals, practices, and the very structure of their internal organization. To keep the vital processes, the essential variables, of a political system alive, as it were, a system may remodel its structures and processes to the point where they are unrecognizable. A democracy may become transformed into an unmitigated dictatorship, a traditional system into a wholly modern one. No human biological system has yet been able to emulate this kind of self-transforming feat; although with modern computer technology and with a growing knowledge of the genetic structure, controlled mutation is well within the realm of probability. It may open up a modest range of internal reorganization of the

---

[14] I have dealt with "equilibrium" as a central theoretical concept in *The Political System, ad hoc* and in "Limits of the Equilibrium Model in Social Research," *Behavioral Science* 1 (1956), 96-104.

human anatomy and physiological processes that will bring the biological system closer to the self-regulative potentials of a social system.

What is implied in these remarks is the presence of a capacity to call up a variety of responses in defense of the essential variable. What has been obscured is that tne selection of alternatives from the repertoires is not necessarily given. The members may be able to make choices and vary their strategies within the limits permitted by circumstances. In one system an outbreak of violence may be the response to stress from deep and intransigent economic crises; in another system similar or even more severe economic disorganization may lead only to expressions of discontent in acceptable styles, accompanied by an intensification of corrective policies.

Not only is there freedom to select from a range of alternative strategies, but in many systems, at least those not bound by traditional practices, the members may consciously set out to devise new methods for meeting new or old crises. In this event they will be adding to their store of responses through innovation. In the last analysis as many alternative responses would be available to meet a stressful situation as can be suggested by the ingenuity of man. In this sense, once again, unlike the implications of the equilibrium model of political processes, the members of a system need not simply absorb a disturbance and mechanically seek to reestablish some old point of stability in the political system or move on to a new one. To accept a conceptualization of this sort would indeed be to leave the system in the hands of some invisible political hand. Members of a system have options, and within the range of these options alternative consequences for the persistence of the system may ensue. As one of these choices, and a central one for social systems, the members may search out entirely new avenues for meeting even old kinds of stresses. Adaptation, if one wishes to attach this label to this process, becomes a creative and constructive task, informed with goals and direction. . . .

HERBERT MARCUSE

Like Erich Fromm, Herbert Marcuse was born in Germany at the turn of the twentieth century and migrated to the United States later in his life under the impact of historical events in Europe. At the present time, Marcuse is one of the most influential radical thinkers in the world. By "radical," we mean a person who believes that basic changes in the organization of human life are necessary before a desirable individual and social existence can be brought into being. Many political theorists, however, maintain that there is a radical tradition in political thought that includes the works of Marx and perhaps the American Abolitionists, among other proponents of systemic change. Radicals often disagree about what changes are basic and about what constitutes a good social and individual existence. Radical psychological theorists tend to think that personality changes are most important, while radical systems theorists usually favor changes in the principles upon which social organizations function. These generalizations, of course, merely represent tendencies. Radical psychological theorists may call for changes in social structures, while radical systems theorists may advocate changes in consciousness.

Marcuse has exercised a great influence on many theorists of the New Left. Like Fromm, he has attempted to combine the insights of Freudian psychoanalysis and Marxian socioeconomic analysis. From Freud he has taken the ideal of a "nonrepressive" civilization in which human beings will no longer be needlessly frustrated and will be able to love and create. From Marx he has taken the point of view that critical analysis should include investigation of general principles of social organization, particularly the ways in which production is managed. Like Rousseau, Marcuse identifies two types of societies, two-dimensional and one-dimensional. Civil societies in the past have been two-dimensional in that they were characterized by a realm of material production and reproduction and a mental domain in which human beings could exercise their imaginations. The existence of an imaginative realm insured that the possibility of people recognizing their current misery and planning for a better future would never be wholly lost. Imagination provided the means for human beings to compare their actual existence to their ideal possibilities. When they saw a wide gap between the ideal and the actual, they might attempt to force social changes in the direction of the ideal. In other words, two-dimensional society provided the conditions for what we earlier called the critical approach. The advanced technological societies of today, Marcuse believes, have lost the two-dimensional quality. They are one-dimensional on the level of material production. The conditions for criticism have been abolished by the alleviation of material misery through modern industry and the manipulation of basic human needs through the media of mass communication. A sense of despair persists among people because their needs to love and express themselves are frustrated. However, their imaginations have been so enslaved by advertising and propaganda that they cannot understand their predicament, much less find a way out of it. Like Rousseau and Easton, Marcuse is interested in the process of socialization. Unlike Easton, however, he does not look with favor upon the loyalties that are presently being cultivated. Marcuse would assent to Rousseau's comment that men are "everywhere in chains."

Identity, Power, and Change* †

Aggressiveness in Advanced Industrial Society

I propose to consider here the strains and stresses in the so-called "affluent society," a phrase which has (rightly or wrongly) been coined to

---

*The material from the writings of Marcuse has been maintained as a single unit, instead of divided into the three categories—identity, power, and change—used throughout the rest of this book, in accordance with copyright requirements.

†Reprinted from *Negations* by Herbert Marcuse, Chapter 8, copyright © 1968 by Herbert Marcuse, by permission of the Beacon Press and Penguin Press.

describe contemporary American society. Its main characteristics are: (1) an abundant industrial and technical capacity which is to a great extent spent in the production and distribution of luxury goods, gadgets, waste, planned obsolescence, military or semimilitary equipment—in short, in what economists and sociologists used to call "unproductive" goods and services; (2) a rising standard of living, which also extends to previously underprivileged parts of the population; (3) a high degree of concentration of economic and political power, combined with a high degree of organization and government intervention in the economy; (4) scientific and pseudoscientific investigation, control, and manipulation of private and group behavior, both at work and at leisure (including the behavior of the psyche, the soul, the unconscious, and the subconscious) for commercial and political purposes. All these tendencies are interrelated: they make up the syndrome which expresses the normal functioning of the "affluent society." To demonstrate this interrelation is not my task here; I take its existence as the sociological basis for the thesis which I want to submit, namely, that the strains and stresses suffered by the individual in the affluent society are grounded in the normal functioning of this society (and of the individual!) rather than in its disturbances and diseases.

"Normal functioning": I think the definition presents no difficulties for the doctor. The organism functions normally if it functions, without disturbance, in accord with the biological and physiological makeup of the human body. The human faculties and capabilities are certainly very different among the members of the species, and the species itself has changed greatly in the course of its history but these changes have occurred on a biological and physiological basis which has remained largely constant. To be sure, the physician, in making his diagnosis and in proposing treatment, will take into account the patient's environment, upbringing, and occupation; these factors may limit the extent to which normal functioning can be defined and achieved, or they may even make this achievement impossible, but as criterion and goal, normality remains a clear and meaningful concept. As such, it is identical with "health," and the various deviations from it are to various degrees of "disease."

The situation of the psychiatrist seems to be quite different. At first glance, normality seems to be defined along the same lines the physician uses. The normal functioning of the mind (psyche, psyche-soma) is that which enables the individual to perform, to function in accord with his position as child, adolescent, parent, as a single person or married, in accord with his job, profession, status. But this definition contains factors of an entirely new dimension, namely, that of society, and society is a factor of normality in a far more essential sense than that of external influence, so much so that "normal" seems to be a social and institutional rather than individual condition. It is probably easy to agree on what is the normal functioning of the digestive tract, the lungs, and the heart, but what is the normal functioning of the mind in lovemaking, in other interpersonal relations, at work and at leisure, at a meeting of a board of directors, on the golf course, in the slums, in prison, in the army? While the normal functioning of the digestive tract or the lung is likely to be the same in the case of a healthy corporation executive and of a healthy laborer, this does not hold true of their minds. In fact, the one would be very abnormal if he regularly thought, felt, and operated like the other. And what is "normal" lovemaking, a "normal" family, a "normal" occupation?

The psychiatrist might proceed like the general physician and direct therapy to making the patient function within his family, in his job or environment, while trying to influence and even change the environmental factors as much as this is in his power. The limits will soon make themselves felt, for example, if the mental strains and stresses of the patient are caused, not merely by certain bad conditions in his job, in his neighborhood, in his social status, but by the very *nature* of the job, the neighborhood, the status itself—in their normal condition. Then making him normal for this condition would mean normalizing the strains and stresses, or to put it more brutally: making him capable of being sick, of living his sickness as health, without his noticing that he is sick precisely when he sees himself and is seen as healthy and normal. This would be the case if his work is, by its very nature, "deadening," stupefying, wasteful (even though the job pays well and is "socially" necessary), or if the person belongs to a minority group which is underprivileged in the established society, traditionally poor and occupied mainly in menial and "dirty" physical labor. But this would also be the case (in very different forms) on the other side of the fence among the tycoons of business and politics, where efficient and profitable performance requires (and reproduces) the qualities of smart ruthlessness, moral indifference, and persistent aggressiveness. In such cases, "normal" functioning would be tantamount to a distortion and mutilation of a human being—no matter how modestly one may define the human qualities of a human being. Erich Fromm wrote *The Sane Society;* it deals, not with the established, but with a future, society, the implication being that the established society is *not* sane but insane. Is not the individual who functions normally, adequately, and healthily as a citizen of a sick society—is not such an individual himself sick? And would not a sick society require an antagonistic concept of mental health, a meta-concept designating (and preserving) mental qualities which are tabooed, arrested, or distorted by the "sanity" prevalent in the sick society? (For example, mental health equals the ability to live as a dissenter, to live a nonadjusted life.)

As a tentative definition of "sick society" we can say that a society is sick when its basic institutions and relations, its structure, are such that they do not permit the use of the available material and intellectual resources for the optimal development and satisfaction of individual needs.

The larger the discrepancy between the potential and the actual human condition, the greater the social need for what I term "surplus-repression," that is, repression necessitated not by the growth and preservation of civilization but by the vested interest in maintaining an established society. Such surplus-repression introduces (over and above, or rather underneath, the social conflicts) new strains and stresses in the individuals. Usually handled by the normal working of the social process, which assures adjustment and submission (fear of loss of job or status, ostracism, and so forth), no special enforcement policies with respect to the mind are required. But in the contemporary affluent society, the discrepancy between the established modes of existence and the real possibilities of human freedom is so great that, in order to prevent an explosion, society has to insure a more effective mental coordination of individuals: in its unconscious as well as conscious dimensions, the psyche is opened up and subjected to systematic manipulation and control.

When I speak of the surplus-repression "required" for the maintenance of a society, or of the need for systematic manipulation and control, I do not refer to individually experienced social needs and consciously inaugurated policies: they may be thus experienced and inaugurated or they may not. I rather speak of *tendencies,* forces which can be identified by an analysis of the existing society and which assert themselves even if the policy makers are not aware of them. They express the requirements of the established apparatus of production, distribution, and consumption— economic, technical, political, mental requirements which have to be fulfilled in order to assure the continued functioning of the apparatus on which the population depends, and the continuing function of the social relationships derived from the organization of the apparatus. These objective tendencies become manifest in the trend of the economy, in technological change, in the domestic and foreign policy of a nation or group of nations, and they generate common, supraindividual needs and goals in the different social classes, pressure groups, and parties. Under the normal conditions of social cohesion, the objective tendencies override or absorb individual interests and goals without exploding the society; however, the particular interest is not simply determined by the universal: the former has its own range of freedom, and contributes, in accordance with its social position, to the shaping of the general interest—but short of a revolution, the particular needs and goals will remain defined by the predominant objective tendencies. Marx believed that they assert themselves "behind the back" of the individuals; in the advanced societies of today, management of enterprise and human relations, and manipulation of instinctual needs are practiced on the policy-making level and testify to the degree of awareness within the general blindness.

As for the systematic manipulation and control of the psyche in the advanced industrial society, manipulation and control for what, and by whom? Over and above all particular manipulation in the interest of certain businesses, policies, lobbies—the general objective purpose is to reconcile the individual with the mode of existence which his society imposes on him. Because of the high degree of surplus-repression involved in such reconciliation, it is necessary to achieve a libidinal cathexis of the merchandise the individual has to buy (or sell), the services he has to use (or perform), the fun he has to enjoy, the status symbols he has to carry—necessary, because the existence of the society depends on their uninterrupted production and consumption. In other words, social needs must become individual needs, instinctual needs. And to the degree to which the productivity of this society requires mass production and mass consumption, these needs must be standardized, coordinated, generalized. Certainly, these controls are not a conspiracy, they are not centralized in any agency or group of agencies (although the trend toward centralization is gaining momentum); they are rather diffused throughout the society, exercised by the neighbors, the community, the peer groups, mass media, corporations, and (perhaps least) by the government. But they are exercised with the help of, in fact rendered possible by science, by the social and behavioral sciences, and especially by sociology and psychology. As industrial sociology and psychology, or, more euphemistically, as "science of human relations," these scientific efforts have become an indispensable tool in the hands of the powers that be.

These brief remarks are suggestive of the depth of society's ingression into the psyche, the extent to which mental health, normality, is not that of the individual but of his society. Such a harmony between the individual and society would be highly desirable if the society offered the individual the conditions for his development as a human being in accord with the available possibilities of freedom, peace, and happiness (that is in accord with the possible liberation of his life instincts), but it is highly destructive to the individual if these conditions do not prevail. Where they do not prevail, the healthy and normal individual is a human being equipped with all the qualities which enable him to get along with others in his society, and these very same qualities are the marks of repression, the marks of a mutilated human being, who collaborates in his own repression, in the containment of potential individual and social freedom, in the release of aggression. And this situation cannot be solved within the framework of individual psychology and therapy, nor within the framework of any psychology—a solution can be envisaged only on the political level: in the struggle against society. To be sure, therapy could demonstrate this situation and prepare the mental ground for such a struggle—but then psychiatry would be a subversive undertaking.

The question now is whether the strains in contemporary American society, in the affluent society, suggest the prevalence of conditions essentially negative to individual development in the sense just discussed. Or, to formulate the question in terms more indicative of the approach I propose to take: Do these strains vitiate the very possibility of "healthy" individual development—healthy defined in terms of optimal development of one's intellectual and emotional faculties? The question calls for an affirmative answer, that is, this society vitiates individual developments, if the prevailing strains are related to the very structure of this society and if they activate in its members instinctual needs and satisfactions which set the individuals against themselves so that they reproduce and intensify their own repression.

At first glance, the strains in our society seem to be those characteristic of any society which develops under the impact of great technological changes: they initiate new modes of work and of leisure and thereby affect all social relationships, and bring about a thorough transvaluation of values. Since physical labor tends to become increasingly unnecessary and even wasteful, since the work of salaried employees too becomes increasingly "automatic" and that of the politicians and administrators increasingly questionable, the traditional content of the struggle for existence appears more meaningless and without substance the more it appears as unnecessary necessity. But the future alternative, namely, the possible abolition of (alienated) labor seems equally meaningless, nay, frightening. And indeed, if one envisages this alternative as the progress and development of the *established* system, then the dislocation of the content of life to free time suggests the shape of a nightmare: massive self-realization, fun, sport in a steadily shrinking space.

But the threat of the "bogey of automation" is itself ideology. On the one hand it serves the perpetuation and reproduction of technically obsolete and unnecessary jobs and occupations (unemployment as normal condition, even if comfortable, seems worse than stupefying routine work); on the other hand it justifies and promotes the education and training of the managers and organization men of leisure time, that is to say, it serves to prolong and enlarge control and manipulation.

The real danger for the established system is not the abolition of labor but the possibility of nonalienated labor as the basis of the reproduction of society. Not that people are no longer compelled to work, but that they might be compelled to work for a very different life and in very different relations, that they might be given very different goals and values, that they might have to live with a very different morality—this is the "definite negation" of the established system, the liberating alternative. For example, socially necessary labor might be organized for such efforts as the rebuilding of cities and towns, the relocation of the places of work (so that people learn again how to walk), the construction of industries which produce goods without built-in obsolescence, without profitable waste and poor quality, and the subjection of the environment to the vital aesthetic needs of the organism. To be sure, to translate this possibility into reality would mean to eliminate the power of the dominant interests which, by their very function in the society, are opposed to a development that would reduce private enterprise to a minor role, that would do away with the market economy, and with the policy of military preparedness, expansion, and intervention—in other words: a development that would reverse the entire prevailing trend. There is little evidence for such a development. In the meantime, and with the new and terribly effective and total means provided by technical progress, the population is physically and mentally mobilized against this eventuality: they must continue the struggle for existence in painful, costly, and obsolete forms.

This is the real contradiction which translates itself from the social structure into the mental structure of the individuals. There, it activates and aggravates destructive tendencies which, in a hardly sublimated mode, are made socially useful in the behavior of the individuals, on the private as well as political level—in the behavior of the nation as a whole. Destructive energy becomes socially useful aggressive energy, and the aggressive behavior impels growth—growth of economic, political, and technical power. Just as in the contemporary scientific enterprise, so in the economic enterprise and in that of the nation as a whole, constructive and destructive achievements, work for life and work for death, procreating and killing are inextricably united. To restrict the exploitation of nuclear energy would mean to restrict its peaceful as well as military potential; the amelioration and protection of life appear as by-products of the scientific work on the annihilation of life; to restrict procreation would also mean to restrict potential manpower and the number of potential customers and clients. Now the (more or less sublimated) transformation of destructive into socially useful aggressive (and thereby constructive) energy is, according to Freud (on whose instinct-theory I base my interpretation) a normal and indispensable process. It is part of the same dynamic by which libido, erotic energy, is sublimated and made socially useful; the two opposite impulses are forced together and, united in this twofold transformation, they become the mental and organic vehicles of civilization. But no matter how close and effective their union, their respective quality remains unchanged and contrary: aggression activates destruction which "aims" at death, while libido seeks the preservation, protection, and amelioration of life. Therefore, it is only as long as destruction works in the service of Eros that it serves civilization and the individual; if aggression becomes stronger than its erotic counterpart, the trend is reversed. Moreover, in the Freudian conception, destructive energy cannot become stronger without reducing erotic energy: the balance between the two primary impulses is a quantitative one; the instinctual dynamic is mechanistic, distributing an available quantum of energy between the two antagonists.

I have briefly restated Freud's conception inasmuch as I shall use it to discuss the depth and character of the strains prevalent in American society. I suggest that the strains derive from the basic contradiction between the capabilities of this society, which could produce essentially new forms of freedom amounting to a subversion of the established institutions on the one hand, and the repressive use of these capabilities on the other. The contradiction explodes—and is at the same time "resolved," "contained"—in the ubiquitous aggression prevalent in this society. Its most conspicuous (but by no means isolated) manifestation is the military mobilization and its effect on the mental behavior of the individuals, but within the context of the basic contradiction, aggressiveness is fed by many sources. The following seem to be foremost:

(1) *The dehumanization of the process of production and consumption.* Technical progress is identical with the increasing elimination of personal initiative, inclination, taste, and need from the provision of goods and services. This tendency is liberating if the available resources and techniques are used for freeing the individual from labor and recreation which are required for the reproduction of the established institutions but are parasitic, wasteful, and dehumanizing in terms of the existing technical and intellectual capabilities. The same tendency often gratifies hostility.

(2) *The conditions of crowding, noise, and overtness characteristic of mass society.* As René Dubos has said, the need for "quiet, privacy, independence, initiative, and some open space" are not "frills or luxuries but constitute real biological necessities." Their lack injures the instinctual structure itself. Freud has emphasized the "asocial" character of Eros—the mass society achieves an "oversocialization" to which the individual reacts "with all sorts of frustrations, repressions, aggressions, and fears which soon develop into genuine neuroses."

I mentioned, as the most conspicuous social mobilization of aggressiveness, the militarization of the affluent society. This mobilization goes far beyond the actual draft of manpower and the buildup of the armament industry: its totalitarian aspects show forth in the daily mass media which feed "public opinion." The brutalization of language and image, the presentation of killing, burning, and poisoning and torture inflicted upon the victims of neocolonial slaughter is made in a common-sensible, factual, sometimes humorous style which integrates these horrors with the pranks of juvenile delinquents, football contests, accidents, stock market reports, and the weatherman. This is no longer the "classical" heroizing of killing in the national interest, but rather its reduction to the level of natural events and contingencies of daily life.

The consequence is a "psychological habituation of war" which is administered to a people protected from the actuality of war, a people who, by virtue of this habituation, easily familiarizes itself with the "kill rate" as it is already familiar with other "rates" (such as those of business or traffic or unemployment). The people are conditioned to live "with the hazards, the brutalities, and the mounting casualties of the war in Vietnam, just as one learns gradually to live with the everyday hazards and casualties of smoking, of smog, or of traffic." The photos which appear in the daily newspapers and in magazines with mass circulation, often in nice and glossy color, show rows of prisoners laid out or stood up for "interrogation," little children dragged through the dust behind armored cars, mutilated women. They are nothing new ("such things happen in a war"), but it is the setting that makes the difference: their appearance in the regular program, in togetherness with the commercials, sports, local politics, and reports on the social set. And the brutality of power is further normalized by its extension to the beloved automobile: the manufacturers sell a Thunderbird, Fury, Tempest, and the oil industry puts "a tiger in your tank."

However, the administered language is rigidly discriminating: a specific vocabulary of hate, resentment, and defamation is reserved for opposition to the aggressive policies and for the enemy. The pattern constantly repeats itself. Thus, when students demonstrate against the war, it is a "mob" swelled by "bearded advocates of sexual freedom," by unwashed juveniles, and by "hoodlums and street urchins" who "tramp" the streets, while the counterdemonstrations consist of citizens who gather. In Vietnam, "typical criminal communist violence" is perpetrated against American "strategic operations." The Reds have the impertinence to launch a "sneak attack" (presumably they are supposed to announce it beforehand and to deploy in the open); they are "evading a death trap" (presumably they should have stayed in). The Vietcong attack American barracks "in the dead of night" and kill American boys (presumably, Americans only attack in broad daylight, don't disturb the sleep of the enemy, and don't kill Vietnamese boys). The massacre of hundred thousands of communists (in Indonesia) is called "impressive"—a comparable "killing rate" suffered by the other side would hardly have been honored with such an adjective. To the Chinese, the presence of American troops in East Asia is a threat to their "ideology," while presumably the presence of Chinese troops in Central or South America would be a real, and not only ideological, threat to the United States.

The loaded language proceeds according to the Orwellian recipe of the identity of opposites: in the mouth of the enemy, peace means war, and defense is attack, while on the righteous side, escalation is restraint, and saturation bombing prepares for peace. Organized in this discriminatory fashion, language designates a priori the enemy as evil in his entirety and in all his actions and intentions.

Such mobilization of aggressiveness cannot be explained by the magnitude of the communist threat: the image of the ostensible enemy is inflated out of all proportion to reality. What is at stake is rather the continued stability and growth of a system which is threatened by its own irrationality—by the narrow base on which its prosperity rests, by the dehumanization which its wasteful and parasitic affluence demands. The senseless war is itself part of this irrationality and thus of the essence of the system. What may have been a minor involvement at the beginning, almost an accident, a contingency of foreign policy, has become a test case for the productivity, competitiveness, and prestige of the whole. The billions of dollars spent for the war effort are a political as well as economic stimulus (or cure): a big way of absorbing part of the economic surplus, and of keeping the people in line. Defeat in Vietnam may well be the signal for other wars of liberation closer to home—and perhaps even for rebellion at home.

To be sure, the social utilization of aggressiveness belongs to the historical structure of civilization and has been a powerful vehicle of progress. However, here too, there is a stage where quantity may turn into quality and subvert the normal balance between the two primary instincts in favor of destruction. I mentioned the "bogey man" of auto-mation. In fact the real spectre for the affluent society is the possible reduction of labor to a level where the human organism need no longer function as an instrument of labor. The mere quantitative decline in need-ed human labor power militates against the maintenance of the capitalist mode of production (as of all other exploitative modes of production). The system reacts by stepping up the production of goods and services which either do not enlarge individual consumption at all, or enlarge it with luxuries—luxuries in the face of persistent poverty, but luxuries which are necessities for occupying a labor force sufficient to reproduce the estab-lished economic and political institutions. To the degree to which this sort of work appears as superfluous, senseless, and unnecessary while necessary for earning a living, frustration is built into the very productivity of this society, and aggressiveness is activated. And to the degree to which the society in its very structure becomes aggressive, the mental structure of its citizens adjusts itself: the individual becomes at one and the same time more aggressive and more pliable and submissive, for he submits to a society which, by virtue of its affluence and power, satisfies his deepest (and otherwise greatly repressed) instinctual needs. And these instinctual needs apparently find their libidinal reflection in the representatives of the people. The chairman of the Armed Services Committee of the United States Senate, Senator Russell of Georgia, was struck by this fact. He is quoted as saying:

> There is something about preparing for destruction that causes men to be more careless in spending money than they would be if they were building for constructive purposes. Why that is, I do not know; but I have observed, over a period of almost thirty years in the Senate, that there is something about buying arms with which to kill, to destroy, to wipe out cities, and to obliterate great transportation systems which causes men not to reckon the dollar cost as closely as they do when they think about proper hous-ing and the care of the health of human beings.

I have argued elsewhere the question of how one can possibly gauge and historically compare the aggression prevalent in a specific society; instead of restating the case, I want now to focus on different aspects, on the specific forms in which aggression today is released and satisfied.

The most telling one, and the one which distinguishes the new from the traditional forms, is what I call *technological aggression and satisfaction*. The phenomenon is quickly described: the act of aggression is physically carried out by a mechanism with a high degree of automatism, of far greater power than the individual human being who sets it in motion, keeps it in motion, and determines its end or target. The most extreme case is the rocket or missile; the most ordinary example the automobile. This means that the energy, the power activated and consummated is the mechanical, electrical, or nuclear energy of "things" rather than the instinctual energy of a human being. Aggression is, as it were, transferred from a subject to an object, or is at least "mediated" by an object, and the target is destroyed by a thing rather than by a person. This change in the relation between human and material energy, and between the physical and mental part of aggression (man becomes the subject and agent of aggression by virtue of his mental rather than physical faculties) must also affect the mental dynamic. I submit a hypothesis which is suggested by the inner logic of the process: with the "delegation" of destruction to a more or less automated thing or group and system of things, the instinctual satisfaction of the human person is "interrupted," reduced, frustrated, "supersublimated." And such frustration makes for repetition and escalation: increasing violence, speed, enlarged scope. At the same time, personal responsibility, conscience, and the sense of guilt is weakened, or rather diffused, displaced from the actual context in which the aggression was committed (i.e. bombing raids), and relocated in a more or less innocuous context (impoliteness, sexual inadequacy, etc.). In this reaction too, the effect is a considerable weakening of the sense of guilt, and the defense (hatred, resentment) is also redirected from the real responsible subject (the commanding officer, the government) to a substitute person: not I as a (morally and physically) acting person did it, but the thing, the machine. The machine: the word suggests that an apparatus consisting of human beings may be substituted for the mechanical apparatus: the bureaucracy, the administration, the party, or organization is the responsible agent; I, the individual person, was only the instrumentality. And an instrument cannot, in any moral sense, be responsible or be in a state of guilt. In this way, another barrier against aggression, which civilization had erected in a long and violent process of discipline is removed. And the expansion of advanced capitalism becomes involved in a fateful psychical dialectic which enters into and propels its economic and political dynamic: the more powerful and "technological" aggression becomes, the less is it apt to satisfy and pacify the primary impulse, and the more it tends toward repetition and escalation.

To be sure, the use of instruments of aggression is as old as civilization itself, but there is a decisive difference between technological aggression and the more primitive forms. The latter were not only quantitatively different (weaker): they required activation and *engagement* of the body to a much higher degree than the automated or semiautomated instruments of aggression. The knife, the "blunt instrument," even the revolver are far more "part" of the individual who uses them and they associate him more closely with his target. Moreover, and most important, their use, unless effectively sublimated and in the service of the life instincts (as in the case of the surgeon, household, etc.), is criminal—individual crime—and as such subject to severe punishment. In contrast, technological aggression is not a crime. The speeding driver of an automobile or motor boat is not called a murderer even if he is one; and certainly the missile-firing engineers are not.

Technological aggression releases a mental dynamic which aggravates the destructive, antierotic tendencies of the puritan complex. The new models of aggression destroy without getting one's hands dirty, one's body soiled, one's mind incriminated. The killer remains clean, physically as well as mentally. The purity of his deadly work obtains added sanction if it is directed against the national enemy in the national interest.

The (anonymous) lead article in *Les Temps Modernes* (January 1966) links the war in Vietnam with the puritan tradition in the United States. The image of the enemy is that of dirt in its most repulsive forms; the unclean jungle is his natural habitat, disembowelment and beheading are his natural ways of action. Consequently, the burning of his refuge, defoliation, and the poisoning of his foodstuff are not only strategic but also moral operations; removing of contagious dirt, cleaning the way for the order of political hygiene and righteousness. And the mass purging of the good conscience from all rational inhibitions leads to the atrophy of the last rebellion of sanity against the madhouse: no satire, no ridicule attends the moralists who organize and defend the crime. Thus one of them can, without becoming a laughingstock, publicly praise as the "greatest performance in our nation's history," the indeed historical achievement of the richest, most powerful, and most advanced country of the world unleashing the destructive force of its technical superiority on one of the poorest, weakest, and most helpless countries of the world.

The decline of responsibility and guilt, their absorption by the omnipotent technical and political apparatus also tends to invalidate other values which were to restrain and sublimate aggression. While the militarization of society remains the most conspicuous and destructive manifestation of this tendency, its less ostensible effects in the cultural dimension should not be minimized. One of these effects is the disintegration of the value of *truth*. The media enjoy a large dispensation from the commitment to truth, and in a very special way. The point is not that the media lie ("lie" presupposes commitment to truth), they rather mingle truth and half-truth with omission, factual reporting with commentary and evaluation, information with publicity and propaganda—all this made into an overwhelming whole through editorializing. The editorially unpleasant truths (and how many of the most decisive truths are not unpleasant?) retreat between the lines, or hide, or mingle harmoniously with nonsense, fun, and so-called human interest stories. And the consumer is readily inclined to take all this for granted—he buys it even if he knows better. Now the commitment to the truth has always been precarious, hedged with strong qualifications, suspended, or suppressed—it is only in the context of the general and democratic activation of aggressiveness that the devaluation of truth assumes special significance. For truth is a value in a strict sense inasmuch as it serves the protection and amelioration of life, as a guide in man's struggle with nature and with himself, with his own weakness and his own destructiveness. In this function, truth is indeed a matter of the sublimated life instincts. Eros, of intelligence becoming responsible and autonomous, striving to liberate life from dependence on unmastered and repressive forces. And with respect to this protective and liberating function of truth, its devaluation removes another effective barrier against destruction.

The encroachment of aggression on the domain of the life instincts also devalues the aesthetic dimension. In *Eros and Civilization* I have tried to show the erotic component in this dimension. Nonfunctional, that is to say, not committed to the function of a repressive society, the aesthetic values have been strong protectors of Eros in civilization. Nature is a part of this dimension. Eros seeks, in polymorphous forms, its own sensuous world of fulfillment, its own "natural" environment. But only in a protected world—protected from daily business, from noise, crowds, waste, only thus can it satisfy the biological need for happiness. The aggressive business practices which turn ever more spaces of protective nature into a medium of commercial fulfillment and fun thus do not merely offend beauty—they repress biological necessities.

Once we agree to discuss the hypothesis that, in advanced industrial society surplus-aggression is released in quite unsuspected and "normal" behavior, we may see it even in areas which are far removed from the more familiar manifestations of aggression, for instance the style of publicity and information practiced by the mass media. Characteristic is the permanent repetition: the same commercial with the same text or picture broadcast or televised again and again; the same phrases and clichés poured out by the purveyors and makers of information again and again. Freud arrived at his concept of the death instinct in the context of his analysis of the "repetition compulsion": he associated with it the striving for a state of complete inertia, absence of tension, return to the womb, annihilation. Hitler knew well the extreme function of repetition: the biggest lie, often enough repeated, will be acted upon and accepted as truth. Even in its less extreme use, constant repetition, imposed upon more or less captive audiences, may be destructive: destroying mental autonomy, freedom of thought, responsibility and conducive to inertia, submission, rejection of change. The established society, the master of repetition, becomes the great womb for its citizens. To be sure, this road to inertia and this reduction of tension is one of high and not very satisfactory sublimation: it does not lead to an instinctual nirvana of satisfaction. However, it may well reduce the stress of intelligence, the pain and tension which accompany autonomous mental activity—thus it may be an effective aggression against the mind in its socially disturbing, critical functions.

These are highly speculative hypotheses on the socially and mentally fateful character of aggression in our society. Aggression is (in most cases) socially useful destructiveness—and yet fateful because of its self-propelling character and scope. In this respect too, it is badly sublimated and not very satisfying. If Freud's theory is correct, and the destructive impulse strives for the annihilation of the individual's own life no matter how long the "detour" via other lives and targets, then we may indeed speak of a suicidal tendency on a truly social scale, and the national and international play with total destruction may well have found a firm basis in the instinctual structure of individuals.

3

Conflict Theories

Thus far, we have described two different ways of looking at public life, each of which turns the investigator's attention to a particular phase of politics. Psychological theories orient inquiry in the direction of relating public problems to basic patterns in the individual personality, and systems theories direct inquiry toward relating public and even personal problems to significant patterns in the social structure. Essentially, psychological theories and systems theories of public life balance one another very neatly. Debates between theorists representing the two points of view have sparked some of the most exciting controversies in the history of Western thought. Disputes about the relative importance, in both the prescriptive and descriptive senses, of the "individual" and the "state" have grown out of the question of whether or not sets of public roles or general principles of social organization take precedence over individual interests and passions. Such controversies are painfully familiar to Americans, who are continually being told to consider the virtues of individualism and the vices of collectivism, the strengths of "free enterprise" and the weaknesses of "communism," the good of the "people" and the evil of the "system." The striking distinction which Rousseau made between the spontaneous and precious individual and the predictable and impersonal civil society guides much academic and popular thought about public affairs in contemporary America. People of the New Left view the events of current political history as a struggle between the claims of the whole personality and the demands of repressive organizations. People of the "New Right" view these same events as a struggle between the claims of the common man and the demands of the "briefcase-toting bureaucrats." Men of the Left and Right may vigorously disagree about the principles that are at work in society, but both sides stress the importance of the distinction between the people and the organization. Even moderates are caught up in the tension between individual and organization. They are concerned with the merits of such concepts as participation, decentralization, expert administration, and organizational efficiency.

A political theorist who was not committed to either the psychological point of view or the systems perspective might look at the pattern of public debate in the West and conclude that neither of the two compelling theories was entirely correct. Having reached this judgment, he would have several courses open to him. He could become an eclectic theorist and, when it seemed appropriate to do so, employ the personality as a major organizing concept and use the system as a concept of interpretation when that appeared to be the best way to further understanding of public problems. He could also attempt to synthesize the two points of view into one coherent scheme. As we have pointed out, all significant political theorists try to develop such syntheses. However, they usually end up emphasizing either the psychological or the systems perspective. Finally, the uncommitted theorist could, after studying the various heated controversies, decide that neither the psychological nor the systems frameworks, nor a combination of the two, was adequate for the understanding of public life. He might be much more impressed with the vigor of the debates between the various opponents than with the actual positions that they were furthering. He might conclude that the processes of strife and agreement have a far greater significance in the conduct of public affairs than the actual things for which the people contest. If he reached these kinds of conclusions, he would be well on his way to becoming a conflict theorist.

While psychological theories refer events in public life to the personality, and systems theories connect the conduct of public affairs to principles of social organization, conflict theories view public activities as manifestations of highly general processes that can be observed in the dynamics of human relations. Thus, the primary unit of analysis for conflict theorists is the relationship between people rather than the concrete human being with a social character or the social structure with a set of roles or an organizing principle. For conflict theorists, human relationships are dynamic—they depend upon exchanges or interactions among people. This dynamic aspect of conflict theories has led to their frequently being called theories of the "political process." An understanding of the term "process" as it applies to the description of public affairs is necessary before the full implications of conflict theory can be grasped.

The word "process" is derived from the Latin verb *procedere,* which means "to proceed." Like method, approach, and system, process often refers to an ordered pattern of steps leading to the realization of a goal. For example, when we speak of someone being "in the process" of making a sale, we mean that he is following the procedures appropriate to concluding the transaction. However, while method, approach, and, in this usage, system refer to conscious practices, process can refer to any ordered pattern of development involving successive changes. Thus, when political theorists talk about processes in public life, they are making reference to general patterns that they observe in the development of relationships among people. The individuals involved in the relationships may or may not be aware of the pattern that the political theorist believes he observes. This distinction between what people who participate in public life think about their activities and the ways in which political theorists interpret these activities has been basic throughout our discussion of the various theories. The American philosopher William James thought that this distinction was the most important one to keep in mind when one investigated human affairs. He coined the term "psychologist's fallacy" to refer to the mistake many theorists make when they assume that the people they observe are aware of the theories that are supposed to describe their actions.

Most of the processes in human relationships which conflict theorists have identified are familiar to anyone who has learned ordinary language. The terms "conflict," "competition," "compromise," "cooperation," and "consensus" are used in day-to-day social exchanges as well as in the disciplined investigation of public affairs. Thus, there is an important sense in which conflict theory is easier to understand than either psychological theory or systems theory. Conflict theorists do not ordinarily attach specialized meanings to the concepts they use, and their descriptions of public life frequently accord with our common-sense notions about politics more than do the descriptions of other theorists. This conformance to common sense has both advantages and dangers. The obvious advantage is that the student of conflict theory does not have to master a new vocabulary or shift his normal conceptions of public life. The chief danger is that the student will read his preconceptions into what the conflict theorist is saying and, therefore, miss a great many new insights.

As one would expect, the most important concept that conflict theorists consider is "conflict." The word "conflict" is derived from the Latin term *conflictus*, which means "a striking together." The Latin root provides a vivid image of what makes the study of conflict so intriguing for many political theorists. The excitement, or tragic sense, of ignorant armies clashing by night or of great debates about great issues, is one of the primary emotional motives that impels many people to study politics. The picture of liberals "fighting the good fight" against the forces of reaction or of conservatives "standing up for America" against its enemies within and without may be ennobling or sickening, depending upon one's point of view. Few would say that it is not interesting. However, once the ubiquity and excitement of conflict have been taken for granted, the problem of understanding this process remains.

Perhaps the best way to treat conflict is to consider it as a process of active disagreement between people. Thus, there is no political conflict when people disagree with one another and do nothing about this disagreement with reference to each other. To have political conflict, people must disagree about the conduct of the affairs of an entire community and translate this disagreement into action aimed at ordering public life to their satisfaction. For example, when two or more people disagree about the proper conduct of specific public affairs and attempt to shape events surrounding those matters to accord with their preferences, they are in conflict with one another. Conflicts can be classified in a wide variety of ways. First, conflicts may be categorized by their intensity. We are all aware of the differences among wars, diplomatic conferences, contested elections, debates, court cases, and confrontations between protest groups and law enforcement officials. We can classify conflicts in terms of their intensity on a continuum from mutual organized violence to mutual attempts at persuasion in accordance with the canons of reasonable debate. Between these poles, we can identify such conflict situations as organized violence opposing passive resistance, mutual attempts at fraud, attempts at fraud opposing attempts at rational persuasion, disorganized violence opposing efforts at economic deprivation, and as many other combinations as can be made of the different means through which people actively express their disagreements. Second, conflicts vary in terms of what the contestants disagree about. Conflict theorists such as Hobbes and Robert Dahl claim that most conflicts can be traced to disagreements about the proper distribution of scarce resources. For example, the amount of economic goods produced in any society is finite. Not all people agree about how these goods should be distributed. Veterans would like to claim more goods by demanding higher government pensions, farmers would like to claim more goods by receiving higher price supports, and students would like to claim more goods by having their tuitions lowered. Others have their own claims to make, and the result is a measure of conflict over the distribution of goods. Conflicts also take place over such scarce resources as status and power. That part of the "black power" movement which emphasizes black history, the gaining of self-respect by black people, and the creation of a black identity is, to some extent, engaged in an attempt to improve the "status" of black people within American society. Whites who ridicule these phases of the black power movement may be doing so, in part, to deny black people the status they seek. Status, or the respect conferred upon individuals and groups, has become increasingly important in contemporary societies where rigid definitions of social position have broken down. In the foreseeable future we may expect status conflicts, especially those between professional experts and people without sophisticated technical skills, to become more intense and frequent. Finally, almost everyone is familiar with conflicts about the distribution of power. In many life situations, decisions must be made that affect groups of people rather than single individuals. The question of who is to make such decisions generates daily power struggles within families, businesses, religious organizations, and governments. Generally, although not inevitably, people seek to control the situations in which they find themselves. Since one's situation usually includes other human beings, the conditions for conflicts over power are frequently met in social life.

Aside from conflicts over the distribution of scarce resources, there are also active disagreements about the uses to which resources should be put. The continuing debate about whether the exploration of space is more important than the improvement of urban areas is a prime example of a conflict over goals. Perhaps the deepest conflict over goals in American society concerns the ways in which social and individual life might be organized in the future. Some people feel that a future society should embody the ideals of advancement by merit, efficient organization, widespread technical competence, and maximum production of economic goods. Others believe that a future society should strive primarily to attain the goals of respect and love for all human beings, decentralization, competence in the art of living, and free creation. Again, this conflict is a reflection of Rousseau's two ideals. One of the major questions of our age is: Can these two ideals be made compatible, or must one be sacrificed to attain the other?

While conflicts over the method of distribution of scarce resources and over what is to be distributed exhaust most of the conflicts that take place in public life, there is yet another kind of conflict that has occurred in human communities. We are all familiar with conflicts over ideas, or conflicts over what should go on in the "minds and hearts of the people." Such ideological conflicts are frequently attached to disagreements about goals and distribution, but sometimes they are engaged in for their own sakes. Political theorists in the seventeenth and eighteenth centuries were particularly interested in ideological conflicts. They wondered how people could presume to try to force their fellowmen to believe and feel things. It seemed impossible to coerce what went on in the mind and heart of an individual. Surely, if one could control anything, it was his interior life. Today, we are no longer as confident about the inviolability of the subjective as were the men of the seventeenth and eighteenth centuries. Discoveries in the fields of psychology and sociology, the consequences of propaganda and advertising, and widespread doubts about the existence of objective standards of truth and morality have combined to cause many people to feel uncertain of their control over their internal lives. The twentieth century has been marked by many efforts to coerce beliefs and feelings, usually for some ulterior purpose. The "Great Proletarian Cultural Revolution" in China, the various anticommunist "crusades" in the United States, the efforts to create a "new socialist man" throughout the Soviet bloc, and the numerous proposals and programs of groups influenced by psychological theorists are examples of such endeavors. Of course, religious groups have always attempted to work changes in the mind and heart, ideally through peaceful persuasion and sometimes through the use of force. Whenever resistance is met in an effort by a person or group to alter the ideas of another, the process of ideological conflict becomes operative. A great many members of the currently maturing generation have experienced direct ideological conflict with their parents and other adults. Often, such mutual attempts to change ideas are undertaken with the aim of eventually altering the other's behavior or obtaining some concrete satisfaction. Sometimes, tragically, the aim is merely to change the other's internal life—to make the other "happier" or to see that he or she has the "right" opinions.

Most human conflicts are limited in both intensity and substance, that is, very few conflicts over distribution of resources, ultimate goals, and beliefs take place in a context of mutual, organized violence. The observed limitations on human conflicts have led most conflict theorists to conclude that disagreements are normally circumscribed by consensus. Whereas conflict refers to a process of active disagreement between people or groups, consensus refers to a process of active agreement. Again, we must beware of committing the "psychologist's fallacy" when we discuss consensus. If an investigator discovers that a number of people agree about something, and that they carry their beliefs into action, this does not mean that the people themselves are aware of this agreement. Perhaps with the general publication and diffusion of public opinion polls and social science research, people will become more aware of their agreements and disagreements. However, there is no assurance that this will be the case.

Consensus can be analyzed in much the same way as conflict. First, and most important to conflict theorists, there may be consensus about the limits that should be placed on the intensity of a conflict, or the means that should be used in prosecuting the conflict. The one-time de facto agreement not to employ poison gases in wars and, in the United States, the agreement not to contest the results of an election with violence, are examples of consensus regarding intensity. There may also be consensus about goals—even if there is conflict over the distribution of goods. For example, black militants and automotive executives may agree that more cars should be produced, while they may disagree about who should get those cars. Moreover, there may be consensus about distribution of goods and about beliefs. It is well known that many politicians attempt, with varying results, to create a wide-ranging consensus about the desirability of their policies.

Conflict theory adds an important dimension to the study of public affairs that was missing from psychological and systems theories. While it is undeniable that both social character and social structure exert a profound influence upon public life, neither of these concepts can fully account for the dynamic activity that we witness in the political world. People with different characters and those with different roles interact. Through these interactions, relationships appear that are characterized by various processes. Among these processes, active agreement and active disagreement are of particular importance. In fact, it is a rare human relationship that is not characterized, in some respects, by both conflict and consensus. Around the core of any struggle, there is usually a fringe of agreement, even if the participants refuse to be aware of it. In any situation of "sweetness and light," there is apt to be a penumbra of active disagreement, even if the participants force themselves to forget about it. While conflict theory may not tell us why we want certain things rather than others, it does try to describe how we go about satisfying our wants. This dimension of process is the lasting contribution of conflict theory to disciplined thought about public life.

HOBBES

Thomas Hobbes, who was born in England in 1588, produced the first rigorous statement of modern conflict theory. Living in a time marked by the turmoil of the English civil wars and the ascendancy of Newtonian physics in natural science, Hobbes' political thought was profoundly influenced by both of these factors. From the political events that were taking place around him he gained the idea that the process of conflict was the most significant element in the conduct of public affairs. From advances in the physical sciences he drew the notion that the study of politics could be made into a deductive science in which explanations of the events in public life could be derived from a few propositions about human nature. Hobbes was a materialist who believed that the human sciences were simply branches of the study of bodies and their movements. He divided the human sciences into ethics, which he defined as the investigation of movements in the nervous system, and politics, which he defined as the study of the effects of nervous systems upon one another. Thus, his theory of public life stressed the processes which take place in human relationships.

For Hobbes, political behavior could be understood in terms of two natural laws of motion. The first law of motion described the tendency of every organic body to preserve and assert itself. Part of preservation and assertion consisted in each individual's attempt to gain control over his environment and eliminate dangers to his person. Since the individual's environment included other people striving for control, however, conflict was inevitable. The second natural law circumscribed universal conflict by describing a tendency in men to give up some of their self-assertion as long as other men did the same. Thus, Hobbes allowed for consensus on limitations to the intensity of conflict over power, wealth, and status. He thought, however, that the consensus could only be implemented by a sovereign who had a monopoly of coercive power. While Hobbes has been known for his doctrine of absolute sovereignty, for our purposes his basic treatment of conflict and consensus as interwoven processes is far more significant. To Hobbes' credit, he outlined a theory of the causes of conflict that is still in use in contemporary sociology and political science. He held that "in the nature of man we find three principal causes of quarrel: first, competition; secondly, diffidence; thirdly, glory." By competition, he meant the struggle between men who "desire the same thing, which nevertheless they cannot both enjoy." In other words, he identified conflict over the distribution of goods. By diffidence, he meant the fear that one's power was not great enough to protect him. For Hobbes, the condition of diffidence caused people to indulge in a ceaseless quest for "power after power" at one another's expense. Finally, by glory, Hobbes meant what we term status. "For every man looks that his companion should value him at the same rate he sets upon himself; and upon all signs of contempt . . . endeavors . . . to extort a greater value from his contemners by damage and from others by the example." It should be clear that our own discussion of conflict theory was greatly influenced by Hobbes, just as our analyses of psychological and systems theories were influenced by Plato and Rousseau, respectively.

Identity*

Of Power, Worth, Dignity Honor, and Worthiness

Power. The Power of a man, to take it universally, is his present means to obtain some future apparent good, and is either *original* or *instrumental.*

Natural power is the eminence of the faculties of body or mind, as extraordinary strength, form, prudence, arts, eloquence, liberality, nobility. *Instrumental* are those powers which, acquired by these or by fortune, are means and instruments to acquire more, as riches, reputation, friends, and the secret working of God, which men call good luck. For the nature of power is in this point like to fame, increasing as it proceeds; or like the motion of heavy bodies, which, the further they go, make still the more haste.

*From Thomas Hobbes, *Leviathan,* copyright © 1968, by The Liberal Arts Press, Inc. Reprinted by permission of the Liberal Arts Press Division of The Bobbs-Merrill Company, Inc., Indianapolis, Indiana.

The greatest of human powers is that which is compounded of the powers of most men united by consent in one person, natural or civil, that has the use of all their powers depending on his will, such as is the power of a commonwealth; or depending on the wills of each particular, such as is the power of a faction or of divers factions leagued. Therefore to have servants is power; to have friends is power: for they are strengths united.

Also riches joined with liberality is power, because it procures friends and servants; without liberality, not so, because in this case they defend not, but expose men to envy, as a prey.

Reputation of power is power, because it draws with it the adherence of those that need protection.

So is reputation of love of a man's country, called popularity, for the same reason.

Also, what quality soever makes a man beloved or feared of many, or the reputation of such quality, is power, because it is a means to have the assistance and service of many.

Good success is power, because it makes reputation of wisdom or good fortune, which makes men either fear him or rely on him.

Affability of men already in power is increase of power, because it gains love.

Reputation of prudence in the conduct of peace or war is power, because to prudent men we commit the government of ourselves more willingly than to others.

Nobility is power, not in all places, but only in those commonwealths where it has privileges, for in such privileges consists their power.

Eloquence is power, because it is seeming prudence.

Form is power, because, being a promise of good, it recommends men to the favor of women and strangers.

The sciences are small power, because not eminent and therefore not acknowledged in any man; nor are at all but in a few, and in them but of a few things. For science is of that nature as none can understand it to be but such as in a good measure have attained it.

Arts of public use—as fortification, making of engines, and other instruments of war—because they confer to defense and victory, are power and though the true mother of them be science—namely, the mathematics—yet, because they are brought into the light by the hand of the artificer, they be esteemed—the midwife passing with the vulgar for the mother—as his issue.

Worth. The *value* or Worth of a man is, as of all other things, his price—that is to say, so much as would be given for the use of his power—and therefore is not absolute but a thing dependent on the need and judgment of another. An able conductor of soldiers is of great price in time of war present or imminent, but in peace not so. A learned and uncorrupt judge is much worth in time of peace, but not so much in war. And as in other things so in men, not the seller but the buyer determines the price. For let a man, as most men do, rate themselves at the highest value they can, yet their true value is no more than it is esteemed by others.

The manifestation of the value we set on one another is that which is commonly called honoring and dishonoring. To value a man at a high rate is to *honor* him, at a low rate is to *dishonor* him. But high and low, in this case, is to be understood by comparison to the rate that each man sets on himself.

Dignity. The public worth of a man, which is the value set on him by the commonwealth, is that which men commonly call Dignity. And this value of him by the commonwealth is understood by offices of command, judicature, public employment, or by names and titles introduced for distinction of such value. . . .

Of the Natural Condition of Mankind as Concerning Their Felicity and Misery

Men by nature equal. Nature has made men so equal in the faculties of the body and mind as that, though there be found one man sometimes manifestly stronger in body or of quicker mind than another, yet, when all is reckoned together, the difference between man and man is not so considerable as that one man can thereupon claim to himself any benefit to which another may not pretend as well as he. For as to the strength of body, the weakest has strength enough to kill the strongest, either by secret machination or by confederacy with others that are in the same danger with himself.

And as to the faculties of the mind, setting aside the arts grounded upon words, and especially that skill of proceeding upon general and infallible rules called science—which very few have and but in few things, as being not a native faculty born with us, nor attained, as prudence, while we look after somewhat else—I find yet a greater equality among men than that of strength. For prudence is but experience, which equal time equally bestows on all men in those things they equally apply themselves unto. That which may perhaps make such equality incredible is but a vain conceit of one's own wisdom, which almost all men think they have in a greater degree than the vulgar—that is, than all men but themselves and a few others whom, by fame or for concurring with themselves, they approve. For such is the nature of men that howsoever they may acknowledge many others to be more witty or more eloquent or more learned, yet they will hardly believe there be many so wise as themselves; for they see their own wit at hand and other men's at a distance. But this proves rather that men are in that point equal than unequal. For there is not ordinarily a greater sign of the equal distribution of anything than that every man is contented with his share.

From equality proceeds diffidence. From this equality of ability arises equality of hope in the attaining of our ends. And therefore if any two men desire the same thing, which nevertheless they cannot both enjoy, they become enemies; and in the way to their end, which is principally their own conservation, and sometimes their delectation only, endeavor to destroy or subdue one another. And from hence it comes to pass that where an invader has no more to fear than another man's single power, if one plant, sow, build, or possess a convenient seat, others may probably be expected to come prepared with forces united to dispossess and deprive him, not only of the fruit of his labor, but also of his life or liberty. And the invader again is in the like danger of another.

From diffidence war. And from this diffidence of one another there is no way for any man to secure himself so reasonable as anticipation—that is, by force or wiles to master the persons of all men he can, so long till he see no other power great enough to endanger him; and this is no more than his own conservation requires, and is generally allowed. Also, because there be some that take pleasure in contemplating their own power in the acts of conquest, which they pursue farther than their security requires, if others that otherwise would be glad to be at ease within modest bounds should not by invasion increase their power, they would not be able, long time, by standing only on their defense, to subsist. And by consequence, such augmentation of dominion over men being necessary to a man's conservation, it ought to be allowed him.

Again, men have no pleasure, but on the contrary a great deal of grief, in keeping company where there is no power able to overawe them all. For every man looks that his companion should value him at the same rate he sets upon himself; and upon all signs of contempt or undervaluing naturally endeavors, as far as he dares (which among them that have no common power to keep them in quiet is far enough to make them destroy each other), to extort a greater value from his contemners by damage and from others by the example.

So that in the nature of man we find three principal causes of quarrel: first, competition; secondly, diffidence; thirdly, glory.

The first makes men invade for gain, the second for safety, and the third for reputation. The first use violence to make themselves masters of other men's persons, wives, children, and cattle; the second, to defend them; the third, for trifles, as a word, a smile, a different opinion, and any other sign of undervalue, either direct in their persons or by reflection in their kindred, their friends, their nation, their profession, or their name.

Out of civil states, there is always war of every one against every one.
Hereby it is manifest that, during the time men live without a common
power to keep them all in awe, they are in that condition which is called
war, and such a war as is of every man against every man. For War consists not in battle only, or the act of fighting, but in a tract of time
wherein the will to contend by battle is sufficiently known; and therefore
the notion of *time* is to be considered in the nature of war as it is in the
nature of weather. For as the nature of foul weather lies not in a shower
or two of rain but in an inclination thereto of many days together, so the
nature of war consists not in actual fighting but in the known disposition
thereto during all the time there is no assurance to the contrary. All other
time is Peace.

The incommodities of such a war. Whatsoever, therefore, is consequent to
a time of war where every man is enemy to every man, the same is consequent to the time wherein men live without other security than what
their own strength and their own invention shall furnish them withal. In
such condition there is no place for industry, because the fruit thereof is
uncertain: and consequently no culture of the earth; no navigation nor use
of the commodities that may be imported by sea; no commodious building; no instruments of moving and removing such things as require much
force; no knowledge of the face of the earth; no account of time; no
arts; no letters; no society; and, which is worst of all, continual fear and
danger of violent death; and the life of man solitary, poor, nasty, brutish,
and short.

It may seem strange to some man that has not well weighed these things
that nature should thus dissociate and render men apt to invade and
destroy one another; and he may therefore, not trusting to this inference
made from the passions, desire perhaps to have the same confirmed by
experience. Let him therefore consider with himself—when taking a journey
he arms himself and seeks to go well accompanied, when going to sleep
he locks his doors, when even in his house he locks his chests, and this
when he knows there be laws and public officers, armed, to revenge all
injuries shall be done him—what opinion he has of his fellow subjects
when he rides armed, of his fellow citizens when he locks his doors, and
of his children and servants when he locks his chests. Does he not there
as much accuse mankind by his actions as I do by my words? But neither
of us accuse man's nature in it. The desires and other passions of man
are in themselves no sin. No more are the actions that proceed from
those passions till they know a law that forbids them, which, till laws be
made, they cannot know, nor can any law be made till they have agreed
upon the person that shall make it.

It may peradventure be thought there was never such a time nor condition of war as this, and I believe it was never generally so over all the
world; but there are many places where they live so now. For the savage

people in many places of America, except the government of small families, the concord whereof depends on natural lust, have no government at all and live at this day in that brutish manner as I said before. Howsoever, it may be perceived what manner of life there would be where there were no common power to fear by the manner of life which men that have formerly lived under a peaceful government use to degenerate into in a civil war.

But though there had never been any time wherein particular men were in a condition of war one against another, yet in all times kings and persons of sovereign authority, because of their independency, are in continual jealousies and in the state and posture of gladiators, having their weapons pointing and their eyes fixed on one another—that is, their forts, garrisons, and guns upon the frontiers of their kingdoms, and continual spies upon their neighbors—which is a posture of war. But because they uphold thereby the industry of their subjects, there does not follow from it that misery which accompanies the liberty of particular men.

In such a war nothing is unjust. To this war of every man against every man, this also is consequent: that nothing can be unjust. The notions of right and wrong, justice and injustice, have there no place. Where there is no common power, there is no law; where no law, no injustice. Force and fraud are in war the two cardinal virtues. Justice and injustice are none of the faculties neither of the body nor mind. If they were, they might be in a man that were alone in the world, as well as his senses and passions. They are qualities that relate to men in society, not in solitude. It is consequent also to the same condition that there be no propriety, no dominion, no *mine* and *thine* distinct; but only that to be every man's that he can get, and for so long as he can keep it. And thus much for the ill condition which man by mere nature is actually placed in, though with a possibility to come out of it consisting partly in the passions, partly in his reason.

The passions that incline men to peace. The passions that incline men to peace are fear of death, desire of such things as are necessary to commodious living, and a hope by their industry to obtain them. And reason suggests convenient articles of peace, upon which men may be drawn to agreement. . . .

Power

Of the Liberty of Subjects

Liberty, what. Liberty, or freedom, signifies properly the absence of opposition—by opposition I mean external impediments of motion—and may be applied no less to irrational and inanimate creatures than to rational. For whatsoever is so tied or environed as it cannot move but within a certain space, which space is determined by the opposition of some external body, we say it has not liberty to go farther. And so of all living creatures while they are imprisoned or restrained with walls or chains, and of the water while it is kept in by banks or vessels that otherwise would spread itself into a larger space, we use to say they are not at liberty to move in such manner as without those external impediments they would. But when the impediment of motion is in the constitution of the thing itself, we use not to say it wants the liberty but the power to move—as when a stone lies still or a man is fastened to his bed by sickness.

What it is to be free. And according to this proper and generally received meaning of the word, a Freeman *is he that in those things which by his strength and wit he is able to do is not hindered to do what he has a will to.* But when the words *free* and *liberty* are applied to anything but *bodies,* they are abused, for that which is not subject to motion is not subject to impediments and therefore, when it is said, for example, the way is free, no liberty of the way is signified but of those that walk in it without stop. And when we say a gift is free, there is not meant any liberty of the gift but of the giver, that was not bound by any law or covenant to give it. So when we *speak freely,* it is not the liberty of voice or pronunciation but of the man, whom no law has obliged to speak otherwise than he did. Lastly, from the use of the word *free will,* no liberty can be inferred of the will, desire, or inclination but the liberty of the man, which consists in this: that he finds no stop in doing what he has the will, desire, or inclination to do.

Fear and liberty consistent. Fear and liberty are consistent, as when a man throws his goods into the sea for *fear* the ship should sink, he does it nevertheless very willingly, and may refuse to do it if he will: it is therefore the action of one that was *free*; so a man sometimes pays his debt only for *fear* of imprisonment, which, because nobody hindered him from detaining, was the action of a man at *liberty.* And generally all actions which men do in commonwealths for *fear* of the law are actions which the doers had *liberty* to omit.

Liberty and necessity consistent. Liberty and *necessity* are consistent, as in the water that has not only *liberty* but a *necessity* of descending by the channel; so likewise in the actions which men voluntarily do, which, because they proceed from their will, proceed from *liberty,* and yet—because every act of man's will and every desire and inclination proceeds from some cause, and that from another cause, in a continual chain whose first link is in the hand of God, the first of all causes—proceed from *necessity.* So that to him that could see the connection of those causes the *necessity* of all men's voluntary actions would appear manifest. And therefore God, that sees and disposes all things, sees also that the *liberty* of man in doing what he will is accompanied with the *necessity* of doing that which God will, and no more nor less. For though men may do many things which God does not command, nor is therefore author of them, yet they can have no passion nor appetite to anything of which appetite God's will is not the cause. And did not his will assure the *necessity* of man's will, and consequently of all that on man's will depends, the *liberty* of men would be a contradiction and impediment to the omnipotence and *liberty* of God. And this shall suffice, as to the matter in hand, of that natural *liberty* which only is properly called *liberty*.

Artificial bonds or covenants. But as men, for the attaining of peace and conservation of themselves thereby, have made an artificial man, which we call a commonwealth, so also have they made artificial chains, called *civil laws,* which they themselves, by mutual covenants, have fastened at one end to the lips of that man or assembly to whom they have given the sovereign power, and at the other end to their own ears. These bonds, in their own nature but weak, may nevertheless be made to hold by the danger, though not by the difficulty, of breaking them.

Liberty of subjects consists in liberty from covenants. In relation to these bonds only it is that I am to speak now of the *liberty* of *subjects*. For seeing there is no commonwealth in the world wherein there be rules enough set down for the regulating of all the actions and words of men, as being a thing impossible, it follows necessarily that in all kinds of actions by the laws pretermitted men have the liberty of doing what their own reasons shall suggest for the most profitable to themselves. For if we take liberty in the proper sense for corporal liberty—that is to say, freedom from chains and prison—it were very absurd for men to clamor as they do for the liberty they so manifestly enjoy. Again, if we take liberty for an exemption from laws, it is no less absurd for men to demand as they do that liberty by which all other men may be masters of their lives. And yet, as absurd as it is, this is it they demand, not knowing that the laws are of no power to protect them without a sword in the hands of a man or men to cause those laws to be put in execution. The liberty of a subject lies, therefore, only in those things which, in regulating their actions, the sovereign has pretermitted: such as is the liberty to buy and sell and otherwise contract with one another; to choose their own abode, their own diet, their own trade of life, and institute their children as they themselves think fit, and the like.

Liberty of the subject consistent with the unlimited power of the sovereign. Nevertheless we are not to understand that by such liberty the sovereign power of life and death is either abolished or limited. For it has been already shown that nothing the sovereign representative can do to a subject, on what pretense soever, can properly be called injustice or injury, because every subject is author of every act the sovereign does, so that he never wants right to anything otherwise than as he himself is the subject of God and bound thereby to observe the laws of nature. And therefore it may and does often happen in commonwealths that a subject may be put to death by the command of the sovereign power and yet neither do the other wrong—as when Jephtha caused his daughter to be sacrificed;[1] in which, and the like cases, he that so dies, had liberty to do the action for which he is nevertheless without injury put to death. And the same holds also in a sovereign prince that puts to death an innocent subject. For though the action be against the law of nature as being contrary to equity, as was the killing of Uriah by David,[2] yet it was not an injury to Uriah but to God. Not to Uriah, because the right to do what he pleased was given him by Uriah himself; and yet to God, because David was God's subject and prohibited all iniquity by the law of nature, which distinction David himself, when he repented the fact, evidently confirmed, saying, *To thee only have I sinned.*[3] In the same manner, the people of Athens, when they banished the most potent of their commonwealth for ten years, thought they committed no injustice; and yet they never questioned what crime he had done, but what hurt he would do—nay, they commanded the banishment of they knew not whom, and, every citizen bringing his oystershell into the market place written with the name of him he desired should be banished, without actually accusing him, sometimes banished an Aristides for his reputation of justice, and sometimes a scurrilous jester, as Hyperbolus, to make a jest of it. And yet a man cannot say the sovereign people of Athens wanted right to banish them, or an Athenian the liberty to jest or to be just.[4]

The liberty which writers praise is the liberty of sovereigns, not of private men. The liberty whereof there is so frequent and honorable mention in the histories and philosophy of the ancient Greeks and Romans, and in the writings and discourse of those that from them have received all their learning in the politics, is not the liberty of particular men but the liberty of the commonwealth—which is the same with that which every man then should have if there were no civil laws nor commonwealth at all. And the effects of it also be the same. For as among masterless men there is

---

[1] [Judg. 11.]

[2] [II Sam. 11.]

[3] [Ps. 51:4.]

[4] [In the 5th century B.C., Athenians had the practice of expelling men who, though guilty of no crime, were considered dangerous to the state. Citizens inscribed the names of men they wanted expelled on pieces of broken pottery, *ostraca*. Aristides, an outstanding general and statesman, was ostracized in 483 B.C. but recalled two years later. The demagogue Hyperbolus was ostracized in 417 B.C.]

perpetual war of every man against his neighbor—no inheritance to transmit to the son nor to expect from the father, no propriety of goods or lands, no security, but a full and absolute liberty in every particular man—so in states and commonwealths not dependent on one another every commonwealth, not every man, has an absolute liberty to do what it shall judge—that is to say, what that man or assembly that represents it shall judge—most conducing to their benefit. But withal they live in the condition of a perpetual war and upon the confines of battle, with their frontiers armed and cannons planted against their neighbors round about. The Athenians and Romans were free—that is, free commonwealths; not that any particular men had the liberty to resist their own representative, but that their representative had the liberty to resist or invade other people. There is written on the turrets of the city of Lucca in great characters at this day the word LIBERTAS, yet no man can thence infer that a particular man has more liberty or immunity from the service of the commonwealth there than in Constantinople. Whether a commonwealth be monarchial or popular, the freedom is still the same.

But it is an easy thing for men to be deceived by the specious name of liberty and, for want of judgment to distinguish, mistake that for their private inheritance and birthright which is the right of the public only. And when the same error is confirmed by the authority of men in reputation for their writings on this subject, it is no wonder if it produce sedition and change of government. In these western parts of the world, we are made to receive our opinions concerning the institution and rights of commonwealths from Aristotle, Cicero, and other men, Greeks and Romans that, living under popular states, derived those rights not from the principles of nature but transcribed them into their books out of the practice of their own commonwealths which were popular—as the grammarians describe the rules of language out of the practice of the time, or the rules of poetry out of the poems of Homer and Virgil. And because the Athenians were taught, to keep them from desire of changing their government, that they were freemen and all that lived under monarchy were slaves, therefore Aristotle puts it down in his *Politics* (lib. 6. cap. 2): *In democracy,* LIBERTY *is to be supposed; for it is commonly held that no man is* FREE *in any other government.* And as Aristotle, so Cicero and other writers have grounded their civil doctrine on the opinions of the Romans, who were taught to hate monarchy at first by them that, having deposed their sovereign, shared among them the sovereignty of Rome, and afterwards by their successors. And by reading of these Greek and Latin authors, men from their childhood have gotten a habit, under a false show of liberty, of favoring tumults and of licentious controlling the actions of their sovereigns and again of controlling those controllers, with the effusion of so much blood as I think I may truly say there was never anything so dearly bought as these western parts have bought the learning of the Greek and Latin tongues.

Liberty of subjects how to be measured. To come now to the particulars of the true liberty of a subject—that is to say, what are the things which, though commanded by the sovereign, he may nevertheless without injustice refuse to do—we are to consider what rights we pass away when we make a commonwealth, or, which is all one, what liberty we deny ourselves by owning all the actions, without exception, of the man or assembly we make our sovereign. For in the act of our *submission* consists both our *obligation* and our *liberty,* which must therefore be inferred by arguments taken from thence, there being no obligation on any man which arises not from some act of his own, for all men equally are by nature free. And because such arguments must either be drawn from the express words, *I authorize all his actions,* or from the intention of him that submits himself to his power, which intention is to be understood by the end for which he so submits, the obligation and liberty of the subject is to be derived either from those words or others equivalent, or else from the end of the institution of sovereignty—namely, the peace of the subjects within themselves and their defense against a common enemy.

Subjects have liberty to defend their own bodies, even against them that lawfully invade them. First, therefore, seeing sovereignty by institution is by covenant of every one to every one, and sovereignty by acquisition by covenants of the vanquished to the victor or child to the parent, it is manifest that every subject has liberty in all those things the right whereof cannot by covenant be transferred. I have shown before in the fourteenth chapter that covenants not to defend a man's own body are void.

Are not bound to hurt themselves. Therefore, if the sovereign command a man, though justly condemned, to kill, wound, or maim himself, or not to resist those that assault him or to abstain from the use of food, air, medicine, or any other thing without which he cannot live, yet has that man the liberty to disobey.

If a man be interrogated by the sovereign or his authority concerning a crime done by himself, he is not bound, without assurance of pardon, to confess it; because no man, as I have shown in the same chapter, can be obliged by covenant to accuse himself.

Again, the consent of a subject to sovereign power is contained in these words: *I authorize, or take upon men, all his actions;* in which there is no restriction at all of his own former natural liberty, for by allowing him to *kill me* I am not bound to kill myself when he commands me. It is one thing to say: *kill me, or my fellow, if you please;* another thing to say, *I will kill myself, or my fellow.* It follows therefore, that—

No man is bound by the words themselves either to kill himself or any other man, and consequently that the obligation a man may sometimes have, upon the command of the sovereign, to execute any dangerous or dishonorable office depends not on the words of our submission but on the intention, which is to be understood by the end thereof. When, therefore, our refusal to obey frustrates the end for which the sovereignty was ordained, then there is no liberty to refuse; otherwise there is.

Nor to warfare, unless they voluntarily undertake it.   Upon this ground, a man that is commanded as a soldier to fight against the enemy, though his sovereign have right enough to punish his refusal with death, may nevertheless in many cases refuse, without injustice—as when he substitutes a sufficient soldier in his place, for in this case he deserts not the service of the commonwealth. And there is allowance to be made for natural timorousness, not only to women, of whom no such dangerous duty is expected, but also to men of feminine courage. When armies fight, there is on one side or both a running away; yet when they do it not out of treachery but fear, they are not esteemed to do it unjustly but dishonorably. For the same reason, to avoid battle is not injustice but cowardice. But he that enrolls himself a soldier, or takes impressed money, takes away the excuse of a timorous nature, and is obliged not only to go to the battle but also not to run from it without his captain's leave. And when the defense of the commonwealth requires at once the help of all that are able to bear arms, everyone is obliged; because otherwise the institution of the commonwealth, which they have not the purpose or courage to preserve, was in vain.

To resist the sword of the commonwealth in defense of another man, guilty or innocent, no man has liberty; because such liberty takes away from the sovereign the means of protecting us, and is therefore destructive of the very essence of government. But in case a great many men together have already resisted the sovereign power unjustly, or committed some capital crime for which every one of them expects death, whether have they not the liberty then to join together and assist and defend one another? Certainly they have, for they but defend their lives, which the guilty man may as well do as the innocent. There was indeed injustice in the first breach of their duty; their bearing of arms subsequent to it, though it be to maintain what they have done, is no new unjust act. And if it be only to defend their persons, it is not unjust at all. But the offer of pardon takes from them to whom it is offered the plea of self-defense, and makes their perseverance in assisting or defending the rest unlawful.

The greatest liberty of subjects depends on the silence of the law.   As for other liberties, they depend on the silence of the law. In cases where the sovereign has prescribed no rule, there the subject has the liberty to do or forbear according to his own discretion. And therefore such liberty is in some places more and in some less, and in some times more, in other times less, according as they that have the sovereignty shall think most convenient. As, for example, there was a time when in England a man might enter into his own land and dispossess such as wrongfully possessed it by force. But in aftertimes that liberty of forcible entry was taken away by a statute made by the king in parliament. And in some places of the world men have the liberty of many wives; in other places such liberty is not allowed. . . .

Change

Of Those Things That Weaken or Tend to the Dissolution of a Commonwealth

Dissolution of commonwealths proceeds from their imperfect institution. Though nothing can be immortal which mortals make, yet if men had the use of reason they pretend to their commonwealths might be secured at least from perishing by internal diseases. For by the nature of their institution they are designed to live as long as mankind, or as the laws of nature, or as justice itself, which gives them life. Therefore when they come to be dissolved, not by external violence but intestine disorder, the fault is not in men as they are the *matter* but as they are the *makers* and orderers of them. For men, as they become at last weary of irregular jostling and hewing one another and desire with all their hearts to conform themselves into one firm and lasting edifice, so for want both of the art of making fit laws to square their actions by, and also of humility and patience to suffer the rude and cumbersome points of their present greatness to be taken off, they cannot without the help of a very able architect be compiled into any other than a crazy building, such as, hardly lasting out their own time, must assuredly fall upon the heads of their posterity.

Among the *infirmities,* therefore, of a commonwealth, I will reckon in the first place those that arise from an imperfect institution and resemble the diseases of a natural body which proceed from a defectuous procreation.

Want of absolute power. Of which this is one: *that a man, to obtain a kingdom, is sometimes content with less power than to the peace and defense of the commonwealth is necessarily required.* From whence it comes to pass that when the exercise of the power laid by is for the public safety to be resumed, it has the resemblance of an unjust act, which disposes great numbers of men, when occasion is presented, to rebel; in the same manner as the bodies of children, gotten by diseased parents, are subject either to untimely death or to purge the ill quality derived from their vicious conception by breaking out into biles and scabs. And when kings deny themselves some such necessary power, it is not always, though sometimes, out of ignorance of what is necessary to the office they undertake, but many times out of a hope to recover the same again at their pleasure.

Wherein they reason not well, because such as will hold them to their promises shall be maintained against them by foreign commonwealths, who in order to the good of their own subjects let slip few occasions to *weaken* the estate of their neighbors. So was Thomas Becket, archbishop of Canterbury, supported against Henry the Second by the Pope, the subjection of ecclesiastics to the commonwealth having been dispensed with by William the Conqueror at his reception when he took an oath not to infringe the liberty of the church. And so were the barons, whose power was by William Rufus, to have their help in transferring the succession from his elder brother to himself, increased to a degree inconsistent with the sovereign power, maintained in their rebellion against King John by the French.

Nor does this happen in monarchy only. For whereas the style of the ancient Roman commonwealth was *The Senate and People of Rome,* neither senate nor people pretended to the whole power; which first caused the seditions of Tiberius Gracchus, Caius Gracchus, Lucius Saturninus, and others, and afterwards the wars between the senate and the people under Marius and Sulla, and again under Pompey and Caesar, to the extinction of their democracy and the setting up of monarchy.

The people of Athens bound themselves but from one only action, which was that no man on pain of death should propound the renewing of the war for the island of Salamis; and yet thereby—if Solon had not caused to be given out he was mad, and afterwards in gesture and habit of a madman, and in verse, propounded it to the people that flocked about him—they had had an enemy perpetually in readiness, even at the gates of their city; such damage or shifts are all commonwealths forced to, that have their power never so little limited.

Private judgment of good and evil. In the second place, I observe the *diseases* of a commonwealth that proceed from the poison of seditious doctrines, whereof one is *that every private man is judge of good and evil actions.* This is true in the condition of mere nature, where there are no civil laws; and also under civil government in such cases as are not determined by the law. But otherwise, it is manifest that the measure of good and evil actions is the civil law, and the judge the legislator, who is always representative of the commonwealth. From this false doctrine, men are disposed to debate with themselves and dispute the commands of the commonwealth, and afterwards to obey or disobey them as in their private judgments they shall think fit, whereby the commonwealth is distracted and *weakened.*

Erroneous conscience. Another doctrine repugnant to civil society is *that whatsoever a man does against his conscience is sin;* and it depends on the presumption of making himself judge of good and evil. For a man's conscience and his judgment is the same thing, and as the judgment, so also the conscience may be erroneous. Therefore, though he that is subject to no civil law sins in all he does against his conscience because he has no other rule to follow but his own reason, yet it is not so with him that lives in a commonwealth, because the law is the public conscience by which he has already undertaken to be guided. Otherwise in such diversity as there is of private consciences, which are but private opinions, the commonwealth must needs be distracted, and no man dare to obey the sovereign power further than it shall seem good in his own eyes.

Pretense of inspiration. It has been also commonly taught *that faith and sanctity are not to be attained by study and reason, but by supernatural inspiration or infusion.* Which granted, I see not why any man should render a reason of his faith, or why every Christian should not be also a prophet, or why any man should take the law of his country rather than his own inspiration for the rule of his action. And thus we fall again in the fault of taking upon us to judge of good and evil, or to make judges of it such private men as pretend to be supernaturally inspired, to the dissolution of all civil government. Faith comes by hearing, and hearing by those accidents which guide us into the presence of them that speak to us; which accidents are all contrived by God Almighty, and yet are not supernatural but only, for the great number of them that concur to every effect, unobservable. Faith and sanctity are indeed not very frequent, but yet they are not miracles, but brought to pass by education, discipline, correction, and other natural ways by which God works them in his elect at such times as he thinks fit. And these three opinions, pernicious to peace and government, have in this part of the world proceeded chiefly from the tongues and pens of unlearned divines, who, joining the words of Holy Scripture together otherwise than is agreeable to reason, do what they can to make men think that sanctity and natural reason cannot stand together.

Subjecting the sovereign power to civil laws. A fourth opinion repugnant to the nature of a commonwealth is this: *that he that has the sovereign power is subject to the civil laws.* It is true that sovereigns are all subject to the laws of nature, because such laws be divine and cannot by any man or commonwealth be abrogated. But to those laws which the sovereign himself—that is, which the commonwealth—makes he is not subject. For to be subject to laws is to be subject to the commonwealth—that is, to the sovereign representative—that is, to himself, which is not subjection but freedom from the laws. Which error, because it sets the laws above the sovereign, sets also a judge above him and a power to punish him, which is to make a new sovereign, and again for the same reason a third to punish the second, and so continually without end to the confusion and dissolution of the commonwealth.

Attributing of absolute propriety to subjects. A fifth doctrine that tends to the dissolution of a commonwealth is *that every private man has an absolute propriety in his goods such as excludes the right of the sovereign.* Every man has indeed a propriety that excludes the right of every other subject, and he has it only from the sovereign power, without the protection whereof every other man should have equal right to the same. But if the right of the sovereign also be excluded, he cannot perform the office they have put him into, which is to defend them both from foreign enemies and from the injuries of one another; and consequently there is no longer a commonwealth.

And if the propriety of subjects exclude not the right of the sovereign representative to their goods, much less to their offices of judicature or execution in which they represent the sovereign himself.

Dividing of the sovereign power. There is a sixth doctrine plainly and directly against the essence of a commonwealth, and it is this: *that the sovereign power may be divided.* For what is it to divide the power of a commonwealth but to dissolve it, for powers divided mutually destroy each other. And for these doctrines men are chiefly beholding to some of those that, making profession of the laws, endeavor to make them depend upon their own learning and not upon the legislative power.

Imitation of neighbor nations. And as false doctrine, so also oftentimes the example of different government in a neighboring nation disposes men to alteration of the form already settled. So the people of the Jews were stirred up to reject God and to call upon the prophet Samuel for a king after the manner of the nations;[5] so also the lesser cities of Greece were continually disturbed with seditions of the aristocratical and democratical factions, one part of almost every commonwealth desiring to imitate the Lacedemonians, the other, the Athenians. And I doubt not but many men have been contented to see the late troubles in England[6] out of an imitation of the Low Countries, supposing there needed no more to grow rich than to change, as they had done, the form of their government.[7] For the constitution of man's nature is of itself subject to desire novelty. When, therefore, they are provoked to the same by the neighborhood also

---

[5] [I Sam. 8:4-7.]

[6] [Reference is to the Civil War. Cf. Editor's Introduction.]

[7] [Prompted by a variety of religious, economic, and particularistic motives, the provinces of the Low Countries revolted in 1572 against their overlord, Philip II of Spain. The northern provinces, of which Holland was the chief, succeeded in 1579 in establishing themselves as an independent republic. In Hobbes's time, the Dutch republic was enjoying its golden age. Engaged in constant warfare, it was one of the great powers of Europe, maintaining a powerful navy and carving out an extensive colonial empire. Its commercial prosperity was unequaled, and it was also the center of a flourishing intellectual and artistic life.]

of those that have been enriched by it, it is almost impossible for them not to be content with those that solicit them to change, and love the first beginnings though they be grieved with the continuance of disorder, like hotbloods that, having gotten the itch, tear themselves with their own nails till they can endure the smart no longer.

Imitation of the Greeks and Romans. And as to rebellion in particular against monarchy, one of the most frequent causes of it is the reading of the books of policy and histories of the ancient Greeks and Romans, from which young men and all other that are unprovided of the antidote of solid reason, receiving a strong and delightful impression of the great exploits of war archieved by the conductors of their armies, receive withal a pleasing idea of all they have done besides, and imagine their great prosperity not to have proceeded from the emulation of particular men but from the virtue of their popular form of government, not considering the frequent seditions and civil wars produced by the imperfection of their policy, From the reading, I say, of such books, men have undertaken to kill their kings, because the Greek and Latin writers, in their books and discourses of policy, make it lawful and laudable for any man so to do, provided before he do it he call him tyrant. For they say not *regicide*—that is, killing a king—but *tyrannicide*—that is, killing of a tyrant—is lawful. From the same books, they that live under a monarch conceive an opinion that the subjects in a popular commonwealth enjoy liberty but that in a monarchy they are all slaves. I say, they that live under a monarchy conceive such an opinion, not they that live under a popular government, for they find no such matter. In sum, I cannot imagine how anything can be more prejudicial to a monarchy than the allowing of such books to be publicly read without present applying such correctives of discreet masters as are fit to take away their venom; which venom I will not doubt to compare to the biting of a mad dog, which is a disease the physicians call *hydrophobia* or *fear of water*. For as he that is so bitten has a continual torment of thirst and yet abhors water, and is in such an estate as if the poison endeavored to convert him into a dog, so when a monarchy is once bitten to the quick by those democratical writers that continually snarl at that estate, it wants nothing more than a strong monarch, which nevertheless, out of a certain *tyrannophobia* or fear of being strongly governed, when they have him they abhor.

As there have been doctors that hold there be three souls in a man, so there be also that think there may be more souls—that is, more sovereigns—than one in a commonwealth, and set up a *supremacy* against the *sovereignty, canons* against *laws,* and a *ghostly authority* against the *civil,* working on men's minds with words and distinctions that of themselves signify nothing but betray by their obscurity that there walks, as some think, invisibly another kingdom—as it were, a kingdom of fairies—in the dark. Now seeing it is manifest that the civil power and the power of the commonwealth is the same thing, and that supremacy and the power of making canons and granting faculties implies a commonwealth, it follows that where one is sovereign, another supreme, where one can make laws and another make canons, there must needs be two commonwealths of one and the same subjects, which is a kingdom divided in itself, and cannot stand. For notwithstanding the insignificant distinction of *temporal* and *ghostly,* they are still two kingdoms and every subject is subject to two masters. For seeing the *ghostly* power challenges the right to declare what is sin, it challenges by consequence to declare what is law, sin being nothing but the transgression of the law; and again, the civil power challenging to declare what is law, every subject must obey two masters who both will have their commands be observed as law, which is impossible. Or, if it be but one kingdom, either the *civil,* which is the power of the commonwealth, must be subordinate to the *ghostly,* and then there is no sovereignty but the *ghostly,* or the *ghostly* must be subordinate to the *temporal,* and then there is no *supremacy* but the *temporal.* When, therefore, these two powers oppose one another, the commonwealth cannot but be in great danger of civil war and dissolution. For the *civil* authority being more visible, and standing in the clearer light of natural reason, cannot choose but draw to it in all times a very considerable part of the people; and the *spiritual,* though it stand in the darkness of School distinctions and hard words, yet because the fear of darkness and ghosts is greater than other fears, cannot want a party sufficient to trouble and sometimes to destroy a commonwealth. And this is a disease which not unfitly may be compared to the epilepsy or falling sickness, which the Jews took to be one kind of possession by spirits in the body natural. For as in this disease there is an unnatural spirit or wind in the head that obstructs the roots of the nerves and, moving them violently, takes away the motion which naturally they should have from the power of the soul in the brain and thereby causes violent and irregular motions—which men call convulsions—in the parts, insomuch as he that is seized therewith falls down sometimes into the water and sometimes into the fire, as a man deprived of his senses; so also in the body politic, when the spiritual power moves the members of a commonwealth by the terror of punishments and hope of rewards—which are the nerves of it—otherwise than by the civil power—which is the soul of the commonwealth—they ought to be moved, and by strange and hard words suffocates their understanding, it must needs thereby distract the people and either overwhelm the commonwealth with oppression or cast it into the fire of a civil war.

Mixed government. Sometimes also in the merely civil government there be more than one soul: as when the power of levying money, which is the nutritive faculty, has depended on a general assembly; the power of conduct and command, which is the motive faculty, on one man; and the power of making laws, which is the rational faculty, on the accidental consent not only of those two but also of a third; this endangers the commonwealth, sometimes for want of consent to good laws, but most often for want of such nourishment as is necessary to life and motion. For although few perceive that such government is not government but division of the commonwealth into three factions, and call it mixed monarchy, yet the truth is that it is not one independent commonwealth but three independent factions, nor one representative person but three. In the kingdom of God, there may be three persons independent without breach of unity in God that reigns; but where men reign, that be subject to diversity of opinions, it cannot be so. And therefore if the king bear the person of the people, and the general assembly bear also the person of the people, and another assembly bear the person of a part of the people, they are not one person nor one sovereign, but three persons and three sovereigns.

To what disease in the natural body of man I may exactly compare this irregularity of a commonwealth I know not. But I have seen a man that had another man growing out of his side, with a head, arms, breast, and stomach of his own; if he had had another man growing out of his other side, the comparison might then have been exact.

Want of money. Hitherto I have named such diseases of a commonwealth as are of the greatest and most present danger. There be other not so great which nevertheless are not unfit to be observed. At first, the difficulty of raising money for the necessary uses of the commonwealth, especially in the approach of war. This difficulty arises from the opinion that every subject has a propriety in his lands and goods exclusive of the sovereign's right to the use of the same. From whence it comes to pass that the sovereign power, which foresees the necessities and dangers of the commonwealth, finding the passage of money to the public treasury obstructed by the tenacity of the people, whereas it ought to extend itself to encounter and prevent such dangers in their beginnings, contracts itself as long as it can, and when it cannot longer, struggles with the people by stratagems of law to obtain little sums, which not sufficing, he is fain at last violently to open the way for present supply or perish; and being put often to these extremities, at last reduces the people to their due temper, or else the commonwealth must perish. Insomuch as we may compare this distemper very aptly to an ague, wherein the fleshy parts being congealed or by venomous matter obstructed, the veins which by their natural course empty themselves into the heart are not, as they ought to be, supplied from the arteries, whereby there succeeds at first a cold contraction and trembling of the limbs, and afterward a hot and strong endeavor of the heart, to force a passage for the blood; and before it can do that, contents itself with the small refreshments of such things as cool for a time till, if nature be strong enough, it break at last the contumacy of the parts obstructed and dissipates the venom into sweat; or, if nature be too weak, the patient dies.

Monopolies, and abuses of publicans. Again, there is sometimes in a commonwealth a disease which resembles the pleurisy; and that is when the treasure of the commonwealth, flowing out of its due course, is gathered together in too much abundance in one or a few private men by monopolies or by farms of the public revenues; in the same manner as the blood in a pleurisy, getting into the membrane of the breast, breeds there an inflammation accompanied with a fever and painful stitches.

Popular men. Also, the popularity of a potent subject, unless the commonwealth have very good caution of his fidelity, is a dangerous disease; because the people, which should receive their motion from the authority of the sovereign, by the flattery and by the reputation of an ambitious man are drawn away from their obedience to the laws to follow a man of whose virtues and designs they have no knowledge. And this is commonly of more danger in a popular government than in a monarchy, because an army is of so great force and multitude as it may easily be made believe they are the people. By this means it was that Julius Caesar, who was set up by the people against the senate, having won to himself the affections of his army, made himself master both of senate and people. And this proceeding of popular and ambitious men is plain rebellion, and may be resembled to the effects of witchcraft.

Excessive greatness of a town, multitude of corporations. Another infirmity of a commonwealth is the immoderate greatness of a town, when it is able to furnish out of its own circuit the number and expense of a great army; as also the great number of corporations, which are as it were many lesser commonwealths in the bowels of a greater, like worms in the entrails of a natural man.

Liberty of disputing against sovereign power. To which may be added the liberty of disputing against absolute power by pretenders to political prudence, which, though bred for the most part in the lees of the people, yet animated by false doctrines are perpetually medding with the fundamental laws to the molestation of the commonwealth, like the little worms which physicians call *ascarides*.

We may further add the insatiable appetite, or $\beta o \upsilon \lambda \iota \mu \acute{\iota} a$, of enlarging dominion, with the incurable *wounds* thereby many times received from the enemy, and the *wens* of ununited conquests which are many times a burden and with less danger lost than kept; as also the *lethargy* of ease and *consumption* of riot and vain expense.

Dissolution of the commonwealth. Lastly, when in a war foreign or intestine the enemies get a final victory so as, the forces the commonwealth keeping the field no longer, there is no further protection of subjects in their loyalty, then is the commonwealth DISSOLVED and every man at liberty to protect himself by such courses as his own discretion shall suggest unto him. For the sovereign is the public soul, giving life and motion to the commonwealth; which expiring, the members are governed by it no more than the carcase of a man by his departed though immortal soul. For though the right of a sovereign monarch cannot be extinguished by the act of another, yet the obligation of the members may. For he that wants protection may seek it anywhere, and when he has it is obliged, without fraudulent pretense of having submitted himself out of fear, to protect his protection as long as he is able. But when the power of an assembly is once suppressed, the right of the same perishes utterly; because the assembly itself is extinct, and consequently there is no possibility for the sovereignty to re-enter.

ROBERT DAHL

Robert Dahl is a contemporary American political theorist who has aligned himself with those favoring the behavioral approach to the study of public affairs. While Lasswell has exerted an important influence on American political science through his pioneering efforts to apply new concepts and methods to the study of politics, and Easton has gained recognition because of his attempts to provide a descriptive theory of public life, Dahl's importance rests in his studies of working democracy in the United States. Dahl is usually identified as one of the leading exponents of the "pluralist theory of politics." "Pluralism"' is essentially a body of descriptive statements that constitutes an attempt to answer the question, "Who governs?"

Generally, there are two answers that can be given to this question. The "elitist" response is to state that an identifiable group of people, who usually hold high positions in particular institutions, make the significant decisions that affect entire communities of human beings. Normally, elitists claim that this power group governs in accordance with its own particular interests. An example of elitist thinking would be the claim that a "military-industrial complex" composed of high-ranking military officers, top civilian administrators in the Pentagon, and the managers and owners of defense contracting firms make the most important decisions about the distribution of scarce resources in American society and the goals that American society should fulfill. The pluralist response to the question, "Who governs?" is to claim that no single identifiable group makes all of the significant community-wide decisions. Instead, the pluralists feel, policies are the result of a continuous conflict between a multitude of groups, each of which is dedicated to the satisfaction of some specific interest. This conflict, of course, is bounded by a broad consensus that includes the agreement that groups should not resort to physical violence as a normal tactic in furthering their interests.

Recently, the pluralist theory of American democracy has been subjected to strong criticism. Claims are made that some groups in the United States have never had many of their interests satisfied via the competitive struggles. A case in point has been the black people, who even recently have not been conspicuously successful in gaining the kinds of privileges that farmers, skilled laborers, owners and managers of corporations, and subsidized middle-class college students take for granted. For pluralism to work, every sizable group must be satisfied that its most important demands have been taken into account and that a reasonable effort has been made to meet them. In fact, this is the bare minimum condition for pluralism; frequently groups will demand much more than "reasonable efforts" on their behalf. The violent conflicts, the instances of civil disobedience, and the appearance of strong political movements outside of the two-party system in recent years give some indication that pluralist descriptions of American democracy may be partially inaccurate. Whether or not this is the case, the conflict theory of pluralism continues to dominate American political science.

Identity*

On the Species Homo Politicus

. . . Let us start with man himself: with his opportunities and resources for gaining influence and the way he exploits—or more often neglects to exploit—his political potentialities.

Homo Civicus

Civic man is, at heart, simply man; man is the child grown up; the child is the human species after millions of years of evolution. In spite of ideas and ideals, the human organism still relentlessly insists on its primordial quest for gratifications and release from pain. The child and the youth learn various forms of gratifying experience; they learn of love, and food, of play, work, and rest, of the pursuit of curiosity, the perception of order and pattern, sex, friendship, self-esteem, social esteem. Throughout man's life, experiences like these channel his efforts, his energies, his attention. They represent his hungers, his needs, his wants.

The child, the budding civic man, learns all too soon that he cannot indulge himself without stint. Constraints are imposed on his liberty to

---

gratify himself, both by nature herself in the form of physiological, mechanical, and psychological limitations and also by other individuals—his family, to begin with, then playmates, teachers, and later a host of others. The child struggles, resists, and is caught, more or less firmly, in a net woven by himself and his society.

He learns how to delay his gratifying experiences; because of the various barriers imposed on him, the routes he now chooses to his goals are frequently complex and time-consuming, sometimes boring, occasionally painful, at times dangerous.

He discovers that just as others constrain him in his efforts to achieve his primary goals, he too has resources that he can use to influence others to gain his own ends. At first these resources are closely attached to his own person and consist of simple, direct actions and reactions like affection, friendliness, anger, hostility, crying, destructiveness. But the world, as he gradually learns, contains many resources that can be used more indirectly. In our own culture, for example, he soon finds that money has a magical power to induce the compliance of many different people for many different purposes.

Thus *homo civicus* begins to develop strategies, ways of using his resources to achieve his goals. Even in choosing strategies, he discovers he does not enjoy complete freedom. Some strategies are banned, some are permissible, others are encouraged, many are all but unavoidable. Schooling and a job are presented to him as compulsory strategies; it is made clear that any attempt to depart from these paths will be visited not only by a great loss in his capacity to attain his goals but possibly even by outright punishment. Schooling is considered instrumental in gaining knowledge, and knowledge is a resource of widespread applicability; a job is instrumental in acquiring income and social standing, resources that are important for a variety of ends.

Young *homo civicus* learns that his choices are constrained by laws enforced by the police, by courts, and by many other officials. He learns of clusters of institutions and men called governments, toward some of which he develops sentiments of loyalty or cynicism. He may accept the constraints on his choices flowing from the actions of these governments, or he may try to evade them, but in either case he gradually learns that the range of permissible strategies in dealing with governments is a good deal wider and includes many subtler alternatives than he had first assumed. Among his resources for influencing officials, *homo civicus* discovers the ballot. Although the prevailing public doctrine of American society places a high value on this resource, and *homo civicus* may himself give lip service to that doctrine, in fact he may doubt its value and rarely if ever employ it, or he may vote merely out of habit and sense of duty. Or he may see the ballot as a useful device for influencing politicians.

Homo civicus has other resources, too. For example, he can forego a movie or two in order to make a contribution to a political campaign; he can forego an evening of television in order to distribute propaganda for a candidate. But the chances are very great that political activity will always seem rather remote from the main focus of his life. Typically, as a source of direct gratifications political activity will appear to *homo civicus* as less attractive than a host of other activities; and, as a strategy to achieve his gratifications indirectly, political action will seem considerably less efficient than working at his job, earning more money, taking out insurance, joining a club, planning a vacation, moving to another neighborhood or city, or coping with an uncertain future in manifold other ways.

Sometimes, however, the actions or inactions of governments may threaten the primary goals of *homo civicus* (as in the cases of Miss Grava and her neighbors when they were threatened by the metal houses, or the New Haven school teachers threatened by declining salaries and poor schools). The *homo civicus* may set out deliberately to use the resources at his disposal in order to influence the actions of governments. But when the danger passes, *homo civicus* may usually be counted on to revert to his normal preoccupation with nonpolitical strategies for attaining his primary goals.

Homo civicus is not, by nature, a political animal.

Homo Politicus

Despite several thousand years of richly insightful speculation, not much can be said with confidence about the factors that shape *homo politicus* out of the apolitical clay of *homo civicus*. Presumably, in the course of development some individuals find that political action is a powerful source of gratifications, both direct and indirect. If and when the primary goals that animate *homo civicus* become durably attached to political action, a new member of the genus *homo politicus* is born. Political man, unlike civic man, deliberately allocates a very sizable share of his resources to the process of gaining and maintaining control over the policies of government. Control over policies usually requires control over officials. And where, as in the United States, key officials are elected by voters, political man usually allocates an important share of his resources to the process of gaining and maintaining influence over voters. Because the acquiescence of *homo civicus* is always a necessary condition for rulership, and to gain his consent is often economical, in all political systems *homo politicus* deliberately employs some resources to influence the choices of *homo civicus*. Political man invariably seeks to influence civic man directly, but even in democratic systems civic man only occasionally seeks to influence political man directly.

Like civic man, political man develops strategies that govern the ways in which he uses the resources at his disposal. Like civic man, political man chooses his strategies from a narrowly limited set. In some political systems, the limits imposed on *homo politicus* are broad; in others the limits are relatively narrow. In pluralistic, democratic political systems with wide political consensus the range of acceptable strategies is narrowed by beliefs and habits rooted in traditions of legality, constitutionality, and legitimacy that are constantly reinforced by a great variety of social processes for generating agreement on and adherence to political norms. Whoever departs from these acceptable strategies incurs a high risk of defeat, for the resources that will be mounted against the political deviant are almost certain to be vastly greater than the resources the political deviant can himself muster. Even *homo civicus* (under the prodding of rival political leaders) can be counted on to rise briefly out of his preoccupation with apolitical goals and employ some of his resources to smite down the political man who begins to deviate noticeably in his choice of strategies from the norms prescribed in the political culture.

Resources

The resources available to political man for influencing others are limited, though not permanently fixed. For our purposes in this book, a resource is anything that can be used to sway the specific choices or the strategies of another individual. Or, to use different language, whatever may be used as an inducement is a resource.

How one classifies resources is to some extent arbitrary. It would be possible to list resources in great detail, distinguishing one from the other with the utmost subtlety or to deal in very broad categories. One could search for a comprehensive and logically exhaustive classification or simply list resources according to the dictates of common sense. One could employ elaborate psychological categories derived from theories of modern psychology, or one could use more commonplace terms to classify resources. To the extent that we can explain the patterns of influence in New Haven, it will do, I think, to use categories dictated by common sense; to do more at this stage of our knowledge would be pseudoscientific window dressing.

Some resources can be used more or less directly as inducements. Or, put another way, the kinds of effective and cognitive experiences mentioned a moment ago as peculiarly fundamental and universal depend rather directly on some kinds of resources and more indirectly on others.

A list of resources in the American political system might include an individual's own time; access to money, credit, and wealth; control over jobs; control over information; esteem or social standing; the possession of charisma, popularity, legitimacy, legality; and the rights pertaining to public office. The list might also include solidarity: the capacity of a member of one segment of society to evoke support from others who identify him as like themselves because of similarities in occupation, social standing, religion, ethnic origin, or racial stock. The list would include the right to vote, intelligence, education, and perhaps even one's energy level.

One could easily think of refinements and additions to this list; it is not intended as an exhaustive list so much as an illustration of the richness and variety of political resources. All too often, attempts to explain the distribution and patterns of influence in political systems begin with an a priori assumption that everything can be explained by reference to only one kind of resource. On the contrary, the various manifestations of influence in New Haven described in earlier chapters can be explained, as we shall see, only by taking into account a number of different political resources.

Although the kinds and amounts of resources available to political man are always limited and at any given moment fixed, they are not, as was pointed out a moment ago, permanently fixed as to either kind or amount. Political man can use his resources to gain influence, and he can then use his influence to gain more resources. Political resources can be pyramided in much the same way that a man who starts out in business sometimes pyramids a small investment into a large corporate empire. To the political entrepreneur who has skill and drive, the political system offers unusual opportunities for pyramiding a small amount of initial resources into a sizable political holding. This possibility will prove to be highly important, as we shall see, in accounting for changes in influence in New Haven. . . .

Power

When one examines a political decision—that is, a decision determining the policies enforced by governmental officials—or what persons become officials—one usually finds that for any particular sector of policy only a small number of persons ever initiate alternatives or veto the proposals of others. These individuals are leaders or policy makers. One may say that they have the greatest *direct* influence on decisions. A larger number of persons, subleaders, generally have moderate influence. But most citizens usually have little or no *direct* influence in this sense: they never initiate or veto any alternatives.

One is also likely to find, however, that some leaders are extremely sensitive to the attitudes and preferences of individuals and groups who do not directly initiate or veto alternatives. Often this indirect influence is *anticipatory:* a leader initiates or vetoes a particular alternative because he anticipates rewards for choosing from one set of alternatives, or sanctions if he chooses from a different set. In this way, persons or groups who are not leaders may exert great indirect influence on the choice of alternatives even though they never directly initiate or veto.

In New Haven, for example, the present mayor has not until this present year ever advocated an increase in taxes, although he has done almost everything else to raise money. Why has he not tried to increase taxes? It was not, I think, because someone said, "Mayor Lee, don't you dare raise taxes!" For the mayor grew up in New Haven; he knows enough about the city to know that raising taxes is politically risky. He *anticipated* what might happen to him in the next election if he should raise taxes. If the decision to take the risk is made, at least it is a fact that the risk involved has been anticipated.

Indirect influence, which is often anticipatory in character, is very important for some kinds of leaders, particularly those who have to win elections. Yet even when indirect influence of this sort is taken into account, the distribution of influence in most sectors of policy is very far indeed from the perfect equality that some democratic theorists would regard as ideal.

One of the main reasons why the system does not very closely approximate political equality is the unequal distribution of access to political resources—that is, to inducements of all kinds. One's influence is partly a function of the political resources to which one has access—labor time, money and credit, jobs, information, popularity, wealth, social standing, legality, and the like. An examination of any one of these political resources will show that some persons have much greater access to it than others. So long as this is the case, political equality is not likely to be approximated. This is hardly a novel conclusion, for a great many writers on politics have said in one way or another that a high degree of equality in the distribution of political resources is a necessary—though by no means a sufficient—condition for a high degree of equality of control over political decisions. This was, for example, one of Tocqueville's key propositions in his analysis of democracy in America.

In appraising inequality in political resources, it is important not to make the mistake of assuming that what we are trying to judge is a ruling elite masquerading in the name of democracy. For if citizens do not rule the system as political equals neither does a unified elite control decisions, at least not in New Haven. There may be exceptions in specific communities, but I am inclined to think that most cities and states, and certainly the national government, are in this respect rather like New Haven.

To condemn our political system for inequality is one thing; to condemn it for being dominated by a ruling elite is another. In my view, appraisal is infinitely more complicated, precisely because the political system is neither a democracy in which citizens share equally in all important decisions nor an oligarchy ruled by an elite. Rather, it combines elements of both.

In the American system (insofar as New Haven is a fair prototype), though political equality is certainly not attained and political resources are unequally distributed, democracy is not wholly subverted into oligarchy because the growth of oligarchy is inhibited both by the *patterns* according to which political resources are allocated and by the ways in which resources are actually *used*.

Let me try to make my point clearer first by some abstract considerations on the nature of power and influence. Abstractly, there is no reason to assume that the relative influence different individuals or groups exert on the decisions of one another is simply and solely a function of the "size" of their resources, that is, of the inducements they have at their disposal.

In the first place, an individual need not *use* his political resources to gain direct or indirect influence over officials of government. To be sure, the extent to which one is willing to use his political resources for political ends, depends *in part* on the magnitude of his resources; for example a millionaire who contributed $100 to a political campaign gives up fewer alternative opportunities than a poor man. But the extent to which a person uses his political resources will depend on other factors as well, including his confidence in the success of his effort, the extent to which he has alternative ways of gaining his ends other than through politics, and the extent to which he expects he will be benefited or injured by government policies. In New Haven, we have found variations attributable to each of these factors.

For example, Negroes in New Haven, a minority of probably 10 or 12 percent of the population, operate at a much higher level of political participation than any other single isolated group in the community. What is the reason for this? The political arena is one area where Negroes are not thwarted and blocked by substantial discrimination. They can get jobs, patronage, and city contracts; they have their votes; their votes are legitimate, and they are counted; and so it has been for a century. This isn't true in the other sectors of community life; so Negroes work harder in the political arena to compensate for their disadvantages.

In the second place, one individual may use his political resources more *skillfully* than another—a variation known to students of politics for several centuries. By a skillful use of limited resources, in fact, a political entrepreneur—Machiavelli's Prince—can increase his resources and thus his influence.

In the third place, the relative influence of different potential coalitions will depend in part on the extent to which individuals and groups actually *combine* their resources. The combined political resources of a very numerous group of individuals who are not very well off may easily exceed the combined political resources of a small elite, each member of which is, individually, very well off. The extent to which people in a group actually combine their resources depends, of course, on the degree of political unity among them. There is no a priori reason for supposing that the rich will display more unity than the poor; and even if they do, it does not follow that combined resources of the well-off strata will inevitably exceed the combined resources of the badly-off strata of a society.

Now, when we turn from these abstract considerations to the way in which different kinds of inducements—political resources—are actually distributed in New Haven we discover that a most significant change seems to have taken place during the last century and a half. In 1800, the citizens of New Haven were not only very unequal in access to political resources of all kinds but their inequalities were *cumulative*. That is, the same tiny elite possessed the highest social standing, wealth, dominance in economic affairs, superior education, control over educational and religious institutions, a monopoly of public offices, evidently a large measure of legitimacy, and perhaps (though this is more doubtful) even popularity. Today, however, inequalities that exist with respect to all these resources tend to be noncumulative or *dispersed*. I can find no single elite at the top of the heap; instead there are many different varieties of political resources, with a somewhat different elite at the top of each. I am inclined to think that this pattern is not peculiar to New Haven but is common throughout the United States, though one would doubtless find exceptions to it here and there.

Moreover, I am tempted toward the hypothesis that the pattern of dispersed inequalities is a likely product of an advanced industrial society, at least if it operates with the kinds of political institutions that most of us would call democratic. The impact of Marx and Weber on habits of thought about industrial society has been very great, even among non-Marxists and non-Weberians, and both men lead us to expect that an advanced industrial society will be rather neatly and consistently stratified along lines shaped by economic class or bureaucratic position. I believe we should entertain the hypothesis that any industrial society in an advanced stage enters on a profound change that can be held back, if at all, only by a most vigorous and oppressive centralized regime. In a moderately free political system, at this stage, increasing affluence, widespread education, impersonal standards of recruitment, incredible specialization of functions and skills, the varieties of popularity, prestige, and achievement, standardization of consumer goods, social and geographical mobility, and probably many other factors, all tend to produce a pattern of dispersed rather than cumulative inequalities. The advance of industrial society may somewhat reduce inequalities in political resources; it does not, however, erase them. Nonetheless, in New Haven, and I think in American society generally, these inequalities are no longer cumulative.

To the extent that inequalities persist, tendencies toward oligarchy also exist in advanced industrial societies. But to the extent that inequalities are dispersed rather than cumulative—as I am suggesting they are in the United States—the growth of a unified oligarchy is inhibited. For the pattern of dispersed inequalities means that an individual or a group at a disadvantage with respect to one resource may compensate for his handicap by exploiting his superior access to a different resource. In New Haven, for example, for the past half century men whose main political resources were popularity and ethnic solidarity have been able to win elections. Very few individuals or groups in New Haven, and I believe this to be true in the United States, are totally lacking in political resources *of some kind.*

The possibility of turning to alternative kinds of resources would be less significant if one kind of resource—say wealth or social standing—dominated all the others, in the sense that a person or group superior in the one resource would invariably exert superior influence in a conflict with persons who drew on other political resources. Yet—and this is the second great limit on the growth of oligarchy—this is simply not the case, despite a tradition of economic determinism that runs in a straight line from Madison to Veblen, Beard, the Lynds, and C. Wright Mills. Surely if the New Deal demonstrated anything, it proved that leaders with popularity and votes can—even if they do not always do so—carry out their policies despite the opposition of leaders supported by men of wealth and social standing. This is a point that was perfectly obvious to both Aristotle and Tocqueville, who considered the problem in the light of observations made on radically different sorts of political systems.

In the third place, individuals or groups who are at a disadvantage in their access to resources can sometimes compensate by using their resources at a relatively high level. In New Haven, Negroes who, as I said before, are more active politically than any other identifiable ethnic group in the city, have overcome some of the disadvantages imposed by their incomes, status, and occupations.

Fourth, an individual or group at a disadvantage in resources may compensate by developing a high level of political skill. Fortunately the skills required in electioneering and party politics are by no means a monopoly of any stratum in the community; one might even conclude that leaders drawn from the well-to-do tend to be somewhat less likely to develop these skills to a high peak of proficiency than leaders drawn from the less-well-off strata of the community. In fact, many sorts of politicking run more sharply counter to the norms of the upper strata than of the lower or lower-middle strata.

Fifth, a group of citizens each of whom is weak in political resources may compensate by combining resources so that in the aggregate these are formidable. One resource that can be most easily aggregated by the less-well-off strata is the ballot. In New Haven, historically the least well-off citizens in the community have been Negroes and members of various immigrant groups whose circumstances produce a unity at the polls that declines as assimilation progresses. This unity among the poor has enabled them—or more accurately, perhaps, their leaders—to influence nominations, elections, and policies (often, to be sure, covert rather than overt policies) despite their lowly status, their low incomes, and their poverty in many other political resources.

Sixth, competitive elections insure that elected officials attempt to shape their covert and overt policies so as to win elections, hence to maximize votes, or at any rate to gain more votes than any rival. Consequently, whenever the many are believed to hold views on government policies at odds with the views held among the few, there exists one set of persons, elected politicians, who are strongly impelled to win votes by shaping or seeming to shape governmental policies according to the views of the many.

The system would be easier to judge either if it did not fall so far short of the goal of political equality—or, ironically, if it fell much shorter than it does. In the first case one might conclude that we possess a reasonable approximation of political equality, and approve the fact; in the other, one might conclude that we have an oligarchy, and condemn it roundly. But in my view the facts do not permit either judgment.

Some of you might draw comfort from the belief that the American system, if I have described it rightly, comes close to the mixture of democracy and oligarchy that Aristotle concluded was "the best constitution and the best way of life for the *majority* of states and men," and which he called a polity, I cannot forbear quoting here a few lines from Barker's translation of *The Politics.*

> . . . . It is a good criterion of a proper mixture of democracy and oligarchy that a mixed constitution should be able to be described indifferently as either. . . . A properly mixed "polity" should look as if it contained both democratic and oligarchical elements—and as if it contained neither. It should owe its stability to its own intrinsic strength, and not to external support; and its intrinsic strength should be derived from the fact, not that a majority are in favor of its continuance. . . , but rather that there is no single section in all the state which would favor a change to a different constitution. . . . It is clear from our argument, first, that the best form of political society is one where power is vested in the middle class, and secondly, that good government is attainable in those states where there is a large middle class—large enough, if possible, to be stronger than both of the other classes, but at any rate large enough to be stronger than either of them singly. (pp. 177, 178, 180)

You will recall also Aristotle's observation that polities of this kind were in fact rather rare, because in most states the middle class was small, and both the masses and the rich sought to install the constitution most favorable to them, either democracy or oligarchy.

For those who do not want to yield up the marvelous Utopian objective that animated the Declaration of Independence and the Gettysburg address, Aristotle's words will scarcely give complete comfort. Unless we abandon the ideal of political equality, and with it the American Dream, I do not see how we can live comfortably with the inequalities of power and political resources that we find around us. Can anyone who holds democratic beliefs remain satisfied with the American political system simply because it is not an oligarchy?

Unfortunately, however, solutions to the problem of political inequality are not as simple as they may have seemed to many hopeful democrats a century or more ago. In order to eliminate large inequalities in direct influence on governmental policies we should have to make far-reaching, indeed revolutionary, alterations in the character of modern society, such as the destruction of the national state and the elimination of all forms of bureaucratic organization including the business corporation. It would also require a world at peace. Even then, so long as individuals had different motives, interests, and skills, sizable differences in direct influence undoubtedly would appear. I do not believe that enough people are interested in these changes—which would generate their own train of uncertainties and impose great costs to other values we all hold—to make it worth the effort to explore them here, even though attempts to think through these problems realistically should continue.

Nor should one be misled by glib solutions. It might be argued, for example, that if inequalities in direct influence are inevitable, at least we should insure that there is equal opportunity to *gain* influence. Many persons are handicapped in the contest for office and influence by inequalities in resources that can be reduced, such as handicaps stemming from gross differences in income and inherited wealth, handicaps arising from inadequate opportunities for education, and handicaps arising from discriminatory practices based on race, ethnic group, religion, or social class. To the extent that these are remediable, surely we should not rest on our oars until the race is won.

But we must not be beguiled into assuming that equality of opportunity to *gain* influence will produce equality of *influence*. In fact, we are reducing and probably in the future will reduce even more many old inequalities in opportunities. But this merely insures that individuals will start out more or less even in a race for unequal influence. Even a modern dictatorship can achieve that. In fact some dictatorships seem to do a tolerably good job of it. It might be thought, too, that inequalities in direct influence over government policies could be reduced solely to *legitimate* differences in the relative influence of government officials, particularly elected officials, and ordinary citizens. No one, I suppose, would quarrel with the proposition that the President or the Secretary of State should have much greater influence over foreign policies, because of official position, than any other citizen. Yet it would be misleading to suppose that we are likely to reach a state of affairs in which reality corresponds to the simple model of democratic representation whereby appointive officials are merely the agents of elected officials, and elected officials are merely the agents of the majority. For in many sectors of policy, including most of the highly critical ones, elected and appointive officials have enormous leeway; public opinion and voting often provide only the vaguest sort of guide as to what is preferred by or even acceptable to a majority of voters. Views are often highly plastic: it is not so much the elected officials who are the agents of a majority as the other way round—voters wait for their trusted leaders to indicate what lines of policy should be followed.

If we are not likely—at least in the present state of national and world organization—to reduce very greatly the enormous differences that now exist with respect to direct influences on government policies, the problem of indirect influence is somewhat more manageable. The most promising means for providing an equal though indirect influence on policies is, surely, through participation in nominations, campaigns, and elections. Here the situation strikes me as a very hopeful one, for political self-confidence and participation are so much a function of education that the wide diffusion of educational opportunities is likely to reduce to insignificance many of the differences in political participation that stem from socio-economic position rather than differences in personality. (Perhaps it is just as well that the differences in personality still elude control.)

Even in the case of campaigns and elections, however, wide participation is no cure-all. A formidable problem arises because of the enormous differences in opportunities for influencing the voters themselves. The problem is much more serious at the national than at the local level, for it is incomparably more expensive and more difficult to obtain a national hearing than a local one. Political theory has barely been extended to cover this problem; in particular, liberal democratic theory has often started with the assumption that the preferences of individuals, whether voters or consumers, should be taken as given, as autonomous to the individual rather than socially determined. To be sure, Tocqueville, Mill, and Bryce all looked beyond the individual to the towering influence of majority opinion on the views of the individual; and critics at the right and left have looked beyond the majority to the influence on its opinions wielded by key minorities of wealth, status, and skill. There have been some innovations, like equal time, and more recently the famous TV debates between the presidential candidates. But clearly we have barely begun to grapple with this problem.

There can be no doubt, then, that our political system falls far short of the high standards of performance indicated by the criterion of political equality. No one who places a high value on political equality can afford to be complacent about the achievements of the American political system.

Nonetheless, it is misleading in the extreme to interpret the inequalities of power that mark our political life as signs of oligarchy. For in our system of dispersed inequalities, almost every group, as said before, has access to some resources that it can exploit to gain influence. Consequently, any group that feels itself badly abused is likely to possess both the resources it needs to halt the abuse and the incentive to use these resources at a high enough level to bring about changes. Nearly every group has enough potential influence to mitigate harsh injustice to its members, though not necessarily enough influence to attain a full measure of justice. The system thus tends to be self-corrective, at least in a limited fashion. If equality and justice are rarely attained, harsh and persistent oppression is almost always avoided. To this extent, the system attains one of the important ends of political equality without the means. . . .

Change

Alternative Strategies for Political Activists

The American political system does not encourage or even facilitate revolutionary changes; obviously no stable political systems do. Comprehensive changes in government policies do sometimes occur in the United States, as in the period of Republican innovation during and after the Civil War or in the New Deal period of the 1930s. But even comprehensive changes are, as we have seen, uncommon. The typical pattern of American politics is one of stability, moderate conflict, and incremental change.

Suppose then, that a body of American citizens wishes to bring about changes in government policies by peaceful and democratic methods. How can such a body proceed?

There are, roughly speaking, four strategies available to a political movement in the United States:

1. The movement can organize a separate political party of its own.
2. The movement can form a new coalition party by combining with another group or movement that has similar, overlapping, but not identical objectives.
3. Although it remains neutral between the two major parties, the movement can act as a pressure group to secure favorable legislation and the nomination and election of sympathetic candidates.
4. By entering into one of the existing parties, the movement can become an element in a major party coalition; it can then use its bargaining power to gain influence for the movement within the party.

Each of these alternatives has its own inner logic, its special advantages and disadvantages. Perhaps this is why all four strategies have been tried so often. The first strategy has been tried by Free Soilers, Socialists, Greenbackers, Communists, Prohibitionists, Single Taxers, America Firsters, Vegetarians, and the Church of God party, among others. The first strategy enables a movement to maintain its ideological purity and avoid compromising its goals. Yet the usual price is political isolation, defeat, and ineffectuality. The second strategy helps a movement break out of its isolation; but in doing so the movement may lose at least some of its purity and still fail to become a major party. The second strategy was that of the Populists, until they went all the way in 1896 and backed the Democratic candidate, Bryan. It was also the strategy of Progressive movements in 1924 and 1948. The third strategy may yield high pay-off if the goals of the movement are narrow and group-oriented. But as a price, the movement must do nothing to alienate the major parties. This is the strategy of most pressure groups; in some states and localities it has also been the strategy of third parties, like the Liberal party in New York. The fourth strategy may yield a movement more influential over a greater range of goals than the third strategy, a better chance of winning elections than the second strategy. The price, however, is a willingness to negotiate, to bargain, to compromise in order to form a winning coalition, and to run the risk of turning members of the other party into opponents. This is the strategy that some unions have adopted at the state level, like the United Automobile Workers in Michigan. It was also the strategy the Populists were moving toward when they supported Bryan in 1896.

Weighing the advantages and disadvantages of the four alternatives is a recurrent task in American politics. Few choices are so important to the destiny of a political movement. It is instructive, therefore, to examine the experience of a movement that has had to face these four alternatives. An obvious candidate is the American labor movement, for from its earliest years down to the present day the labor movement has debated the pros and cons of the various strategies. As in so many other cases, Americans once again chose a path different from that taken in most European countries. Yet the debate over alternatives is not yet ended; perhaps it never will be. . . .

Every group, every organization, every movement that seeks changes in government policies faces the same alternatives as the labor movement. Weighing the pros and cons of alternative strategies is no easy task. Ideologues are drawn toward the first or second strategy; pragmatists toward the third or fourth. A strong desire to maintain the purity of its aim beckons a movement toward independent political action; a strong desire to be effective beckons a movement toward negotiation and coalition. Idealism cries: Reject compromises! Realism asks: Of what value is ideological purity when it leads merely to political futility?

If success is measured by the ability to win elections, then historically the first strategy has been the least successful. The history of the first strategy is, in plain fact, a record of very nearly total failure. Why this is so should by now be all but self-evident. The first strategy is likely to appeal most to a movement committed to goals which are unacceptable to either of the two major parties. Yet, if the goals of the movement are unacceptable to either of the existing parties, is there not good reason to think that these goals will also be unacceptable to the followings of the major parties and hence to most voters? If one goal of a political movement is to win elections, the first strategy will work only if at least one of the two major parties has fallen down badly on the prime job of the politician: to find out what appeals to voters and to act accordingly. The one clear historical instance of atrophy among the existing parties and the emergence of a new major party is furnished by the birth of the Republican party; the newborn Republican organization rapidly acquired the support of dissident Whigs and Democrats throughout the North and West. Yet this example remains the only case in which a third party has attracted enough support from discontented followers of the major parties to develop into a major party in its own right.

If this is so, why does the first strategy have any appeal at all? Partly, no doubt, because its advocates ignore the historical regularities in American politics; partly because a movement with goals unacceptable to the major parties may simply have no other alternative open to it; and partly, one suspects, because of faith in the "doctrine of the hidden majority." The doctrine of the hidden majority, which is sometimes propounded by movements on both the extreme right and the extreme left, is the belief that a majority of like-minded citizens already exists waiting only to be mobilized, since the two major parties are for some reason ignoring and frustrating that latent majority. Belief in the doctrine of the hidden majority is not always confined to people on the most extreme fringes; in 1964 Senator Goldwater seems to have assumed the validity of the doctrine and to have fashioned his campaign accordingly with disastrous results.[1]

Choice of the first strategy by a movement that is already divorced from the main currents of American opinion may establish a vicious cycle of political alienation: defeat, political isolation, and powerlessness reinforce a sense of political alienation and lack of realism in the movement, while alienation and lack of realism in turn increase the likelihood that the movement will be badly defeated in elections and will remain politically isolated and powerless.

The second strategy has been, at least in national politics, no more successful than the first. The second strategy has some of the appeal of the first, for it enables a group to adhere to most of its goals even though it enters into a coalition with one or two other groups with slightly divergent (but in the main overlapping) goals. The strategy reached its zenith of success in the Populist party; but the needed majority was not forthcoming. Neither "labor" nor "farmers" constituted a homogeneous body of like-minded citizens, and the combination of the two groups created an even more heterogeneous coalition. Bryan and the Populists gained a good deal of support in some farming areas, especially in the South and West. But they lost badly in others and failed to win urban labor. If the American citizen body was already highly heterogeneous in the 1890s, it is probably even more heterogeneous today.

---

[1] Cf. Philip F. Converse, Aage A. Clausen, and Warren E. Miller, "Electoral Myth and Reality: the 1964 Election," *American Political Science Review* (June 1965), pp. 321-336. See also, however, the comment "On Electoral Myth and Reality," by William C. Baum, ibid. (September 1965), p. 693.

FIGURE 1. THE VICIOUS CYCLE OF POLITICAL ALIENATION

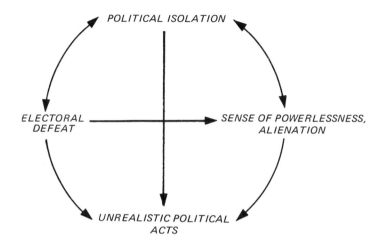

Just as the appeal of the first strategy may lie in the doctrine of the hidden majority, so the appeal of the second may be drawn from the "doctrine of the pure and simple coalition": a belief in the possibility of forming a majority coalition that is *pure,* in the sense that the coalition partners do not need to modify their goals in order to create or maintain a coalition, and that is *simple,* in the sense that it can be formed from only two or three groups, movements, classes, strata, each of which is internally homogeneous. Hence the appeal of a pure and simple coalition of workers and farmers; of the civil rights movement and the peace movement; of conservatives and property owners. . . .

Yet . . . the doctrine of the pure and simple coalition must also be largely mythical. For where are these two or three internally like-minded groups that can combine to form a majority? Blue-collar workers are a minority of the working force, and a declining minority at that. Trade union members are an even smaller minority—a fifth to a quarter of the employed population. The white-collar strata constitute a complex of occupational minorities, from clerical workers to professional men and employers. Professional men and women are a small minority of the working force; doctors are a minority of professionals; psychiatrists, a minority of doctors. The poor are a minority, but so are the rich; the middle-income strata are only a statistical category, not a homogeneous group. Negroes are a minority; so are white Southerners; so are Southerners, white and black. Jews and Catholics are minorities; the Protestant "majority" is largely a fiction, for it is a congeries of minorities as different as Southern Baptists, Lutherans, Episcopalians, and Quakers. What is more, none of the categories just mentioned are, in fact, collections of like-minded people—blue-collar workers, trade union members, white-collar workers, professionals, doctors, psychiatrists, the poor, the rich, the middle-income strata, Negroes, white Southerners, Northerners, Jews, Catholics, Protestants, Democrats, Republicans, liberals, conservatives. . . . No major category of the population defined by a single criterion, whether occupation, income, religion, ethnic group, region, or any other, consists altogether of like-minded voters.

The third strategy offers a fair chance of success for any group smaller than a majority, when the members of the group agree on relatively narrow or specific goals that do not run sharply counter to widely prevailing beliefs. The third strategy is the strategy of the pressure group. For limited purposes it can be highly successful. Farm organizations, representing at most a small and diminishing minority, have used it with enormous success. So, in varying degrees, have literally thousands of other organizations, representing or claiming to represent trade unionists, veterans, businessmen, industrialists, taxpayers, bankers, oil companies, copper importers, doctors, women's clubs, nature-lovers, stream pollutionists, conservationists, foreign policy groups, old people. . . .

But a movement that seeks something more than its own group interests may conclude that as a pure pressure group it will exert too limited an influence over the policies of the American republic. If a movement also has a numerous following of prospective voters, like the labor movement, it may find the fourth strategy more reasonable than the third.

Is the fourth strategy perhaps the "best" all round strategy? Not necessarily. A very small and well organized group without many votes behind it may retain more influence as an independent pressure group. A large group whose members are divided among people loyal to both parties would run the risk of splitting its following if it adopted the fourth strategy. A group with narrow goals more or less acceptable to both parties may succeed better as a pressure group. A group whose goals diverge widely from those supported by both parties could not find a home in either party.

Thus each strategy has its advantages and disadvantages. Since enthusiasts are prone to believe that they can have the advantages of a strategy without its disadvantages, a choice among the four strategies is often a somewhat irrational process colored more by hope and faith than by hardheaded analysis.

It is probably impossible, and in any case not very useful, to lay down a set of hard and fast rules according to which one strategy or the other would always be the most "rational" in the American political system. Instead, let me try to draw the discussion together by pinpointing four fac-

TABLE 1. FOUR FACTORS RELEVANT TO THE CHOICE OF POLITICAL STRATEGIES BY A GROUP

A. GOALS	Goals of the group are:	
1. Breadth	1a. Oriented to NARROW objectives.	1b. Oriented to COMPREHENSIVE objectives.
2. Acceptability	2a. ACCEPTABLE to both major parties.	2b. UNACCEPTABLE to either major party.
	Members of the group are:	
B. MEMBERS		
3. Number	3a. FEW in number	3b. NUMEROUS
4. Homogeneity	4a. HOMOGENEOUS in political outlook.	4b. DIVERSE in political outlook.

tors that seem relevant in choosing among strategies (Table 1).

Theoretically, these factors can be combined, in a number of different ways. For many combinations it might be difficult or impossible to say that one strategy was more "rational" than another. For others, however, one strategy does seem more appropriate than the others. Table 2 shows one type of group for which a particular strategy seems appropriate.

Why is it that every strategy seems to have certain disadvantages? The main source of trouble is an apparently inescapable fact: In the United States, any group of people who have virtually the same views on political questions, the same political loyalties and identifications, is certain to be a *minority*. Whether the group is microscopic or relatively numerous, it will be a minority of the total body of citizens, even a minority of voters, and

TABLE 2. APPROPRIATE STRATEGIES FOR FOUR KINDS OF GROUPS

Thus if a group's

Goals are	Members are	An appropriate strategy would be to:
1. Comprehensive Acceptable to neither party	Few Homogeneous	Form an independent party.
2. Comprehensive Acceptable to neither party	Numerous Diverse	Form a new coalition party.
3. Narrow Acceptable to both parties	Few Diverse	Form a pressure group.
4. Comprehensive Acceptable to one party	Numerous Diverse	Join coalition with existing party.

a rather small minority at that. To make the same point in another way, every aggregate of American citizens large enough to constitute a majority of voters is necessarily a heterogeneous collection of individuals and groups who may agree on some matters but are sure to disagree on others. No group of like-minded citizens can ever win a national election merely by mobilizing themselves and others who think exactly the way they do. To win national elections, even to win influence over national policies, every group must participate somehow in the politics of coalition building. To be sure, it can pursue its own goals; and it must engage in conflict; but it must also conciliate, compromise, negotiate, bargain—and in the process often forego its lesser goals for its greater objectives. In this sense, no single group *can* win national elections—only heterogeneous combination of groups can.

Some people, particularly if they happen to be highly confident of their own political virtue, the rightness of their own goals, and the evils of compromise, find this a most repugnant interpretation of American political life. Either this interpretation is false, they say, and the strict, undiminished pursuit of the goals held by the group, the movement, the cause will one day eventuate in political success uncontaminated by compromise. Or if the view is true, then politics is a dirty and evil business.

This, I think, is too crabbed, too inhuman a view of political life. For it seems obvious that, in a democratic republic, freedom and diversity lead inexorably to conflict. Yet they need not lead to inexorable conflict. For among a people guided, even in their conflicts, by a talent for conciliation and a commitment to the principles and institutions of a democratic republic, both freedom and diversity might flourish.

ALBERT CAMUS

Albert Camus, a Frenchman born in Algeria in 1914, is a major figure on both the literary and philosophical scenes. Along with the writings of Erich Fromm and Herbert Marcuse, his works have been important sources of ideas for the New Left throughout the world. Camus was not a conflict theorist in the same sense as Hobbes or Dahl, in that he did not interpret human activity in terms of striving after wealth, power, or status. Instead, he viewed the human condition as a confrontation between the individual and what he termed "the absurd." According to Camus, the absurdity of existence is revealed to the individual when he attempts to investigate the meaning of his life. The person finds that the world around him has no ultimate meaning that will assure him that his existence is worthwhile or has some significance or overarching purpose. Yet, at the same time, he discovers that he cannot help but demand an explanation of his life. The interplay of the facts that no meaning can be extracted from existence and that the person nevertheless continues to demand such a meaning constitutes the absurd. Once one has become fully aware of the absurd, Camus counsels him to revolt against his condition. In other words, with full knowledge that there is no absolute significance to his life, the person should continue to act. Such action undertaken with the awareness of the absurd allows the individual to mock his condition and, thus, rise above it.

Why should such a doctrine have any political implications? In the first place, recognition of the absurd bars one from accepting any religious or ideological explanations of public life. There is a deep current in Camus' thought that stresses our obligation not to accept the necessity of any unsatisfactory political situation. We are free to attempt to create the conditions for justice, and no one can excuse us from the responsibility of choosing whether or not to make such an effort. Second, Camus was preoccupied with the problem of how the freedom of individuals could be increased in a world of complex organizations. He committed himself to the ideal of an alliance of intellectuals and workers which would struggle against repressive managers and bureaucrats. Camus' overriding interest in expanding the area of freedom through active struggle makes him a conflict theorist. His emphasis on individual initiative has inspired many in the currently maturing generation.

Identity*

The Absurd Man

If Stavrogin believes, he does not think he believes. If he does not believe, he does not think he does not believe.

— The Possessed

"My field," said Goethe, "is time." That is indeed the absurd speech. What, in fact, is the absurd man? He who, without negating it, does nothing for the eternal. Not that nostalgia is foreign to him. But he prefers his courage and his reasoning. The first teaches him to live *without appeal* and to get along with what he has; the second informs him of his limits. Assured of his temporally limited freedom, of his revolt devoid of future, and of his mortal consciousness, he lives out his adventure within the span of his lifetime. That is his field, that is his action, which he shields from any judgment but his own. A greater life cannot mean for him another life. That would be unfair. I am not even speaking here of that paltry eternity that is called posterity. Mme. Roland relied on herself. That rashness was taught a lesson. Posterity is glad to quote her remark, but forgets to judge it. Mme. Roland is indifferent to posterity.

There can be no question of holding forth on ethics. I have seen people behave badly with great morality and I note every day that integrity has

*Pages 203-205 from *The Myth of Sisyphus and Other Essays,* by Albert Camus, trans. by Justin O'Brien. Copyright © 1955 by Alfred A. Knopf, Inc. Reprinted by permission of the publisher. Pages 205-210 from *Resistance, Rebellion, and Death,* by Albert Camus, trans. by Justin O'Brien. Copyright © 1960 by Alfred A. Knopf, Inc. Reprinted by permission of the publisher.

no need of rules. There is but one moral code that the absurd man can accept, the one that is not separated from God: the one that is dictated. But it so happens that he lives outside that God. As for the others (I mean also immoralism), the absurd man sees nothing in them but justifications and he has nothing to justify. I start out here from the principle of his innocence.

That innocence is to be feared. "Everything is permitted," exclaims Ivan Karamazov. That, too, smacks of the absurd. But on condition that it not be taken in the vulgar sense. I don't know whether or not it has been sufficiently pointed out that it is not an outburst of relief or of joy, but rather a bitter acknowledgment of a fact. The certainty of a God giving a meaning to life far surpasses in attractiveness the ability to behave badly with impunity. The choice would not be hard to make. But there is no choice, and that is where the bitterness comes in. The absurd does not liberate; it binds. It does not authorize all actions. "Everything is permitted" does not mean that nothing is forbidden. The absurd merely confers an equivalence on the consequences of those actions. It does not recommend crime, for this would be childish, but it restores to remorse its futility. Likewise, if all experiences are indifferent, that of duty is as legitimate as any other. One can be virtuous through a whim.

All systems of morality are based on the idea that an action has consequences that legitimize or cancel it. A mind imbued with the absurd merely judges that those consequences must be considered calmly. It is ready to pay up. In other words, there may be responsible persons, but there are no guilty ones, in its opinion. At very most, such a mind will consent to use past experience as a basis for its future actions. Time will prolong time, and life will serve life. In this field that is both limited and bulging with possibilities, everything in himself, except his lucidity, seems unforeseeable to him. What rule, then, could emanate from that unreasonable order? The only truth that might seem instructive to him is not formal: it comes to life and unfolds in men. The absurd mind cannot so much expect ethical rules at the end of its reasoning as, rather, illustrations and the breath of human lives. The few following images are of this type. They prolong the absurd reasoning by giving it a specific attitude and their warmth.

Do I need to develop the idea that an example is not necessarily an example to be followed (even less so, if possible, in the absurd world) and that these illustrations are not therefore models? Besides the fact that a certain vocation is required for this, one becomes ridiculous, with all due allowance, when drawing from Rousseau the conclusion that one must walk on all fours and from Nietzsche that one must maltreat one's mother. "It is essential to be absurd," writes a modern author, "it is not essential to be a dupe." The attitudes of which I shall treat can assume their whole meaning only through consideration of their contraries. A subclerk in the post office is the equal of a conqueror if consciousness is common to them. All experiences are indifferent in this regard. There are some that do either a service or a disservice to man. They do him a service if he is conscious. Otherwise, that has no importance: a man's failures imply judgment, not of circumstances, but of himself.

I am choosing solely men who aim only to expend themselves or whom I see to be expending themselves. That has no further implications. For the moment I want to speak only of a world in which thoughts, like lives, are devoid of future. Everything that makes man work and get excited utilizes hope. The sole thought that is not mendacious is therefore a sterile thought. In the absurd world the value of a notion or of a life is measured by its sterility. . . .

Power And Change

Bread and Freedom

If we add up the examples of breach of faith and extortion which have just been pointed out to us, we can foresee a time when, in a Europe of concentration camps, the only people at liberty will be prison guards who will then have to lock up one another. When only one remains, he will be called the "supreme guard" and that will be the ideal society in which problems of opposition, the headache of all twentieth-century governments, will be settled once and for all.

Of course, this is but a prophecy and, although governments and police forces throughout the world are striving, with great good will, to achieve such a happy situation, we have not yet gone that far. Among us, for instance, in Western Europe, freedom is officially approved. But such freedom makes me think of those poor female cousins in certain middle-class families. She has become a widow; she has lost her natural protector. So she has been taken in, given a room on the top floor, and is welcome in the kitchen. She is occasionally paraded publicly on Sunday, to prove that one is virtuous and not a dirty dog. But for everything else, and especially on state occasions, she is requested to keep her mouth shut. And even if some policeman idly takes liberties with her in dark corners, one doesn't make a fuss about it, for she has seen such things before, especially with the master of the house, and, after all, it is not worth getting in bad with the legal authorities. In the East, it must be admitted, they are more forthright. They have settled the business of the female cousin once and for all by locking her up in a cupboard with two solid bolts on the door. It seems that she will be taken out fifty years from now, more or less, when the ideal society is definitively established. Then there will be celebrations in her honor. But in my opinion she may then be somewhat moth-eaten and I am very much afraid that it may be impossible to make use of her. When we stop to think that these two conceptions of freedom, the one in the cupboard and the other in the kitchen, have decided to force themselves on each other and are obliged in all that hullabaloo to reduce still further the female cousin's activity, it will be readily seen that our history is rather one of slavery than of freedom and that the world we live in is the one that has just been described, which leaps out at us from the newspaper every morning to make of our days and our weeks a single day of revolt and disgust.

The simplest, and hence most tempting, thing is to accuse governments or some obscure powers of such wicked behavior. Besides, it is indeed true that they are guilty and that their guilt is so solidly established that we have lost sight of its beginnings. But they are not the only ones responsible. After all, if freedom had always had to rely on governments to encourage her growth, she would probably still be in her infancy or else definitively buried with the inscription "another angel in heaven." The society of money and exploitation has never been charged, so far as I know, with assuring the triumph of freedom and justice. Police states have never been suspected of opening schools of law in the cellars where they interrogate their subjects. So, when they oppress and exploit, they are merely doing their job, and whoever blindly entrusts them with the care of freedom has no right to be surprised when she is immediately dishonored. If freedom is humiliated or in chains today, this is not because her enemies had recourse to treachery. It is simply because she has lost her natural protector. Yes, freedom is widowed, but it must be added because it is true: she is widowed of all of us.

Freedom is the concern of the oppressed, and her natural protectors have always come from among the oppressed. In feudal Europe the communes maintained the ferments of freedom; those who assured her fleeting triumph in 1789 were the inhabitants of towns and cities; and since the nineteenth century the workers' movements have assumed responsibility for the double honor of freedom and justice, without ever dreaming of saying that they were irreconcilable. Laborers, both manual and intellectual, are the ones who gave a body to freedom and helped her progress in the world until she has become the very basis of our thought, the air we cannot do without, that we breathe without even noticing it until the time comes when, deprived of it, we feel that we are dying. And if freedom is regressing today, throughout such a large part of the world, this is probably because the devices for enslavement have never been so cynical nor better equipped, but also because her real defenders, through fatigue, through despair, or through a false idea of strategy and efficiency, have turned away from her. Yes, the great event of the twentieth century was the forsaking of the values of freedom by the revolutionary movement, the progressive retreat of socialism based on freedom before the attacks of a Caesarian and military socialism. Since that moment, a certain hope has disappeared from the world and a solitude has begun for each and every free man.

When, after Marx, the rumor began to spread and gain strength that freedom was a bourgeois hoax, a single word was misplaced in that definition, and we are still paying for that mistake through the convulsions of our time. For it should have been said merely that bourgeois freedom was a hoax—and not all freedom. It should have been said simply that bourgeois freedom was not freedom or, in the best of cases, was not yet freedom. But that there were liberties to be won and never to be relinquished again. It is quite true that there is no possible freedom for the man tied to his lathe all day long, who, when evening comes, crowds into a single room with his family. But this fact condemns a class, a society and the slavery it assumes, not freedom itself, without which the poorest among us cannot get along. For even if society were suddenly transformed and became decent and comfortable for all, it would still be a barbarous state unless freedom triumphed. And because bourgeois society talks about freedom without practicing it, must the world of workers also give up practicing it and boast merely of not talking about it? Yet the confusion took place and in the revolutionary movement freedom was gradually condemned because bourgeois society used it as a hoax. From a justifiable and healthy distrust of the way that bourgeois society prostituted freedom, people came to distrusting freedom itself. At best, it was postponed to the end of time, with the request that meanwhile it be not talked about. The contention was that we needed justice first and that we would come to freedom later on, as if slaves could ever hope to achieve justice. And dynamic intellectuals announced to the worker that bread alone interested him rather than freedom, as if the worker did not know that his bread depends in part on his freedom. And to be sure, faced with the prolonged injustice of bourgeois society, the temptation to go to such extremes was great. After all, there is probably not one of us here who, either in deed or in thought, did not succumb. But history has progressed and what we have seen must now make us think things over. The revolution brought about by workers succeeded in 1917 and marked the dawn of real freedom and the greatest hope the world has known. But that revolution, surrounded from the outside, threatened within and without, provided itself with a police force. Inheriting a definition and a doctrine that pictured freedom as suspect, the revolution little by little became stronger, and the world's greatest hope hardened into the world's most efficient dictatorship. The false freedom of bourgeois society has not suffered meanwhile. What was killed in the Moscow trials and elsewhere, and in the revolutionary camps, what is assassinated when in Hungary a railway worker is shot for some professional mistake, is not bourgeois freedom but rather the freedom of 1917. Bourgeois freedom can meanwhile have recourse to all possible hoaxes. The trials and perversions of revolutionary society furnish it at one and the same time with a good conscience and with arguments against its enemies.

In conclusion, the characteristic of the world we live in is just that cynical dialectic that sets up injustice against enslavement while strengthening one by the other. When we admit to the palace of culture Franco, the friend of Goebbels and of Himmler, Franco, the real victor of the Second World War—to those who protest that the rights of man inscribed in the charter of U.N.E.S.C.O. are turned to ridicule every day in Franco's prisons, we reply without smiling that Poland figures in U.N.E.S.C.O. too and that as far as public freedom is concerned, one is no better than the other. An idiotic argument, of course! If you were so unfortunate as to marry off your elder daughter to a sergeant in a battalion of ex-convicts, this is no reason why you should marry off her younger sister to the most elegant detective on the society squad; one black sheep in the family is enough. And yet the idiotic argument works, as is proved to us every day. When anyone brings up the slave in the colonies and calls for justice, he is reminded of prisoners in Russian concentration camps, and vice versa. And if you protest against the assassination in Prague of an opposition historian like Kalandra, two or three American Negroes are thrown in your face. In such a disgusting attempt at outbidding, one thing only does not change—the victim, who is always the same. A single value is constantly outraged or prostituted—freedom—and then we notice that everywhere, together with freedom, justice is also profaned.

How then can this infernal circle be broken? Obviously it can be done only by reviving at once, in ourselves and in others, the value of freedom—and by never again agreeing to its being sacrificed, even temporarily, or separated from our demand for justice. The current motto for all of us can only be this: without giving up anything on the plane of justice, yield nothing on the plane of freedom. In particular, the few democratic liberties we still enjoy are not unimportant illusions that we can allow to be taken from us without a protest. They represent exactly what remains to us of the great revolutionary conquests of the last two centuries. Hence they are not, as so many clever demagogues tell us, the negation of true freedom. There is no ideal freedom that will some day be given us all at once, as a pension comes at the end of one's life. There are liberties to be won painfully, one by one, and those we still have are stages, most certainly inadequate, but stages nevertheless on the way to total liberation. If we agree to suppress them, we do not progress nonetheless. On the contrary, we retreat, we go backwards and some day we shall have to re-trace our steps along that road, but that new effort will once more be made in the sweat and blood of men.

No, choosing freedom today does not mean ceasing to be a profiteer of the Soviet regime and becoming a profiteer of the bourgeois regime. For that would amount, instead, to choosing slavery twice and, as a final condemnation, choosing it twice for others. Choosing freedom is not, as we are told, choosing against justice. On the other hand, freedom is chosen today in relation to those who are everywhere suffering and fighting, and this is the only freedom that counts. It is chosen at the same time as justice and, to tell the truth, henceforth we cannot choose one without the other. If someone takes away your bread, he suppresses your freedom at the same time. But if someone takes away your freedom, you may be sure that your bread is threatened, for it no longer depends on you and your struggle but on the whim of a master. Poverty increases insofar as freedom retreats throughout the world, and vice versa. And if this cruel century has taught us anything at all, it has taught that the economic revolution must be free just as liberation must include the economic. The oppressed want to be liberated not only from their hunger but also from their masters. They are well aware that they will be effectively freed of hunger only when they hold their masters, all their masters, at bay.

I shall add in conclusion that separating freedom from justice is tantamount to separating culture and labor, which is the epitome of social sin. The confusion of the workers' movement in Europe springs in part from the fact that it has lost its real home, where it took comfort after all defeats, namely its faith in freedom. But likewise, the confusion of European intellectuals springs from the fact that the double hoax, bourgeois and pseudo-revolutionary, separated them from their sole source of authenticity, the work and suffering of all, cutting them off from their sole natural allies, the workers. For my own part, I have never recognized but two aristocracies, that of labor and that of the intelligence, and I know now that it is mad and criminal to try to make one dominate over the other. I know that the two of them constitute but a single nobility, that their truth and above all their effectiveness lie in union; that, if they are separated, they will allow themselves to be overcome gradually by the forces of tyranny and barbarousness, but that united, on the other hand, they will govern the world. This is why any undertaking which aims to loosen their ties and separate them is directed against man and his loftiest hopes. The first concern of any dictatorship is consequently to subjugate both labor and culture. In fact, both most be gagged or else, as tyrants are well aware, sooner or later one will speak up for the other. Thus, in my opinion, there are at present two ways for an intellectual to betray; in both cases, he betrays because he accepts a single thing—separation between labor and culture. The first way is characteristic of bourgeois intellectuals who are willing that their privileges should be paid for by the enslavement of the workers. They often say that they are defending freedom, but they are defending first of all the privileges freedom gives them, and them alone.[1] The second way is characteristic of intellectuals who think they are leftist and who, through distrust of freedom, are willing that culture and the freedom is presupposes, should be directed, under the vain pretext of serving a future justice. In both cases, the profiteers of injustice and the renegades of freedom ratify and sanction the separation of intellectual and manual labor which condemns both labor and cul-

---

[1] And besides, most of the time they do not even defend freedom as soon as there is any risk in doing so.

ture to impotence. They depreciate at one and the same time both freedom and justice.

It is true that freedom, when it is made up principally of privileges, insults labor and separates it from culture. But freedom is not made up principally of privileges; it is made up especially of duties. And the moment each of us tries to give freedom's duties precedence over its privileges, freedom joins together labor and culture and sets in motion the only force that can effectively serve justice. The rule of our action, the secret of our resistance, can be easily stated: everything that humiliates labor also humiliates the intelligence, and vice versa. And the revolutionary struggle, the centuries-old straining towards liberation can be defined first of all as a double and constant rejection of humiliation.

To tell the truth, we have not yet cast off that humiliation. But the wheel turns, history changes, and a time is coming, I am sure, when we shall cease to be alone. For me, our gathering here today is in itself a sign. The fact that members of unions gather together and crowd around our freedoms to defend them is indeed reason enough for all to come here from all directions to illustrate their union and their hope. The way ahead of us is long. Yet if war does not come and mingle everything in its hideous confusion, we shall have time at last to give a form to the justice and freedom we need. But to achieve that we must henceforth categorically refuse, without anger but irrevocably, the lies with which we have been stuffed. No, freedom is not founded on concentration camps, or on the subjugated peoples of the colonies, or on the workers' poverty! No, the doves of peace do not perch on gallows! No, the forces of freedom cannot mingle the sons of the victims with the executioners of Madrid and elsewhere! Of that, at least, we shall henceforth be sure, as we shall be sure that freedom is not a gift received from a State or a leader but a possession to be won every day by the effort of each and the union of all.

Concluding Remarks

Evaluating Political Theories

Sooner or later the student of political theory asks himself: What were all of my efforts worth? This inevitable query is the result of several factors that characterize inquiry into public affairs. First, throughout the history of political thought there has been profound disagreement over the appropriate approaches and methods by which to study public affairs, the kinds of systems of generalizations through which public life can be understood, and the solutions to the public problems that have been considered significant. All of these disagreements have appeared in the writings of the theorists who are represented in this book. The existence of such diversity, while a source of excitement in one way, has always been a cause of discomfort for people who have looked to theory for guidance in understanding public life or for ways to alter the structures and processes of political affairs. It is important to understand that most political theorists have viewed themselves more as philosophers or scientists than as artists. They have not thought of their work as articulating a private vision of the human universe that readers could accept or reject according to their tastes. Instead, they have believed that they were expressing general truths. The problem has always been, of course, that various theorists have reached different, and often contradictory, conclusions about the same issues. Further, the most serious disagreements have concerned the most important problems. Thus, it is difficult to feel secure in saying, with some, that many of the conflicts between political theorists are merely superficial appearances masking a fundamental consensus. People who make such claims are usually arguing that the basic agreement reflects their particular views.

The bare fact that differences can be observed between political theorists, however, should not, in itself, lead the student of public affairs to doubt whether his inquiry was worthwhile. If some way could be devised to evaluate the "truth" claims of political theorists, "false" doctrines could be separated from "true" propositions. Unfortunately, despite recent intense discussions about the evaluation of theories, no universally accepted standards of judgment have been elaborated. In fact, there are just as many controversies about the proper standards of evaluation as there are about approaches, methods, and results. These debates do, however, take place in a context in which some order can be discerned. In the United States, most political theorists adhere to an "empirical" standard for evaluating theories. In other words, they hold that the truth and falsity of general statements about public affairs can be determined through experimental testing. For example, if a theorist claims that workers are less likely to hold democratic ideas than businessmen, empiricists might test this statement by developing a questionnaire about democratic beliefs and administering it to sample groups of workers and businessmen. While an emphasis on empirical testing is probably the major contribution of contemporary American political scientists to thought on public affairs, strict adherence to this form of evaluation is too limiting to satisfy many people. First, the empirical standard does not allow one to evaluate prescriptive statements. For example, the problem of identity usually takes the form: What kind of person should I be? Although empiricists like Dahl and Easton can enumerate the kinds of people present in public life, the two do not believe that they are capable of deciding what ways of life are better or worse. If one tells them what he wants, they may attempt to identify the most efficient means to attain it. (Of course, the problem of identity arises in the first place because people are not sure of what they want.) Second, the empirical standard does not allow one to make statements about what is going on directly within the consciousness of human beings. Empiricists may attempt to investigate the inner life by asking people questions about their thoughts, feelings, and judgments, but they are wary of making statements based on investigation of their own experiences. Some people believe that the stress that empiricists place on observed and observable behavior excludes them from studying the most significant aspects of public life. While the individual's confrontation with organized power can be described partially in terms of observable activities, such as compulsive conformity to rules, the formation of protest movements, and the rates of alcoholism and drug addiction, it is also a situation that is associated with a wide range of subtle feelings and judgments. Whether or not a questionnaire can elicit such feelings and judgments, which are often semi-conscious or even unconscious, has not yet been determined. Finally, and perhaps most important, the empirical standard has not proven very useful in evaluating the "truth" claims of general propositions about public life. Empirical theorists have long been divided over the choice among theories which propose that public problems are essentially private dilemmas, theories which state that private problems can be understood in terms of public affairs, and theories which claim that private and public problems can be reduced to the processes of human relations. The weakness of the empirical standard in evaluating entire theories may not plague it forever. If enough descriptive generalizations about public affairs can be experimentally verified, the choice between competing theories might become possible. For the person who is interested in analyzing political change today, however, such promises for the future are somewhat hollow. The empirical standard provides little or no guidance for the person trying to decide whether to commit himself to changing consciousness, structures, or relationships.

Dissatisfaction with the empirical standard has led many thinkers to explore intuitive, subjective, or so-called phenomenological modes of evaluation. In these cases, general statements are usually referred to the individual reader or listener for judgment. The theorist attempts to describe the essential characteristics of a situation or a sentiment, and the reader or listener judges whether the essential description brings his own experience into clearer awareness. The Spanish philosopher Ortega y Gasset suggested a phenomenological standard for evaluating his essay on love. "I hope my readers now love or have loved something or someone, and can capture their feeling by its translucent wings and hold it steadily before their inner gaze. . . . The reader will judge whether or not my analysis matches what he finds within himself." In the case of descriptions of public affairs, one might ask whether Hobbes was correct in stating that the essential characteristics of our relations with other people are fear, desire, and status-seeking; whether Rousseau and Marcuse are correct in arguing that we confront society as an oppressive fact to which we adjust; whether Dahl is correct in contending that few of us have any intrinsic interest in public affairs; whether Lasswell and Fromm are correct in their descriptions of social characters; whether Plato was correct in stating that we seek harmony in our individual and social lives; whether Camus was correct in holding that we confront the absurd, rather than society, as an oppressive fact; or whether Easton is correct in arguing that we can be dissolved into our roles.

Each of these nine theorists can be viewed as describing a fundamental political situation. None of these descriptions is unknown to people who have done the slightest bit of thinking about public affairs. In fact, most of us use one or another of them every day in our discussions. Frequently, we employ different descriptions of the same phenomena, depending upon the point we want to get across at the moment. There is nothing easier to do in any argument than to let a generalization that pretends to solve everything roll off one's lips. Often we employ the description that gives us the best feeling, that we "like" the best. It is comfortable, for example, to believe that, deep down, people are "beautiful," that they have good hearts. Through such means, we drug our thoughts more efficiently than we could ever soothe them by taking narcotics. For people who advocate subjective modes of evaluation, descriptions that help in winning debating points and descriptions of what one would like to believe are tremendous obstacles in the way of political understanding. To use the phenomenological standard in an appropriate manner, one must first disentangle what he would like to believe about public affairs from what he really thinks about them; one must second separate opinions that will advance his concrete interests from the opinions that he holds in the absence of interfering interests. Both of these steps are difficult to perform, as anyone who has ever tried to be "objective" about human relationships can testify. Some theorists believe that the difficulties involved in dispassionate investigations of conscious situations are so overwhelming that such inquiries are nearly impossible. Other theorists hold that even if a person could control his tendencies to mingle the "is" and the "ought," and prevent his concrete interests from interfering with his judgments about the situation, his conclusions would still be so infected by his particular experiences that they would be useless as general descriptions. Finally, still other theorists believe that there can be no reliable knowledge about the inner life just because it *is* private and not open to the observation of anyone but the individual subject.

Each of the three objections to the phenomenological standard is powerful, but not insurmountable. We understand what it means to be dispassionate about states of consciousness just because there have been times when we have suspended our wishes and our interests for the purpose of clearer knowledge. We are also aware that we converse with people about conscious situations and often feel that mutual understanding has occurred. Even if sometimes we have been proved mistaken, mistakes do not invalidate the instances of authentic communication. Finally, much of our ordinary language refers to mental states. When we speak of fear and desire, we are talking about feelings, not behaviors. While we may test a person's claim that he is afraid by observing whether or not he acts in fearful ways, we do not usually feel that such observations are a final test. In fact, we normally test such a claim by putting ourselves into the other's situation imaginatively and deciding whether or not we would experience fear.

Both the empirical and the phenomenological standards of evaluation have strengths and weaknesses. Regarding strengths, the empirical standard yields descriptive generalizations, tested by observation, which can be confirmed by anyone with the time and money to repeat the experiment. Acceptance of the empirical standard in modern science has been partly responsible for the great increases in sophisticated knowledge of nature which have characterized the modern era. The phenomenological standard yields essential descriptions of conscious situations and sentiments which, supposedly, can be confirmed by anyone who is willing to look at his inner life dispassionately. Acceptance of the phenomenological standard by many contemporary critics and, implicitly, by many of the classical thinkers, has been partly responsible for the rich descriptions of thought and feeling which have pushed many contemporary individuals into an awareness of the world around them. We have already discussed the weaknesses of each standard. The empirical standard, though reliable, drastically limits the kinds of data that the political theorist can consider. The phenomenological standard, though liberating in the respect of subject matter, lacks the rigor of the empirical standard. In the same way that people who think about public affairs have not reconciled the conflict between the ideal of individual spontaneity and that of efficient and just organization, which appeared in Rousseau's work, political theorists are still divided over the merits of the empirical and phenomenological standards of evaluation.

The student of political theory who asks himself, "What were all of my efforts worth?" should first decide what standards of evaluation he holds. Most likely, he will be best off applying a mix of three standards, each in its appropriate context. First, he might apply what can most adequately be termed a "logical" standard. In this case, he would check to determine whether or not the theory he was studying was consistent. For example, he would try to find out whether the theorist in question claimed on one page that private problems can be reduced to public problems and, somewhere else, stated that public problems are essentially private. If he found that the theory was consistent in its most significant aspects, he might apply the empirical standard, as far as he could, to determine whether or not the theorist's descriptive generalizations were supported by adequate evidence. He might even attempt to test some of the more important generalizations by conducting research of his own. Finally, if the theory was relatively consistent and the descriptive generalizations reasonably supported, he might apply the phenomenological standard to determine whether the basic political situations described by the theorist accorded with his own experiences of public affairs.

This process is tedious, however. Almost no student of public affairs has ever applied all three standards in this idealized fashion. Instead, each theorist has usually emphasized one of the modes of evaluation over the others. This does not mean, though, that the three standards of evaluation exclude one another. Rather, they mutually support one another, and all of the significant political theorists have been aware of the importance of all three standards even while they were emphasizing only one. Moreover, a group of detached descriptive generalizations is less useful than commonsense knowledge, in which descriptions have some relation to one another. A group of descriptive generalizations about public affairs that seem trivial are usually superficial observations. A brilliant portrayal of a conscious situation that is never manifested in observable human activity has little significance in public life. A completely consistent set of propositions about behaviors that never occur is similarly trivial, though it may substitute for a parlor game. Finally, a formless blob of emotionalism, lacking any vestige of coherence, is perhaps the most frustrating statement of all. The endless disagreements that one encounters in the literature of political theory become less disheartening when one keeps the three standards of evaluation clearly in mind. The greatest mistake that students of political theory make is to believe that their own experiences of public affairs are irrelevant, that they know nothing about public life, and that they cannot judge the consistency of a piece of writing. Once a person gains confidence, rather than pride or diffidence, the study of political theory can bring insights into his conscious life, general information about public affairs, and some order into his thoughts about politics. It is less likely that political theory will provide him with answers to his moral problems. He will, however, have a more intelligent basis on which to make his choices.

Types of Public Situations

For the professional philosopher, the logical standard of evaluation is usually the most important. When he studies a political theory, the philosopher examines the forms of the arguments, tries to discover exactly how the most important concepts are defined, and checks whether conclusions follow from premises. For the political scientist, the empirical standard of evaluation normally takes precedence. When he investigates a political theory, the political scientist tries to discern whether the descriptive generalizations can be experimentally tested, checks to see whether the generalizations are already supported by research findings, and attempts to determine whether the theory provides explanations for hitherto problematic events. For the citizen, or active member of a political community, however, the phenomenological standard of evaluation is the most appropriate. He tries to define the essential characteristics of his relationship to public life, envision a more satisfactory public situation, and bring present circumstances into conformance with the desired condition. Thus, when the active member of a political community studies a political theory, he is looking for a clearer definition of his public situation than he could gain unaided. Finally, the political theorist combines some of the interests of the philosopher, the political scientist, and the citizen. Again, even if his work is dominated by one standard, he is impelled to give some consideration to the other two.

The problems of identity, organized power, and political change are certainly concerns of active members of contemporary political communities, as well as of philosophers, political scientists, and political theorists. It might be well to try to consider the discussions of the problems presented in this book in the light of the phenomenological standard of evaluation. To undertake such an evaluation, it will be necessary to define three public situations in which a person might find himself. Each of these situations will be associated with a type of theory of public life, and each will include aspects of the quest for personal identity, the individual's confrontation with organized power, and the drive for political change. Thus, there will be different public situations associated with psychological theories of public life, systems theories of public affairs, and conflict theories of politics.

The term "public situation" refers to the way in which the individual is related, or relates himself, to the concerns of the community to which he belongs. In this context, "community" means a group of people living under the same laws and regulations, or living within the same institutions. Thus, in the contemporary world, the significant community with respect to the public situation is usually the nation state. Of course, some people consider themselves members of a "world community" that they believe is emerging or should emerge; others, particularly in the Third World, consider themselves members of localized village, or even tribal, communities. Such ambiguity is merely a reflection of the many changes in the structures of human existence that are taking place at the present time. However, whether the relevant community is constituted by humanity in general, one's fellow citizens, or some more limited group, the individual still must have some relationship to it. Even if he does not seek a relationship, one will be imposed upon him merely because he will be expected to conform to the requirements of certain laws and regulations. Moreover, if he wants any gratifications at all, he will probably have to obtain them through existing social institutions unless he is able to create new social institutions through cooperating with others. Thus, to be in a public situation is inescapable. It is part of living as a human being.

Any public situation has several components. First, there is an internal aspect that includes the ways in which the person understands his roles, his relationships, and his personality in their reference to the entire community; the ways in which the individual feels about these roles and relationships, and his identity; and the ways in which the person would like to act to preserve or alter his roles, his relationships, and his personality. Second, there is an external aspect that includes the ways in which the person actually behaves with reference to the entire community. There is no guarantee that a person will act in full accordance with his beliefs, feelings, and evaluations about public life. Further, these beliefs, feelings, and evaluations may be utterly disorganized or contradictory. Third, there is an integrative aspect that includes the ways in which the individual integrates, or fails to integrate, his beliefs, feelings, evaluations, and activities. Fourth, there are general interpretations of the public situation as a whole that seek to relate the internal, external, and integrative dimensions to one another. These interpretations essentially define the public situation, and they are the statements that we will attempt to evaluate with the phenomenological standard.

All people hold beliefs, have feelings, and make judgments about the communities of which they are members. Also, everybody sometimes acts with reference to his community. Finally, social psychologists, political scientists, and most contemporary social philosophers tell us that people usually attempt to integrate their internal and external dimensions. However, very few people step outside of themselves and try to relate the subjective, objective, and integrative activities. In a sense, if one attempts to give general descriptions of public situations, he is a political theorist. But, it is a mistake to believe that everyone is an amateur political theorist, just as it is a mistake to think that everyone is an amateur theologian. Most people are afraid to look dispassionately at the patterns of their public and religious lives, which may be one reason why political theory and theology are so often considered irrelevant or boring. One need not face up to things that he has convinced himself are trivial or dull. Each individual must choose for himself whether or not he wants to live in a fog. No political theorist can cause the fog to lift, although descriptions of public situations can provide the interested person with means to disperse the clouds of rationalization. Again, before an individual can adequately evaluate a description of a public situation, he must make an attempt to suspend temporarily both his wishes about what he would like public life to be and his concrete interests in public affairs.

Public Situations: Are Public Problems Private Dilemmas?

The commonsense way of relating oneself to public life is founded on the notion that political events express the needs, motives, and problems of individual human beings. It seems reasonable to affirm, with Plato, that constitutions "cannot come out of sticks and stones." We ordinarily believe that the basic patterns of public life "must result from the preponderance of certain characters which draw the rest of the community in their wake." There is, as many people have remarked, a certain finality to the individual human being. It is the *person* who thinks, feels, and acts rather than the "organization" or the "group." Even if we frequently make statements like "U.S. Steel rolled back its prices today," or "State University defeated Elite College in football this afternoon," we are aware that some individual human beings decided to lower prices, or that some well-defined people performed certain actions on a football field. Thus, our judgments on public affairs often reflect the underlying belief that the structures of politics reflect the structures of personalities. Our newspapers, magazines, and radio and television newscasts are filled with information, often of dubious worth, about the characters of public leaders. We are frequently interested in what kind of person the President is. We feel that if we know something about his background, his tastes, and even his private frustrations we will be able to understand his activities in their relation to the entire community. Frequently, when we become involved in politics ourselves, we interpret our activities in terms of personality. A decision, for example, to risk one's future by joining a protest movement is usually both intense and personal. Even the relatively simple act of voting has a personal dimension. It is only natural for us to believe that others confront their decisions about public life with the same personal involvement, and in a sense we are correct. While many people are "apathetic" about politics, any activities in which they engage that have reference to the entire community are their own. Behind almost every activity that takes place in human societies there is a wealth of subjectivity. This does not mean that most people are fully conscious of the meanings of their activities, or that they always act in accordance with a clear purpose. Rather, it means that there are abundant internal processes accompanying our behavior with reference to other human beings. As Lasswell pointed out, the most significant of these internal processes may be unconscious. As Plato and Fromm argued, we may share the important internal processes with large numbers of other people. However, if our inner lives are somewhat standardized, we still normally believe that public life is the expression of individuals.

Aside from the finality that we usually ascribe to human beings, there are other reasons why the psychological interpretation of the public situation is so widespread. If it is true that a great many people are preoccupied with the problems of identity, power, and change, it is also correct that most concerned individuals look at these problems from a psychological point of view. In the case of identity, of course, the psychological nature of the problem is clear. The question of what distinguishes one as a concrete human being is a query about one's personality. However, the psychological point of view goes much deeper than this. The person seeking an identity usually goes about conducting his quest with the kind of tools that Plato, Lasswell, and Fromm used. For example, the individual may ask, "How can I avoid becoming *homo mechanicus,* addicted to gadgets and living like an automaton? How can I avoid becoming *homo consumens,* passively assimilating material goods and never experiencing genuine human relations?" Or, he may ask, "How can I free myself and take on a democratic character? How can I become flexible and receptive to new and satisfying experiences?" Finally, he may ask, "How can I put my life in order so that my actions conform to my knowledge? How can I rid myself of distorting obsessions?" In each of these cases the individual is asking himself what he can do to gain a satisfying identity. Even if he finally takes his problems to a psychologist, he is still acting as an individual. Thus, the psychological description of the public situation leads to a view that the problem of identity is an individual matter. While proposals for humanistic management, preventive politics, and statesmanlike rule all have an aspect of social organization, they are meant to work directly upon individuals.

When we interpret the problem of organized power, we also tend to take a psychological approach. While the problem of identity is usually defined in terms of whether or not it is possible to repudiate the dominant types of social character and whether or not one should make such a repudiation, the person's confrontation with organized power is normally understood in relation to the kinds of social characters he encounters. The same individual who fears that he is or may become a mechanical man or a pure consumer views the organizations in which he is living as expressions of the technocratic mentality. This is the essential meaning of Fromm's frightening vision of the "technetronic" society of the future, in which human beings will be fully committed to the maxims that "something *ought* to be done because it is technically *possible* to do it" and that there should be *"maximal efficiency and output."* The same individual who seeks an open, flexible, and receptive character, and finds himself frustrated in his efforts to love, views the organizations among which he is living as expressions, perhaps, of the characters of specialists in violence and their allies. This is the essential meaning of Lasswell's terrible vision of a society in which people steel themselves "against deep-lying tendencies to retreat from death and mutilation." Finally, the same individual who seeks a just life, sees petty dictators and opportunists around him. This is the meaning of Plato's vision of despotism. Thus, the concept of social character is fundamental to the psychological description of the public situation. Power, in this view, is organized by certain kinds of men.

The commonsense way of relating ourselves to public life also includes a psychological interpretation of the problem of social change. This is not to say that the ordinary man believes that public life can and should be improved by programs of humanistic management, preventive politics, or enlightened statesmanship. In fact, the ordinary person is apt to be fearful of such schemes and proposals, as are many sophisticated people. However, the kinds of devices for implementing political change that were discussed by Fromm, Lasswell, and Plato have their analogies in day-to-day discourse and practice. Many people believe that a return to "traditional morals" and a new commitment to "religion" would provide the conditions for desirable social changes. Others think that if certain men were elected to public office, beneficial social changes would come about without changing the organizational structures at all. Still others believe that if we sympathized with each other and loved one another enough, many problems would disappear. Finally, there are those who believe that if people were made conscious of the claim that they are being exploited, they would rise up in revolution. Each of these beliefs is merely a crude reflection of the kinds of proposals offered by the psychological theorists. They are applications of the principle that public problems are essentially personal dilemmas. However, are public problems really private dilemmas? Is the public situation one in which social character confronts social character? Must desirable social change come about through action taken directly on individual personalities? If one describes the public situation by answering yes to these three questions, he has committed himself to a view of public life fraught with many difficulties.

The first difficulty of the psychological view of the public situation is a simple fact about our social relations. Each of us holds himself somewhat apart from his social character. There are no perfect examples of the "mechanical man," the "specialist in violence," or the "despot" in ordinary human life, although there are people in mental institutions who come close to these models. While a person may come close to being *homo mechanicus* on his job, he is apt to be a very different person at home. Further, it is likely that he is a different person to himself than he is either in the work or family situation. That people so frequently play roles rather than live them with commitment may lead one to believe that public life is not merely an expression of character. Instead, public life may be in great part an expression of various kinds of people playing roles that have been thrust upon them. People can do things that they heartily dislike, but whatever their feelings, those things get done. Second, the psychological interpretation of the public situation virtually ignores the ways in which organizational rules result in the selection of some types of people for rewards rather than others. While organizations are made up of people, people also find themselves in organizations with preexisting systems of rewards and punishments. Third, the psychological interpretation of the public situation puts great obstacles in the way of social change. Just because people are somewhat separate from their roles, it may be possible to change organizationally defined roles without bothering to alter individual personalities. To change the structure of a person's beliefs, feelings, and moral evaluations requires a long and difficult process. To change the structure of the rewards and punishments that a person receives in his organizational situation is much easier. At least this is the judgment that most successful revolutionaries throughout history have made. The psychological description of the public situation has usually been associated with conservatism. This does not mean that theorists like Lasswell and Fromm are ideological conservatives. Rather, it means that since psychological descriptions of the public situation stress the importance of the personality, they usually emphasize individual changes at the expense of structural changes. Individual changes, while they may be far-reaching, usually work much more slowly than structural changes. Moreover, there is a tendency on the part of many psychological theorists to believe that individuals should be helped to adjust to the existing social structure. Neither Plato, Lasswell, nor Fromm evinced this tendency. In order to avoid it, these men devised proposals to make psychological changes socially efficient. Whether or not such schemes are practicable is another question. Plato dreamed of a time when philosophers would become kings or kings would become philosophers, but he was well aware of the obstacles of power that would have to be overcome before human beings could live in such a time. The same obstacles stand in the way of contemporary programs like those of Lasswell and Fromm.

Public Situations: Are Private Dilemmas Public Problems?

Sometimes a person frees himself from the commonsense world and gains the insight that his actions in public life are not wholly his own. The first step on the path to such intellectual liberation is often the recognition by the person that he is not fully exhausted by his roles. He may realize that every day he is being asked to do things that are based on beliefs that he considers false, that he does not like, and that he judges to be morally wrong. He may discover that he has been performing such unsatisfying actions for a long time, perhaps without even realizing it. If he explores the matter further, the individual may notice that he has been compartmentalizing his life and rationalizing his compromises. Maybe he soothed himself in the past by convincing himself that the dissonance between his internal and external lives was a necessary part of living in an imperfect world. Perhaps he told himself that the only important freedom is subjective; that as long as he could think as he pleased, actions were not important. Most likely he comforted himself by saying that the world is pretty good anyway, and it is improving all the time. The person who awakens from such mental slumber may become terror-stricken. At some time, the thought will cross his mind that not only have his acts been limited by the rules of social organizations, but his very consciousness has been shaped by social roles or general principles of social organization. Thus, starting from the distinction between his "real self" and his behavior in standardized social situations, the person may come to the conclusion that this supposed "real self" is merely a product of his socialization. When he has reached this point of view, which is just as extreme as the notion that public affairs can be reduced to processes of the personality, he may begin to blame his frustrations and problems on the "system," which he feels has created him. He may come to believe that his private problems would be solved if only the social structure could be changed. This belief can take either of two forms. First, the person may decide that his internal and external lives are completely a product of the socialization process through which he has come. This is the position of extreme behaviorists, who view the human being outside of a social environment as indeterminate. Second, the individual may decide that the socialization process has frustrated certain of his basic desires to the point that he may not even know how to express them. This is much more the position of critics like Rousseau and Marcuse. However, whether the person chooses the behavioristic interpretation or the romantic point of view, he will turn his attention to the social structure and the ways in which it can be altered. When a person has reached the conclusion that he is related to public life through his roles, and that his roles have become part of his personality, he has adopted a systems description of the public situation. Of course, it is possible to come to the systems point of view in other ways than the one just outlined. Easton, for example, became a systems theorist because he thought that alternative theories did not adequately explain the facts of public life. The awakening to social limitations, however, is a common way of coming to the systems description of the public situation.

Just as was the case with the public situation viewed from the vantage point of psychological theory, the systems interpretation of the public situation knits the problems of identity, power, and political change into a coherent pattern. The problem of identity is discussed in terms of the socialization process. For the person who asks what distinguishes him as a concrete individual, there is a ready answer. He is the result of the education he has received, the work he has done, the rewards he has enjoyed, and the punishments he has suffered. Thus, Easton attempted to show how the child gradually becomes a good citizen, adopting at different ages the socially approved political attitudes and behaviors. Rousseau was also concerned with education, although he was highly critical of the way it was being conducted. He believed that there was an authentic person who was being frustrated by social institutions. He did not, however, think that the true self could express itself unaided by an altered social environment. Marcuse, of course, was concerned with that part of the socialization process conducted through the mass media. He has argued that needs are implanted in people from the outside in such a subtle way that the persons involved do not even understand what is being done to them. These socially conditioned needs suppress authentic needs and thereby perpetuate unhappiness. Thus, the systems description of the public situation leads to the conclusion that identity is not a personal problem, but a problem traceable to the way in which society is organized.

The systems description of the problem of organized power follows from the treatment of identity. If one's actions with reference to the entire community are functions of his roles or of the general principles of social organization, then organized power is also a function of those roles and principles. Thus, Rousseau distinguishes between societies that are organized to serve particular interests and those that are organized to serve some general interest; Easton defines a system for the authoritative allocation of values; and Marcuse speaks of the "rule of a repressive whole" and "technological control." Just as the psychological description of the public situation interpreted organized power in terms of social character, the systems description of the public situation interprets social character in terms of organized power. When they are not propagandizing for political change, systems theorists are always concerned with making a distinction between the "system" and the individuals who compose it. These individuals, even when they are exploiters, are viewed as being locked into their roles or social positions. Technologies, systems of property ownership, or media of communication organize power and personalities in accordance with some principle. That organization is not carried out consciously, just as the ecological order of a pond is not consciously determined. It is merely the case that both of these systems can be observed and understood.

It is with reference to the problem of social change that systems theorists have attracted the attention of people who desire radical alteration in public life. Since the systems description of the public situation depreciates the importance of the concrete individual, it should allow changes to be effected even if individuals are bypassed. However, there has always been an ambiguity about this point in systems theory. Some systems theorists have maintained that the continued operation of the general principle of social organization that they have identified will itself ensure social change. Many Marxists of the Old Left believed in such a doctrine of the inevitability of revolution. However, most people who have held to a systems description of the public situation, while advocating social change, have also argued that the consciousness of individuals must somehow be altered before structural changes can take place. Whether the person believes that consciousness can be changed most effectively through education, propaganda, or involving people in confrontations with established authority where they "see the evils of the system at work" is unimportant in this context. The important point is that systems theorists have often found it necessary to argue that changes can come about only through direct action upon individuals. In other words, individuals must somehow be brought to the realization of the systems description of the public situation. Once they believe that their private problems are really public problems, they will be ready to direct their efforts toward the social structure.

The weaknesses of the systems interpretation of the public situation are the strengths of the psychological point of view. In fact, the two descriptions can be played off against one another to good advantage. Systems theorists tend to forget that roles are usually not fully absorbed. The personal quest for an identity is not wholly a cruel joke. People can and do create unique styles of living, even if they are often thwarted in their attempts to express them. Furthermore, organized power is not completely impersonal. In the same way that ordinary people frequently attempt to manipulate their roles, the individuals who occupy positions of power in contemporary organizations have some choice among alternatives. It is, of course, debatable whether the decisions of any man in contemporary industrial societies are significant in comparison to the restrictions imposed by organizations. This question is further complicated by the fact that leaders tend to blame circumstances beyond their control for mistakes, while praising themselves for successes. Perhaps one must define what a significant decision is before he can agree or disagree with the systems interpretation. Finally, the fact that most systems theorists recognize the part that the individual plays in social change is some indication that the systems description of the public situation is not sufficient. However, after we have taken all of this into account, the important insight remains that at least some of our private problems are really public problems.

Public Situations: Are Public Problems Relational?

For people who find the processes of conflict in public life more significant than the structures of the personality or the social system, there is an implicit description of the public situation. Under this interpretation, public problems are understood in terms of the relationships among individuals and among their groups. The individual relates himself to public life by demanding, either by himself or through an intermediary group, something from the entire community. Within the bounds set by his agreement with opponents on the proper limitations to political conflict, by his fear of reprisals, or by sheer habit, he attempts to maximize his goals, perhaps at the expense of others. He is caught in a world where he is partially or completely dependent upon others for wealth, status, and power and where he is trapped in a situation in which he is competing with others for these goods. The forms by which the impulses to gain property, protect oneself from harm, and be honored are expressed in the relationships among people and groups constitute the essential factors in public affairs. The public situation as interpreted by conflict theorists sets off an individual, with his desires and his group memberships, from the obstacles to the fulfillment of these desires embodied in opposing groups and individuals. While the resulting conflict is almost always limited by some agreement between the contestants about the maximum intensity that the struggles will be allowed to reach, the public situation is inevitably a type of war of "all against all."

The conflict description of the public situation orders the problems of identity, power, and change into a coherent pattern just as did the psychological and systems interpretations. In the case of identity, the individual must come to terms with his set of desires and interests, which can generally be aggregated under the three major interests in wealth, status, and power that were defined by Hobbes. In addition to these three interests, an interest in opposing a hostile and purposeless universe through the exercise of freedom, that was identified by Camus, may be widespread in certain groups. Whatever desires and interests are identified, though, the person seeking an identity must order them rather than choose among social characters or manipulate roles. The way in which the person finally comes to terms with his desires will determine whether he gains an identity as *homo civicus* or *homo politicus.* These two types of character, as defined by Dahl, are the basic personalities that can be observed in an analysis of conflict processes. Under the conflict description of the public situation, one either lets others decide which interests are going to be satisfied by the entire community or attempts to have some say himself in the determination of who gets what. Of course, in discussing the prescriptive question of whether one should become *homo civicus* or *homo politicus,* conflict theorists have reached a wide variety of answers. Hobbes would say that the ordinary man should remain a civic soul, minding his own private business and obeying the laws of the time. For him, any widespread participation in political conflicts would spell social chaos. Dahl would say that in the interest of political stability the ordinary person should remain a civic man whenever his important interests are being satisfied and are not being threatened. Camus would recommend that the ordinary person become a political man dedicated to the enhancement of freedom. Perhaps this is why he is so much more popular among radicals than either Hobbes or Dahl, even though he is a conflict theorist. There is, of course, an ambiguity in the recommendations of Hobbes and Dahl. From the point of view of tranquility in public affairs, perhaps it is wise to minimize political participation. However, for the concrete individual who is not getting many of his interests satisfied, failure to become *homo politicus* may perpetuate injustice. Further, even the individually satisfied person who wants to take responsibility for what goes on in his community may decide that both bread and freedom are important. This was Camus' point.

Conflict theorists treat the problem of organized power in much the same way as they deal with identity. Power is organized by individuals and groups to serve certain interests. Coalitions and blocs are formed to gain certain benefits, strategies of various types are employed to overcome opponents, and organizations with rules backed up by rewards and punishments are formed to perpetuate advantages that have already been gained or to provide a base from which to seek further advantages. Conflict theorists do not deny that a coalition of groups may succeed in dominating the other groups in a community. However, unlike systems theorists, they do not see such domination as a function of general principles of social organization, and, unlike psychological theorists, they do not see it as a function of the selection of social characters. Instead, conflict theorists view concentrations of organized power as one result of the successful application of the techniques of conflict.

In the conflict description of the public situation, political change is interpreted in terms of the same processes that underlie the formation of concentrations of organized power. Thus, Hobbes provided a list of factors that would work against political stability. Of course, he argued that the authorities should eliminate these factors for the sake of social peace. However, people in favor of social change could just as easily attempt to enhance the importance of disruptive factors. Dahl, also, provided strategies for social change and attempted to evaluate their efficiency. Finally, Camus, in his "Bread and Freedom" and "New Mediterranean Culture" essays, identified the two types of "revolution" that radicals talk about at the present time. In "Bread and Freedom," he defined the "political revolution" which consists of a drive for greater freedom and self-determination for individuals and groups. This is the central meaning of the concept of "participation" which has become so popular during the last several years. In "The New Mediterranean Culture," he defined the "cultural revolution" which consists of a drive for free creation and meaningful expression by individuals and groups. This is the central factor underlying the artistic experimentation and invention of new styles that have been evident recently, as well as the force behind "black culture." In all cases, however, conflict theorists view social change as a matter of either gaining advantages in relations that already exist or creating new relations through political and cultural activities.

Like the psychological and systems points of view, the conflict description of the public situation is weak in what it ignores. Conflict theorists pay little attention to the major aspect of the problem of identity: how diverse interests and desires can be sorted out into some meaningful pattern. They begin their analysis with existing interests, without inquiring how these interests might be ordered into an identity. While the conflict interpretation adds a necessary element of process to the discussion of organized power, it does not take sufficient account of the fact that social structures often limit what individuals and groups can do. Conflict theory is most useful in understanding the problem of social change, especially from the point of view of the person who seeks alterations in the conduct of public affairs. There is little that the ordinary person can do in the way of realizing a program of preventive politics, humanistic management, or enlightened statesmanship. There is next to nothing he can do about changing the general principles of social organization. The individual can, however, make a decision about the kind of public life he would like to see and attempt to promote it by becoming *homo politicus.* In fact, people who have adopted the psychological or systems interpretations of the public situation have normally adopted the conflict point of view with regard to their activities in the pursuit of change. Whether the individual wants to change consciousness, structure, or both, he can only do so by entering the conflict process, most likely as a member of a group that shares his commitments. This is the major contribution of conflict theory for the individual citizen.

Toward a Provisional Synthesis

Is there a description of the public situation that preserves the valuable insights of all three of the above interpretations without embodying their distortions? While this is primarily a question for the reader to think about, some provisional suggestions can be offered. Regarding the problem of identity, psychological interpretations seem to be the strongest. Anyone who seeks an identity quests for something better defined than a set of social roles or an aggregation of interests and desires. While he must realize that the roles that he performs often become parts of his personality and that his interests also play a part in his self-definition, he will want to order these factors into some pattern of his own. It is in this task of ordering that social character becomes important. The person seeking an identity wants more than to have his way from moment to moment. He wants a way of his own; he wants to be a certain kind of person. In developing such a way of his own, he can experiment with various social characters and determine whether any of them satisfy him. He may not, in the end, adopt in its entirety a social character that someone else has defined, but an appreciation of the contours of the different "types of men" that have been defined by psychological theorists will aid him in making his own choices. This does not mean that all public problems are private. Rather, it means that the individual has an area of control over the kind of person he will become.

Turning to the problem of organized power, the systems interpretation seems to be the most persuasive. Once we have awakened from the commonsense attitude, it is impossible to escape an appreciation of the impersonal limitations on our activities. In modern industrial societies, a person confronts primarily the power of organizational rules and people in organizational roles; he meets the power of concrete individuals in only a secondary way. This does not mean that all private problems are public. Rather, it means that organizations have an area of control over the expression of a person's character.

Finally, regarding the problem of social change, the conflict description of the public situation seems to be the most reasonable. The individual with a character to express who is confronted by the demands of his roles has little choice other than to enter the conflict process if he wants to play a part in bringing structures more into accordance with his personal vision. While the types of conflict in which he decides to engage may vary widely in intensity, engagement and commitment are inescapable for the person seeking political change. Again, this does not mean that all public problems are relational. Rather, it means that people can only attack public problems through relational processes. In other words, groups have an area of control over both the expression of the individual's character and the organizations in which he exists.

The integration and synthesis of the psychological, systems, and conflict points of view is a task that may never reach completion. However, our phenomenological evaluation of the three theories should at least have shown that the study of political theory is of value in understanding one's relation to public life, even if one is neither a philosopher nor a political scientist. If we are fated to a relationship with public life, at least we can attempt to both comprehend that relation and, perhaps, change it to accord with our deepest desires.